THE PSYCHOLOGY
OF WRITTEN
COMMUNICATION

The Psychology of Written Communication

SELECTED READINGS

Edited by
JAMES HARTLEY *Keele University, UK*

Kogan Page, London/Nichols Publishing Company, New York

First published in Great Britain in 1980 by
Kogan Page Limited, 120 Pentonville Road, London N1 9JN

First published in the United States of America in 1980 by
Nichols Publishing Company, PO Box 96, New York, NY 10024

Library of Congress Cataloging in Publication Data
Main entry under title:
Psychology of Written Communication
    Includes index.
    1. Authorship-addresses, essays, lectures.
    2. English language-rhetoric-addresses, essays, lectures.
    3. Communication-addresses, essays, lectures. I. Hartley,
        James, Ph.D.
PN149. P75 1980 401'.9 79-27247
ISBN 0-89397-081-6

Printed in Great Britain by
Billing & Sons Ltd, Guildford, London and Worcester
ISBN 0 85038 282 3

Contents

Part 4: Communicating in Print: New Techniques

Part 5: Some Aspects of Scientific Communication

Preface

An issue in psychology apparently becomes respectable when there are international conferences on the topic, the publication of textbooks devoted solely to it, and an increasing number of journal articles on the theme. In these respects we may say that the topic of written communication has arrived — although, of course, writing has been of interest to some people for a very long time.

It is curious, nonetheless, that the topic of writing has never attracted as much attention from psychologists as that of reading. Yet writing is clearly as important, if not more so. Today's turbulent society demands that we and our children produce and process documents of great complexity. We need, therefore, to know a great deal more about good writing. The aim of this book is to indicate what has been done — and what might be done — in this field.

In putting the text together I have tried to cover a broad framework, and to gather a representative set of papers, each of which makes a contrasting contribution. The text is divided into five main parts, and for each part I have written an introductory essay to set the chosen articles in a wider context. The resulting text, I hope, will be of value to psychologists, teachers, editors and printers: indeed, to anyone who is involved in communicating in print.

I am grateful to many people for their assistance in the preparation of this text, not least to my fellow contributors, as well as to their editors and publishers. Philip Kogan and Margaret Conn at Kogan Page deserve my special thanks, and so too do Mavis Phillips, Margaret Woodward, and Hilda Rhodes who, between them, shared the joys of deciphering my own special brand of written communication.

James Hartley
August 1979

Part 1: Reading and Writing: Some Theoretical Issues

1.0 Introduction

It may seem curious in a book on the psychology of written communication to begin with a section on reading. However, people who write usually expect their product to be read: writers work with readers in mind.

But what do we know about reading? About its acquisition? And how skilled adults read? Is it possible to condense the miles of print on reading into something useful for writers? Can our knowledge about reading processes be translated into guidelines for better expression and for better ways of presenting text?

Currently, in the psychology of reading, there seems to be a great divide between researchers who stress perceptual processes and those who stress meaning and comprehension. Those who stress perceptual processes use what is currently called a 'bottom-up' approach to reading, whilst those who stress meaning use a 'top-down' approach.

'Bottom-up' processes, as their name implies, suggest that reading involves discriminating between different symbols, matching sounds to symbols, and fusing sounds into words. (This view, incidentally, so characteristic of the early work of E Gibson, has now been all but abandoned by her: see Gibson, 1977.) Researchers in this area seem to spend a good deal of time making 'chronometric studies' of the time taken to carry out various sub-processes in reading, such as perceiving rapidly presented individual letters, isolated words or nonsense syllables. (See LaBerge and Samuels, 1977.)

It is conventional to say that bottom-up processes are 'text-driven', that is, to argue that it is features of the text that determine what is read. 'Top-down' processes, on the other hand, imply that reading is 'reader-driven': that is to say that what people see when they read is determined by their expectations and past experience. It is argued that skilled readers do not study every individual letter, but sample the text in order to confirm or reject hypotheses about its content. Reading involves processing sentences, clauses and *groups of words* in the search for the author's meaning. By examining readers' errors (when reading aloud) we can detect the expectancies that they have. Different readers, it is argued, may extract different meanings from the same text.

These distinctions between text- and reader-driven processes seem too forced to be taken too literally. It is clear that reading can be both

11

text- and reader-driven. Skilled readers are able to switch from one level to another with great ease. Normally, it is argued, reader-driven strategies predominate: text-driven strategies are so well practised that they are, in effect, automatic. Text-driven strategies predominate only when readers are faced with a difficult new word, or when obvious ambiguities or printing errors occur.

In this book, then, we shall be interested primarily in top-down reader-driven strategies — although there are many ways of using typography to make readers use a text-driven approach if this is deemed necessary (by, for example, italicising a new or difficult word). Generally speaking, however, it is the reader-driven strategies that suggest ways of organizing text that help writers communicate better with their readers.

Paper 1.1, 'The facilitation of meaningful verbal learning in the classroom', presents a summary of the views of David Ausubel. Ausubel has argued for many years that learning involves fitting what is known into what is already known. Ausubel distinguishes between rote and meaningful learning, and between reception and discovery learning. (By reception learning Ausubel means learning passively from someone or something else — eg a teacher or a textbook.) Thus four possibilities are available: rote/reception learning; meaningful/reception learning; rote/discovery learning; and meaningful/discovery learning. Ausubel argues that rote/reception learning occurs all too often in schools; that meaningful/reception learning is the most common form of learning and is the most valuable; that rote/discovery learning can occur (eg discovering a glib right answer without comprehension); and that meaningful/discovery learning — whilst satisfactory in theory — takes too long in practice.

For something to be meaningful it must of course fit in with or relate to one's existing knowledge (or cognitive structure). It is in this context that Ausubel introduces his notion of advance-organizers. Organizers contain material that is given to the learner before the main body of instruction. Expository organizers make explicit the relationships between old and new material: comparative organizers point out the ways in which old and new material differ.

Ausubel has spelt out in detail how to prepare advance-organizers, but most investigators seem to generate their own procedures in this respect. Some studies, for instance, have claimed to use organizers which are only one sentence long (see Meyer, 1979).

Clearly there are other ways of introducing topics to learners as well as organizers. Hartley and Davies (1976) reviewed the then available research on advance-organizers, pre-tests, behavioural objectives and summaries. They concluded that (i) all these methods were useful in different ways but (ii) they only applied to the domain of meaningful/reception learning.

A serious criticism of Ausubel's approach has been made by Macdonald-Ross (1979). Macdonald-Ross argues that Ausubel's underlying assumptions — that the structure of subject matter can be seen as hierarchical, and that readers start at the beginning and read through to the end — do not always fit the facts. Macdonald-Ross suggests that there is a point in placing advance-organizers in a consistent place — because it helps the reader to locate them readily — but this is not the reason advocated by Ausubel for doing so.

Richard Anderson and others have criticized Ausubel's theory on the grounds that advance-organizers can only be useful if the learner has pre-knowledge of some kind — if he has (to use Anderson's terminology) the appropriate schemata or 'slots' into which to classify the incoming information (Anderson *et al*, 1978). Anderson argues that if the learner has no appropriate schemata at the initial stage of learning then devices like advance-organizers or summaries are better positioned at the end of the instruction. New schemata will be developed from the instruction and end-organizers or summaries will serve to reinforce their development.

In Paper 1.2, 'Schema-directed processes in language comprehension', Anderson presents a clear account of what I called earlier the 'top-down' approach to reading. Anderson agrees with Ausubel that the different prior knowledge and experience that readers bring to a text can have a marked effect upon their perception and recall of words, sentences, paragraphs and complete passages, but Anderson argues that text information is interpreted, organized and retrieved in terms of 'high-level schemata', ie mental structures that incorporate general knowledge. His paper concludes — but he is not specific — by suggesting that this approach to reading has clear implications for writing.

If a particular topic has a clear structure — say a beginning, a middle and an end — then that structure will dictate how a writer might present and discuss it. (It is helpful, for instance, to write instructions in the sequence in which they are carried out.) The question of how subject-matter structure on the one hand, and cognitive-structure on the other, might interact has long intrigued psychologists.

If it were possible to devise notational systems for representing the conceptual structure of subject matters, then there would be an enormous contribution to the study of reading, writing and instruction. It would be possible, for example, to relate research on organizers and summaries to the structure of a text independent of its specific meaning. In recent years, therefore, a great deal of interest has been paid to examining text in order to find out ways of depicting its inherent structure. Paper 1.3 by Richard Shavelson and Cathleen Stasz compares and contrasts four such approaches to describing the structure of text. Of these four, the 'microstructure' approaches of Kintsch and of Meyer appear to be receiving most attention at present. These approaches are also discussed by McConkie (1977) and Reder (1978). A detailed account of Kintsch's work is given in Kintsch and Van Dijk (1978).

The criticisms of Shavelson and Stasz concerning these procedures, however, are serious. The notational systems are complex; they are subject to human judgement, and thus to some extent they are unreliable; and, of course, they overlook the contribution of the reader's prior knowledge to their understanding of the text. It would be a pity if the excitement generated by these new approaches caused one to forget the distinction to be drawn between the nominal stimuli (what is there) and the effective stimuli (what is perceived).

Ernst Rothkopf, in a controversial series of papers, has developed and extended the notion of nominal and effective stimuli in the context of what he has called *mathemagenic* behaviours in reading. Mathemagenic is a coined word derived from the Greek *mathein* and *gignesthai* and mathemagenic behaviours are defined as those activities that *give birth to learning* when reading. Typically, Rothkopf has concentrated on assessing the effects on learning of presenting questions before and after paragraphs of information, and how these questions affect the way readers process the text. For Rothkopf these processing strategies determine the nature of what is perceived (the effective stimuli), and these effective stimuli determine what is learned.

The most complete account of Rothkopf's work can be found in his paper 'Writing to teach and reading to learn' (Rothkopf, 1976). In this text, however, I have chosen to present a less well known but more recent extension of Rothkopf's work. Paper 1.4 is concerned with whether or not mathemagenic processes can be related to eye movements during reading.

Eye movement research has told us a great deal about reading processes. The eyes traverse lines of text in jumps, or saccades, and it is in the pauses between the jumps that the text is sampled. Good readers make fewer (and bigger) jumps than poor ones, with less backtracking (or regressions) over the material that has already been covered. The more difficult the text, the greater the number of pauses and regressions. The evidence suggests that readers sample chunks of text which are largely determined by syntactic boundaries — and so making these boundaries clearer to readers is one of the procedures advocated by some writers as a way of simplifying complex text (eg see Frase and Schwartz, 1979; Hartley, Paper 3.1).

The study of eye movements during reading could form a bridge between text-driven and reader-driven research. However, it seems unlikely that this will be the case for the methods of studying eye movements often place severe constraints upon the reader and the material that can be presented to him. Rothkopf's paper in this text describes one approach that avoids these difficulties to a certain extent — but only at a certain cost.

The approach can be criticized because Rothkopf has to infer from his data what is happening: he does not have a system that directly maps on to what the eye is looking at. In addition, despite his disclaimer to the contrary, one has to express some doubt as to how far a normal reading situation compares with being wired up in an experimental situation and reading a series of several hundred slides, each of which contains only a few lines of text.

Despite these comments, however, the point of Rothkopf's research still stands. Rothkopf is able to show that readers follow the instructions he sets them — to read for a specific purpose — but that this purpose is not clearly reflected in their eye movements. Thus both the assumption that eye movement research will tell us much of value about skilled reading, and the design of experiments in this field, need to be carefully considered.

The four papers in Part 1, then, concentrate on 'top-down'

processing in reading. Each, in its own way, has implications for writing. One or two of the implications have been spelled out, but most are left unsaid. Clearly text structure is important, and so too is the approach of the reader. Readers may skim, scan, browse, read carefully or casually. They may read from start to finish at one sitting, or they may read in diverse sequences over a period of weeks. It would be helpful if cognitive psychology could tell us something about how readers with different needs and backgrounds go about reading different kinds of text. Unfortunately, most research on 'top-down' processing does not yet seem to have got that far.

References

Anderson, R C, Spiro, R J and Anderson, M C (1978) Schemata as scaffolding for the representation of information in connected discourse. *American Educational Research Journal* 15 3: 433-46

Frase, L T and Schwartz, B J (1979) Typographical cues that facilitate comprehension. *Journal of Educational Psychology* 71 2: 197-206

Gibson, E J (1977) How perception really develops: a view from outside the network. In D LaBerge and S J Samuels (eds) *Basic Processes in Reading: Perception and Comprehension.* Hillsdale, N J: Erlbaum

Hartley, J and Davies, I K (1976) Pre-instructional strategies: the role of pre-tests, behavioural objectives, overviews and advance organizers. *Review of Educational Research* 46 2: 239-65

Kintsch, W and Van Dijk, T A (1978) Toward a model of text comprehension and production. *Psychological Review* 85 5: 363-94

LaBerge, D and Samuels, S J (eds) (1977) *Basic Processes in Reading: Perception and Comprehension.* Hillsdale, N J: Erlbaum

Macdonald-Ross, M (1979) Language in texts. In L S Shulman (ed) *Review of Research in Education* 6. Itasca, Ill: Peacock

McConkie, G W (1977) Learning from text. In L S Shulman (ed) *Review of Research in Education* 5. Itasca, Ill: Peacock

Meyer, R E (1979) Twenty years of research on advance organisers: assimilation theory is still the best predictor of results. *Instructional Science* 8 123-67

Reder, L M (1978) Comprehension and the retention of prose. Technical Report No 108, Center for the Study of Reading, University of Illinois at Urbana Champaign

Rothkopf, E Z (1976) Writing to teach and reading to learn: a perspective on the psychology of written communication. In N L Gage (ed) *Psychology of Teaching Methods.* Chicago: NSSE

Further Reading

Anderson, R C, Spiro, R J and Montague, W E (eds) (1977) *Schooling and the Acquisition of Knowledge.* Hillsdale, N J: Erlbaum

Macdonald-Ross, M (1979) Language in texts. In L S Shulman (ed) *Review of Research in Education* 6. Itasca, Ill: Peacock

Underwood, G and Holt, P O'B (1979) Cognitive skills in the reading process. *Journal of Research in Reading* 2. 2: 82-94

1.1 The facilitation of meaningful verbal learning in the classroom

DAVID P AUSUBEL

(Excerpt from Ausubel, D P (1978) The facilitation of meaningful verbal learning in the classroom. *Educational Psychologist* 12 2: 251-7. Reproduced with permission of the author and AERA.)
In this excerpt, Ausubel's discussion of his theory of memory is omitted, and so too are his comments on the freedom of educational enquiry in the United States, on the problems of access to research funds, and on editorial policies in educational journals.

In most scholarly disciplines, pupils acquire subject-matter knowledge largely through meaningful reception learning of presented concepts, principles, and factual information. In this paper, therefore, I first propose to distinguish briefly between reception and discovery learning on the one hand, and between meaningful and rote learning on the other. This will lead to a more extended discussion of the nature of meaningful verbal learning (ie an advanced form of meaningful reception learning) and the reasons it is predominant in the acquisition of subject matter; of the manipulable variables that influence its efficacy; and of some of the hazards connected with its use in the classroom setting. Then I will attempt to bolster the theoretical argument by referring to some of the recent supporting studies on short-term prose learning and by replying to some of the criticisms directed at my recent findings and methodology.

Reception versus discovery learning

The distinction between reception and discovery learning is not difficult to understand. In reception learning the principal content of what is to be learned is presented to the learner in more or less final form. The learning does not involve any discovery on his part. He is required only to internalize the material or incorporate it into his cognitive structure so that it is available for reproduction or other use at some future date. The essential feature of discovery learning, on the other hand, is that the principal content of what is to be learned is not given but must be discovered by the learner before he can internalize it: the distinctive and prior learning task, in other words, is to discover something. After this phase is completed, the discovered content is internalized just as in reception learning (Ausubel, 1961a).

Meaningful versus rote learning

Now this distinction between reception and discovery learning is so self-evident that it would be entirely unnecessary to labour the point were it not for the widespread but unwarranted belief that reception learning is invariably rote, and that discovery learning is invariably meaningful. Actually, each distinction constitutes an entirely independent dimension of learning. Thus reception and discovery learning can each be rote or meaningful, depending on the conditions under which learning occurs. In *both* instances meaningful learning takes place if the learning task is related in a non-arbitrary and non-verbatim fashion to the learner's existing structure of knowledge. This presupposes (i) that the learner manifests a *meaningful learning set*, that is, a disposition to relate the new learning task non-arbitrarily and substantively to what he already knows, and (ii) that the *learning task* is *potentially meaningful* to him, namely, relatable to his structure of knowledge on a non-arbitrary and non-verbatim basis. The first criterion, non-arbitrariness, implies some plausible or reasonable basis for establishing the relationship between the new material and existing relevant ideas in cognitive structure. The second criterion, substantiveness or non-verbatimness, implies that the potential meaningfulness of the material is never dependent on the exclusive use of particular words and no others, ie that the same concept or proposition expressed in synonymous language would induce substantially the same meaning (Ausubel, 1963; 1968).

The significance of meaningful learning for acquiring and retaining large bodies of subject matter becomes strikingly evident when we consider that human beings, unlike computers, can incorporate only very limited amounts of arbitrary and verbatim material, and also that they can retain such material only over very short intervals of time unless it is greatly overlearned and frequently reproduced. Hence the tremendous efficiency of meaningful learning as an information-processing and storing mechanism can be largely attributed to the two properties that make learning material potentially meaningful.

First, by non-arbitrarily relating potentially meaningful material to established ideas in his cognitive structure, the learner can effectively exploit his existing knowledge as an ideational and organizational matrix for the understanding, incorporation, and fixation of new knowledge. Non-arbitrary incorporation of a learning task into relevant portions of cognitive structure, so that new meanings are acquired, also implies that newly learned meanings become an integral part of an established ideational system; and because this type of anchorage to cognitive structure is possible, learning and retention are no longer dependent on the frail human capacity for acquiring and retaining arbitrary associations. This anchoring process also protects the newly incorporated material from the interfering effects of previously learned and subsequently encountered similar materials that are so damaging in rote learning. The temporal span of retention is therefore greatly extended.

Second, the substantive or non-verbatim nature of thus relating new material to, and incorporating it within, cognitive structure circumvents the drastic limitations imposed by the short item and time spans of verbatim learning on the processing and storing of information. Much more can obviously be apprehended and retained if the learner is required to assimilate only the substance of ideas rather than the verbatim language used in expressing them.

It is only when we realize that meaningful learning presupposes only the two aforementioned conditions, and that the rote-meaningful and reception-discovery dimensions of learning are entirely separate, that we can appreciate the important role of meaningful reception learning in classroom learning. Although, for various reasons, rote reception learning of subject matter is all too common at all academic levels, this need not be the case if expository teaching is properly conducted. We are gradually beginning to realize not only that good expository teaching can lead to meaningful reception learning, but also that discovery learning or problem solving is no panacea that guarantees meaningful learning. Problem solving in the classroom can be just as rote a process as the outright memorization of a mathematical formula without understanding the meaning of its component terms or their relationships to each other. This is obviously the case, for example, when students simply memorize rotely the sequence of steps involved in solving each of the 'type problems' in a course such as algebra (without having the faintest idea of what they are doing and why), and then apply these steps mechanically to the solution of a given problem, after using various rotely memorized cues to identify it as an exemplar of the problem type in question. They get the right answers and undoubtedly engage in discovery learning. But is this learning any more meaningful than the rote memorization of a geometrical theorem as an arbitrary series of connected words (Ausubel, 1961a; 1961b)?

It is important to bear in mind that the distinction between rote and meaningful learning is not absolute, but rather that the two kinds of learning are at opposite poles of a continuum (Ausubel, 1963). For example, representational learning, in contrast to concept and propositional learning, shares some of the verbatim properties of rote learning in that the name of an object, person, or concept has to be learned identically rather than substantively. Often, too, rote and meaningful learning go on simultaneously as when learning a poem by heart or learning the multiplication table.

In meaningful classroom learning, the balance between reception and discovery learning tends, for several reasons, to be weighted on the reception side. First, because of its inordinate time-cost, discovery learning is generally unfeasible as a *primary* means of acquiring large bodies of subject-matter knowledge. The very fact that the accumulated discoveries of millennia can be transmitted to each new generation in the course of childhood and youth is possibly only because it is so much less time-consuming for teachers to communicate and explain an idea meaningfully to pupils than to have them rediscover it by themselves. Second, although the extent and complexity of meaningful reception learning in pure verbal form is seriously limited in pupils who are either cognitively immature in general or unsophisticated in a particular discipline (Ausubel, 1968), the actual process of discovery *per se* is never required for the meaningful acquisition of knowledge. Typically it is more efficient pedagogy to compensate for such deficiencies by simply incorporating concrete-empirical props into expository teaching techniques. Finally, although the development of problem-solving ability as an end in itself is a legitimate objective of education, it is less central an objective, in my opinion, than that of learning subject matter. The ability to solve problems calls for traits such as flexibility, originality, resourcefulness, and problem-sensitivity that are not only less generously distributed in the population of learners than is the ability to understand and retain verbally presented ideas but are also less teachable. Thus relatively few good problem-solvers can be trained in comparison with the number of persons who can acquire a meaningful grasp of various subject-matter fields.

The nature of meaningful reception learning

Like all learning, reception learning is meaningful when the learning task is related in non-arbitrary and non-verbatim fashion to relevant aspects of what the learner already knows. It follows, therefore, from what was stated above that the first precondition for meaningful reception learning is that it takes place under the auspices of a *meaningful learning set.* Thus irrespective of how much potential meaning may inhere in a given proposition, if the learner's intention is to internalize it as an arbitrary and verbatim series of words, both the learning process and the learning outcome must be rote or meaningless.

One reason why pupils commonly develop a rote-learning set in relation to potentially meaningful subject matter is that they learn from sad experience that substantively correct answers lacking in verbatim correspondence to what they have been taught receive no credit whatsoever from certain teachers. Another reason is that because of a generally high level of anxiety or because of chronic failure experience in a given subject (reflective, in turn, of low aptitude or poor teaching), they lack confidence in their ability to learn meaningfully, and hence they perceive no alternative to panic apart from rote learning. This phenomenon is very familiar to mathematics teachers because of the widespread prevalence of 'number shock' or 'number anxiety'. Lastly, pupils may develop a rote-learning set if they are under excessive pressure to exhibit glibness, or to conceal, rather than admit and gradually remedy, original lack of genuine understanding. Under these circumstances it seems both easier and more important to create a spurious impression of facile comprehension by rotely memorizing a few key terms or sentences than to try to understand what they mean. Teachers frequently forget that pupils become very adept at using abstract terms with apparent appropriateness — when they have to — even though their understanding of the underlying concepts is virtually non-existent.

The second precondition for meaningful reception learning — that the learning task be *potentially meaningful or non-arbitrarily and substantively relatable to the learner's* structure of knowledge — is a somewhat more complex matter than meaningful learning set. At the very least it depends on the two factors involved in establishing this kind of relationship, that is, on the nature of the material to be learned, and on the availability and other properties of relevant content in the particular learner's cognitive structure. Turning first to the nature of the material, it must obviously be sufficiently plausible and reasonable that it could be related on a non-arbitrary and substantive basis to *any* hypothetical cognitive structure exhibiting the necessary ideational background. This is seldom a problem in school learning, since most subject-matter content unquestionably meets these specifications. But inasmuch as meaningful learning or the acquisition of meanings takes place in *particular* human beings, it is not sufficient that the learning task be relatable to relevant ideas simply in the abstract sense of the term. It is also necessary that the cognitive structure of the *particular* learner includes relevant ideational content to which the learning task can be related. Thus, in so far as meaningful learning outcomes in the classroom are concerned, various properties of the learner's cognitive structure constitute the most crucial and variable determinants of potential meaningfulness. These properties will be considered briefly but systematically in the following section.

Another serious problem in more advanced instances is that the learner must possess the necessary cognitive equipment meaningfully to process complex abstract propositions on a purely verbal basis, that is, to relate them to his cognitive structure in non-arbitrary and non-verbatim fashion without making use of concrete-empirical props (Ausubel, 1963; 1968). The existence of this capability, in turn, depends upon certain minimal levels of intellectual maturity and subject-matter sophistication which, generally speaking, cannot be assumed to be present among typical elementary school pupils, older intellectually retarded pupils, or complete neophytes in a given discipline regardless of their degree of general intellectual maturity. In the meaningful reception learning of highly abstract concepts and principles, such learners are therefore dependent upon the concurrent or recent prior availability of concrete and specific exemplars. Teachers who overlook this fact are clearly open to the charge of encouraging pupils to acquire rotely memorized and empty verbalisms.

The role of cognitive structure variables in meaningful verbal learning

Since, as suggested above, the potential meaningfulness of a learning task depends on its relatability to a particular learner's structure of knowledge in a given subject-matter or sub-area, it follows that *cognitive structure itself,* that is, both its substantive content and its major organizational properties, should be the principal factor influencing meaningful reception learning and retention in a classroom setting. According to this reasoning, it is largely by strengthening salient aspects of cognitive structure in the course of prior learning that new subject-matter learning can be facilitated. In principal, such deliberate manipulation of crucial cognitive structure variables — by shaping the content and arrangement of antecedent learning experience — should not meet with undue difficulty. It could be accomplished
(i) *substantively,* by using for organizational and integrative purposes those unifying concepts and principles in a given discipline that have

the greatest inclusiveness, generalizability, and explanatory power, and (ii) *programmatically*, by employing optimally effective methods of ordering the sequence of subject matter, constructing its internal logic and organization, and arranging practice sessions.

Both for research and for practical pedagogic purposes it is important to identify those manipulable properties or variables of existing cognitive structure that influence the meaningful reception learning of subject-matter knowledge. On logical grounds, three such variables seem self-evidently significant: (i) the *availability* in the learner's cognitive structure of relevant and otherwise appropriate ideas to which the new learning material can be non-arbitrarily and substantively related, so as to provide the kind of anchorage necessary for the incorporation and long-term retention of subject matter; (ii) the extent to which such relevant ideas are *discriminable* from similar new ideas to be learned so that the latter can be incorporated and retained as separately identifiable entities in their *own* right; and (iii) the *stability* and *clarity* of relevant anchoring ideas in cognitive structure, which affect both the strength of the anchorage they provide for new learning material and their degree of discriminability from similar new ideas in the learning task.

Availability of relevant anchoring ideas in cognitive structure

One of the principal reasons for rote or inadequately meaningful learning of subject matter is that pupils are frequently required to learn the specifics of an unfamiliar discipline before they have acquired an adequate foundation of relevant and otherwise appropriate anchoring ideas. Because of the unavailability of such ideas in cognitive structure to which the specifics can be non-arbitrarily and substantively related, the latter material tends to lack potential meaningfulness. But this difficulty can largely be avoided if the more general and inclusive ideas of the discipline, that is, those which typically have the most explanatory potential, are presented first and are then progressively differentiated in terms of detail and specificity. When adequately inclusive context is available new ideas can be assimilated into cognitive structure much more efficaciously, thereby facilitating both comprehension and retention of the new material.

In other words, meaningful reception learning and retention occur most readily and efficiently if, by virtue of prior learning, general and inclusive ideas are already available in cognitive structure to play a *subsuming* role relative to the more differentiated learning material that follows. This is the case because such subsuming ideas when established in the learner's structure of knowledge (i) have maximally specific and direct relevance for subsequent learning tasks; (ii) possess enough explanatory power to render otherwise arbitrary factual detail potentially meaningful (ie relatable to cognitive structure on a non-arbitrary basis); (iii) possess sufficient inherent stability to provide the firmest type of anchorage for detailed learning material; and

(iv) organize related new facts around a common theme, thereby integrating the component elements of new knowledge both with each other and with existing knowledge.

This proposition simply restates the principle that subsumptive learning is easier than superordinate learning. The argument for using organizers rests on the same principle. It is appreciated, however, that the learning of certain propositions requires the synthesis of previously acquired subordinate concepts or propositions, that is, superordinate learning (Gagné, 1962). Nevertheless, the need for periodic superordinate learning does not negate the proposition that both the psychological organization of knowledge and the optimal acquisition of subject matter *generally* conform to the pattern of subsumptive learning.

Gagné (1962) also conceives of individual knowledge as a set or hierarchy of intellectual skills or capabilities instead of in the substantive terms conceptualized above as an idiosyncratic body of concepts and propositions in cognitive structure, progressively differentiated from the more to the less inclusive. This, of course, is strictly a problem-solving view of knowledge that essentially repudiates the entire notion of reception learning on which subject-matter learning, in my opinion, largely rests. In a more recent statement, Gagné (1968) does recognize verbalizable knowledge but discounts its importance relative to intellectual skills.

ADVANCE ORGANIZERS

One of the more effective strategies that can be used for implementing the principle of progressive differentiation in the arrangement of subject-matter content involves the use of special introductory materials called 'organizers'. A given organizer is introduced in advance of the new learning task *per se*; is formulated in terms that, among other things, relate it to and take account of generally relevant background ideas already established in cognitive structure; and is presented at an appropriate level of abstraction, generality, and inclusiveness to provide specifically relevant anchoring ideas for the more differentiated and detailed material that is subsequently presented. An additional advantage of the organizer, besides guaranteeing the availability of specifically relevant anchoring ideas in cognitive structure, is that it makes explicit both its own relevance and that of the aforementioned background ideas for the new learning material. This is important because the mere availability of relevant anchoring ideas in cognitive structure does not assure the potential meaningfulness of a learning task unless this relevance is appreciated by the learner.

In short, the principal function of the organizer is to bridge the gap between what the learner already knows and what he needs to know before he can successfully learn the task at hand.

IN DEFENCE OF ORGANIZERS

The most pervasive criticism of advance-organizers is that their definition is vague and therefore that different researchers have varying concepts of what an organizer is and can only rely on intuition in constructing one — since nowhere, it is alleged, is it specified how they are to be constructed. The critics apparently ignore the fact that I have devoted approximately 23 pages in my educational psychology text (Ausubel, 1968) to the nature and definition of an organizer and how it affects information-processing, including a discussion of how to construct an organizer on the topic of biological evolution. The same material also appears in briefer form in each of my major studies (Ausubel, 1960; Ausubel and Fitzgerald, 1961; Ausubel and Fitzgerald, 1962; Ausubel and Youssef, 1963) on advance-organizers. And, apart from describing organizers in general terms with an appropriate example, one cannot be more specific, for the construction of a given organizer always depends on the nature of the learning material, the age of the learner, and his degree of prior familiarity with the learning passage. From the exhaustive and explicit general discussion of the definition, nature and effects of an organizer in my various publications (Ausubel, 1960; Ausubel and Fitzgerald, 1961; Ausubel and Fitzgerald, 1962; Ausubel and Youssef, 1963), plus the description of how to construct an organizer for a particular topic (Ausubel, 1968), there should be no difficulty in different researchers constructing comparable operationalized organizers for particular learning passages and in replicating each others' studies. Joyce and Weil (1972), for example, had no difficulty in operationalizing the distinction between expository and comparative organizers in relation to teaching concepts and facts in multiplication.

Somewhat equivocal findings have been reported for studies involving advance organizers (Hartley and Davies, 1976). In part this is due to failure to adhere to my explicit criteria of what an organizer is (see above), and in part to various methodological deficiencies in research design. One of the commonest misconceptions about the organizer studies stems from Anderson's frequently quoted criticism in his well-known *Annual Review* article (1967). He stated:

> Organizers are reported to contain nothing which could be directly helpful in answering post-test questions. Instead Ausubel believes that organizers facilitate retention in an indirect manner by providing 'ideational scaffolding'. The weak link in the argument is that none of the studies thus far has included controls to show that the organizer alone does not improve performance. Therefore the possibility remains that the organizers have a direct rather than an indirect effect.

Anderson apparently neglected to read the clear statement in the procedure of two of the organizer studies that described the use of a special control group, in addition to the control group studying a non-organizer introduction, that studied the organizer alone without the learning passage.

Still another criticism of organizers (Peeck, 1970) is that they are too time-consuming to be efficient adjunct aids and that, therefore, the time spent on them would be just as well or better spent studying the learning passage itself. To support this argument, Peeck simply understates by half the time actually spent by my subjects on the learning passage that is reported in the research paper he cites

(Ausubel and Fitzgerald, 1962). He also ignores the relative amounts of time spent in studying learning and organizer passages respectively, varying from 5 to 8 to 1 in favour of the former, that are reported in my three other organizer studies (Ausubel, 1961; Ausubel and Fitzgerald, 1961; Ausubel and Youssef, 1963).

In my opinion, our understanding of the effects of organizers would advance much more rapidly (i) if the authors of the numerous critiques would first read the description and criteria of an organizer that has been set forth in numerous of my articles and books before castigating it as vague and intuitive in nature, and (ii) if they would also consult the original primary sources on the research methodology used in the organizer studies, instead of quoting the same inaccurate and misleading secondary sources that bear little relation to the actual experimental procedures employed.

A recent study by Barnes (1972) indicates that organizers exert not only a statistically significant but also a practically important effect on school learning. Statistical analysis of her findings to assess 'practical significance' showed that in 98 per cent of the cases an advance-organizer resulted in a 10 to 18 per cent increase in mean learning score. Compared to groups not using an advance-organizer, the percentage of increase in mean concept transfer score effected by an organizer varied from 16 per cent to 50 per cent depending on the type of learning task involved.

Recent research on the use of adjunct questions in prose learning by Rickards (1976), Rickards and DiVesta (1974) and Rickards and Hatcher (1975) indicates that once the rote-learning methodological bias of requiring verbatim recall of single text phrases is discarded in favour of demanding substantive learning of entire paragraphs, and when the vague and global 'mathemagenic' variable is replaced by differential variables permitting the testing of more specific explanatory hypotheses regarding the facilitating effect of adjunct questions, superordinate concepts in the adjunct questions facilitate the learning of subordinate textual material in much the same way that advance-organizers do. Also, consistent with the findings of the organizer studies, these latter workers found that conceptual *pre*questions yield higher recall and more highly structured memories than conceptual *post*questions, that *conceptual* prequestions unlike *verbatim* postquestions increase *delayed* as well as *immediate* recall, and that meaningful postquestions, like advance-organizers, tend differentially to facilitate the recall of *poor* as opposed to *good* comprehenders.

References

Anderson, R C (1967) Educational psychology. In P R Farnworth, O McNemar and Q McNemar (eds) *Annual Review of Psychology*. Palo Alto, Calif: Annual Reviews
Ausubel, D P (1960) The use of advance organizers in the learning and retention of meaningful verbal material. *Journal of Educational Psychology* 51: 267-72
Ausubel, D P (1961a) In defense of verbal learning. *Educational Theory* 11: 15-25

Ausubel, D P (1961b) Learning by discovery: rationale and mystique. *Bulletin. National Association of Secondary School Principals* 45: 18-58

Ausubel, D P (1963) *The Psychology of Meaningful Verbal Learning.* New York: Grune & Stratton

Ausubel, D P (1968) *Educational Psychology: A Cognitive View.* New York: Holt, Rinehart & Winston

Ausubel, D P and Fitzgerald, D (1961) The role of discriminability in meaningful verbal learning and retention. *Journal of Educational Psychology* 52: 266-74

Ausubel, D P and Fitzgerald, D (1962) Organizer, general background, and antecedent learning variables in sequential verbal learning. *Journal of Educational Psychology* 53: 243-9

Ausubel, D P and Youssef, M (1963) The role of discriminability in meaningful parallel learning. *Journal of Educational Psychology* 54: 331-6

Barnes, Henrietta L (1972) An investigation of the effects of differential instructional material on concept acquisition and transfer. (Doctoral dissertation, Michigan State University, 1972). *Dissertation Abstracts International* 33: 2207

Gagné, R M (1962) The acquisition of knowledge. *Psychological Review* 69: 355-65

Gagné, R M (1968) Learning hierarchies. *Educational Psychologist* 6: 1-3, 6-9

Hartley, J and Davies, I K (1976) Pre-instructional strategies: the role of pre-tests, behavioural objectives, overviews and advance organizers. *Review of Educational Research* 46 2: 239-65

Joyce, B and Weil, M (1972) *Models of Teaching.* New York: Prentice-Hall

Peeck, J (1970) Effect of prequestions on delayed retention of prose material. *Journal of Educational Psychology* 61: 241-6

Rickards, J P (1976) Interaction of position and conceptual level of adjunct questions on immediate and delayed retention of text. *Journal of Educational Psychology* 68 2: 210-17

Rickards, J P and Hatcher, Catherine W (1976) Meaningful learning postquestions as semantic cues for poor readers. Unpublished manuscript. Department of Education, Purdue University

Rickards, J P and DiVesta, F J (1974) Types and frequency of questions in processing textual material. *Journal of Educational Psychology* 66: 354-62

1.2 Schema-directed processes in language comprehension

RICHARD C ANDERSON

(Paper, with the same title, from A Lesgold *et al* (eds) (1978)
Cognitive Psychology and Instruction. New York: Plenum Press.
Reproduced with permission of the author and the publishers.)

This paper will attempt to develop the thesis that the knowledge a
person already possesses has a potent influence on what he or she will
learn and remember from exposure to discourse. It begins by outlining
some assumptions about the characteristics of the structures in which
existing knowledge is packaged. Next, based on these assumptions, it
presents a speculative theoretical treatment of the processes involved
in assimilating the information and ideas in discourse. This is the topic
that will be given most attention in this paper. Data consistent with the
theory will be summarized. It should be emphasized in advance,
however, that the experiments to date show at most that the theoretical
notions are interesting and plausible. The research has not advanced to
the point where there is a firm basis for choosing between competing
accounts. Finally, some observations will be made about the implications
of this research for education.

Schematic knowledge structures

Like many others (Ausubel, 1963; Minsky, 1975; Schank and Abelson,
1975; Bower, 1976; Rumelhart and Ortony, 1977), I find it useful to
postulate that knowledge is incorporated in abstract structures that
have certain properties. These structures will be called *schemata*, in
deference to Piaget (1926) and Bartlett (1932) who introduced the
term to psychology. What follows is an amalgam of my own thinking
and that of other theorists.

   A schema represents generic knowledge; that is, it represents what
is believed to be generally true of a class of things, events, or
situations. A schema is conceived to contain a *slot*, or placeholder, for
each component. For instance, a Face schema (Palmer, 1975) includes
slots for a mouth, nose, eyes, and ears. Encoding a particular object is
conceived to be a matter of filling the slots in the schema with the
features of the object. Part of schematic knowledge is the specification
of the constraints on what normally can fill the slots. An object will be
recognized as a face only if it has features that qualify as eyes, a mouth,
a nose, and so on. To be sure, the constraints on the slots in a Face
schema are flexible enough that we can tolerate considerable variation,

as in a sketchy drawing in a comic strip, the stylized and transformed representation in a cubist painting, or the exaggerated portrayal in a political cartoon (Gombrich, 1972). Nonetheless, there are limits beyond which an object is no longer a face.

The encoded representation of a particular thing or event consists of a copy of the schemata that were brought to bear in interpretation, plus the information inserted in the schemata's slots. Such particularized representations are called *instantiated* schemata (cf Anderson *et al* 1976). The slots in a schema may be instantiated with information that could be said to be 'given' in the situation, or message, but often slots are filled by inference.

A schema is a knowledge 'structure' because it indicates the typical relations among its components. A Face schema will represent the relative spatial positioning of the eyes and nose, for instance. Another attribute of schemata with structural significance is that they exist at various levels of abstraction and embed one within another (Rumelhart and Ortony, 1977). Contrast the knowledge that (a) a face has eyes, (b) an eye has a pupil, (c) a pupil dilates in the dark. It is apparent that these propositions are arranged in decreasing order to importance to face. This variation in importance can be captured by assuming that Eye is a subschema embedded in the Face schema; and that Pupil, in turn, is a subschema of Eye. It is assumed that a person can employ a dominant schema without necessarily accessing the knowledge available in embedded subschemata. On the other hand, should the occasion demand it, the full meaning of a subschema can be unpacked and a deeper interpretation given.

To comprehend a message is to place a construction upon it that gives a coherent formulation of its contents. In schema terms, a 'coherent formulation' means a one-to-one correspondence between the slots in a schema and the 'givens' in the message. It is instructive to examine the comprehension of a sentence devised by Bransford and McCarrell (1974), for which a subsuming schema is not readily apparent: *The notes were sour because the seams split.* The syntax is simple and the individual words are easy, yet the sentence as a whole does not immediately make sense to most people. However, the sentence becomes meaningful as soon as one hears the clue *bagpipe*. Why is this clue effective? An answer is that it enables the conception of a framework that maps on to a possible world. Within the framework, each word in the sentence can be construed to have a referent with a sensible role to play in the possible world. That is to say, the clue allows one to invoke a schema containing slots for the objects, actions, and qualities mentioned in the sentence. The schema gives a good account of the sentence and, therefore, there is the subjective sense that it has been comprehended.

Conceptions of the reading process

According to one view, reading is a 'bottom-up' or 'data-driven' process (Bobrow and Norman, 1975). There is a series of discrete processing stages, each corresponding to a level of linguistic analysis. Analysis proceeds from the most primitive low-order level to the most complex high-order level. As a first step, feature analysers are brought to bear on discriminate horizontal, vertical, and oblique line segments; open and closed loops; intersection with a horizontal plane; and so on. From these, letters are identified. Strings of letters are analysed into clusters with morphophonemic significance. Words are recognized. Strings of words are parsed into phrase constituents. Word meanings are retrieved from the subjective lexicon. Eventually, a semantic interpretation of a sentence is produced. Sentence meaning is conceived to be the deterministic product of the lower-order levels of analysis and, presumably, the meaning of a text is a concatenation of the meanings of its component sentences.

Another view holds that reading is essentially a 'top-down' or 'conceptually driven' process. Rather than analysing a text squiggle by squiggle, the reader samples it to confirm or reject hypotheses about its content. In other words, reading is conceived to be a psycholinguistic guessing game (Goodman, 1976). The reader's expectations represent a form of preprocessing that should expedite and speed up subsequent analysis. Occasionally, expectation would be predicted to override the print, as appears to happen when children make miscues in oral reading, substituting semantically related words in place of those given.

There is an interesting difference between the bottom-up and top-down theories about reading in their treatment of ambiguity. According to the former view, a high-order process does not affect low-order processes. Each stage takes as its input the output from the preceding stage. If an ambiguity arises at any stage, the alternative interpretations are sent forward for resolution at a later point. For instance, it would be supposed that all of the meanings of a homonym are assessed. Eventually, if the message as a whole is not ambiguous, a process operating on syntax, semantics, or pragmatics at the phrase, sentence, or text level, will permit a choice among the homonym's senses.

From the perspective of a bottom-up model, reading is a matter of growing a tree of possible interpretations. Any stage may add new branches, or prune some of those already there. From the perspective of a model that admits of possible top-down influences, on the other hand, not all of the branches need be grafted on to the tree in the first place. Emerging high-order expectations may forestall some interpretations before they occur. With respect to the meaning of a homonym, it might be expected that normally only the contextually most appropriate meaning would be accessed. This is the implication of research by Schvaneveldt, Meyer, and Becker (Note 1), using a lexical decision task. For instance, *money* was identified as a word faster in the sequence *save, bank, money* than in either *river, bank, money,* or the control sequences *save, date, money* or *fig, date, money.* If all senses of a word were activated, *bank* should have primed *money* to some extent, even when preceded by *river,* but this did not happen. Converging evidence has been obtained by Swinney and Hakes (1976) who found, using a phoneme monitoring task, that a disambiguating context of a sentence or two can constrain the interpretation of a subsequently encountered homonym.

Of course, it is surely simplistic to imagine that reading is either a bottom-up or top-down process. Rumelhart (1976) has presented a persuasive case that reading must involve continuous interactions among many levels of analysis. This paper deals with how concepts brought to a text influence comprehension, learning, and recall; but, to assert the obvious, the processes involved in analysing the print itself are also crucial.

Schemata and text interpretation

We have used various devices to get people to bring different schemata into play when reading text. Several studies have employed whole passages that were ambiguous. For instance, Schallert (1976) constructed passages that could be given two distinct interpretations. One of the passages told of a character who was afraid that his best pitchers would crack in the heat. The passage was entitled 'Worries of a baseball manager' or 'Worries of a glassware factory manager'. Scores on a multiple-choice test — constructed so that the interpretation of pitcher and other similarly ambiguous elements could be distinguished — indicated that the interpretation of this and other passages was strongly related to the title.

In the absence of strong contextual cues, such as titles and introductions, the schemata by which people assimilate ambiguous passages can be expected to depend upon their background and life situation. Anderson *et al* (1977) wrote the following passage:

> Every Saturday night four good friends get together. When Jerry, Mike, and Pat arrived, Karen was sitting in her living room writing some notes. She quickly gathered the cards and stood up to greet her friends at the door. They followed her into the living room but as usual they couldn't agree on exactly what to play. Jerry eventually took a stand and set things up. Finally, they began to play. Karen's recorder filled the room with soft and pleasant music. Early in the evening, Mike noticed Pat's hand and the many diamonds. As the night progressed the tempo of play increased. Finally, a lull in the activities occurred. Taking advantage of this, Jerry pondered the arrangement in front of him. Mike interrupted Jerry's reverie and said, 'Let's hear the score.' They listened carefully and commented on their performance. When the comments were all heard, exhausted but happy, Karen's friends went home.

Most people interpret this passage in terms of an evening of cards, but it can be interpreted as being about a rehearsal of a woodwind ensemble. Another passage is usually perceived to be about a convict planning his escape from prison; however, it is possible to see it in terms of a wrestler hoping to break the hold of an opponent. These passages were read by a group of physical education students and by a group of music students. Scores on a multiple-choice test and theme-revealing disambiguations and intrusions in free recall indicated that the interpretations given to passages bore the expected strong relationships to the subject's background. An example of an intrusion showing a card theme was, 'Mike sees that Pat's hand has a lot of hearts.' One showing a music theme was, 'As usual they couldn't decide on the piece of music to play.'

Of special significance to the discussion in this section are responses on a debriefing questionnaire. Subjects were asked whether they became aware of another possible interpretation of either passage. The interesting fact is that 62 per cent reported that another interpretation *never* occurred to them, while an additional 20 per cent said they became aware of an alternative interpretation during the multiple-choice test or when responding to the debriefing questionnaire. Less than 20 per cent said they were aware of a second interpretation while reading a passage. Many people would not wish to place too much stock in retrospective reports. Still, these are the results that would be expected on the basis of top-down, schema-based processing.

Gordon Bower (Note 2) and his co-workers at Stanford have completed several studies that parallel those done in my laboratory. One study involved stories about characters who visit the doctor. An examination is completed and the doctor smiles and says, 'Well, it seems my expectations have been confirmed.' The base story was, in Bower's words, 'a sort of neutral Rorschach card on to which subjects would project their own meanings'. The introduction to one version of the story describes the character as worried about whether she is pregnant. Here subjects tended to recall the doctor's remark as, 'Your fears have been confirmed' or simply, 'You're pregnant.' An alternative introduction described the main character as a wrestler worried about being underweight. Subjects who read this version remembered that the doctor told the character he was gaining weight.

In another study, Bower and his associates used a story about a series of mishaps that happen when a TV commercial involving water skiing is filmed. Alternate introductions were written to cause the reader to identify with either Harry, the boatdriver, or Rich, the water skier. On a recognition test, subjects tended to rate, as explicitly part of the text, statements formulated from the perspective of the character with whom they were led to identify. For instance, more subjects given the water skier the boatdriver introduction identified, 'The handle was torn from Rich's grasp as the boat unexpectedly jumped ahead', as a proposition from the text. The reverse was true of the parallel formulation of the same episode written from the boatdriver's perspective: 'Rich slipped and lost control and the handle went skipping across the water.'

The general point illustrated by these experiments is that the meaning of a text arises in an interaction between the characteristics of the message and the reader's existing knowledge and analysis of context. Ambiguous passages are useful for making transparent the role of world knowledge and context. However, there is every reason to suppose that they are equally important when comprehending material that would be said to be 'unambiguous'. A message has an unambiguous meaning just in case there is consensus in a linguistic community about the schemata that normally will subsume it. The role of knowledge of the world is merely less obvious to the psychologist doing prose memory research in these cases, for the author, reader, and the judges who score the protocols employ complementary schemata, and thus give essentially the same interpretation to the material.

Schemata and the significance of text elements

Since Binet and Henri (1894; also, Thieman and Brewer, in press) worked with French school children at the end of the nineteenth century, it has been known that people are more likely to learn and remember the important than the unimportant elements of a prose passage. No doubt, authors provide linguistic cues to the important points in a text; however, I shall argue that importance is largely a derivative of the schemata the reader imposes on the text.

The schema brought to bear on a text will contain embedded subschemata that generally can be conceived to form a hierarchy. The position of a subschema in the hierarchy is one index of its importance. Significant text information instantiates higher-order slots in the structure. The schema could be said to 'give' such information its importance. It follows that the importance of a text element would vary if readers were caused to invoke schemata in which the text element played a greater or lesser role. This hypothesis has been investigated in two lines of research in my laboratory.

Anderson, Spiro, and Anderson (1977) wrote two passages — one about dining at a fancy restaurant, the other a closely comparable story about shopping at a supermarket. The same 18 items of food, attributed to the same characters, were mentioned in the same order in the two stories. Subjects read one of the stories and then, after an interval, attempted recall.

The first prediction was that the food items would be better learned and recalled when presented in the restaurant narrative. The reasoning was that a dining-at-a-fancy-restaurant schema contains a more finely articulated structure; that is, certain categories of food will be ordered and served. Also, there are constraints on the items that can fit into these categories: hot dogs will not be the main course, nor Koolaid the beverage. Just about any food or beverage fits a supermarket schema. This prediction was confirmed in two experiments.

The second experiment involved food categories determined on the basis of a norming study to have a high or a low probability of being in an individual's restaurant schema. An entrée and a drink during the meal are examples, respectively, of the high and low categories. An entrée is an essential element. No fine meal would be complete without one. A drink during dinner is a less central, perhaps optional, element. Subjects who read the restaurant story recalled substantially more of the foods and beverages from three high probability categories than subjects who read the supermarket story. In contrast, there was no difference between the two passages on items from three low probability categories. This shows that the restaurant narrative did not indiscriminately facilitate performance, as would be expected if it were more interesting, coherent, or memorable overall. Instead, as predicted, there was selective enhancement of items from just those categories that have special importance in a restaurant schema.

The next prediction was that subjects would more accurately ascribe foods to characters when given the restaurant story. Who gets what food has significance within a restaurant schema, whereas it does not matter in a supermarket who throws the brussels sprouts into the shopping cart. In both experiments, the conditional probability of attributing a food item to the correct character, given that the item had been recalled, was higher among subjects who received the restaurant story than the supermarket story.

Finally, it was predicted that order-of-recall of food items would correspond more closely to order-of-mention for subjects who read the restaurant passage. There is not, or need not be, a prescribed sequence for selecting foods in a grocery store, but at a fine restaurant it would be peculiar to have a strawberry parfait before the escargot. In the first experiment, the average correlation between recall order and order of mention was significantly higher for the group that received the restaurant narrative. The trend was in the same direction, but not significant in the second experiment, perhaps because recall was attempted shortly after reading. There had been an hour and a half interval before recall in the first study. Maybe surface order information is available shortly after reading, and this makes the generic order information, inherent in a schema, superfluous.

The experiments just described used the device of weaving the same information into two different narratives in order to get readers to assimilate that information in two different schemata. The device in a second, parallel line of research was to ask subjects to read a narrative from alternative points of view that, presumably, caused them to invoke different schemata. Pichert and Anderson (1977) asked subjects to read stories from one of two perspectives or from no directed perspective. One of the stories ostensibly was about what two boys do when skipping school. They go to one of the boys' homes, since his mother is never home on Thursdays. It is a well-to-do family with a luxuriously appointed home. It has a number of attractive features, such as spacious grounds, a tall hedge that hides the house from the road, and a new stone fireplace. However, it also has some defects, including a musty basement and a leaky roof. The family has many valuable possessions — silverware, a coin collection, a colour TV set. Readers were asked to approach the story from the viewpoint of a burglar or a prospective homebuyer. Obviously, a coin collection is important to a burglar, but unimportant to a homebuyer. The opposite is true of a musty basement or a leaking roof. In a preliminary experiment, the average intercorrelation of rated idea unit importance across three perspectives on each of two stories was determined to be quite low, which is in itself evidence that schemata determine the significance of text elements.

The next experiment manipulated perspective to investigate the effects of schemata on text learning and recall. The previously obtained ratings of idea unit importance were strongly related to immediate recall and, independently, to delayed recall. This was true just of ratings obtained under the perspective the subject was directed to take, not other possible but non-operative perspectives. Ratings of importance under the operative perspective was a significant predictor of recall in five of six stepwise multiple regression analyses (one for each of three perspectives on each of two stories). It was the only significant predictor in four of these analyses.

The past few years have seen increasing refinement of the notion of importance in terms of theories of text structure (cf Kintsch, 1974; Meyer, 1975; Rumelhart, 1975; Mandler and Johnson, 1977). These are more properly regarded as theories of the structure of the schemata by which a linguistic community normally will subsume a message, as some theorists expressly acknowledge. But a text need not be read 'normally'. Depending on the reader's goal, task, or perspective, he or she may override the conventions a linguistic community ordinarily uses to structure a text. When the schema changes, then, so will the importance of text elements.

Possible effects of schemata on encoding and retrieving text information

This section gives a more detailed account of some of the mechanisms by which schemata may affect the processing of text information. The central phenomenon to be explained is the primacy of important text in recall, illustrated in the preceding section.

Significant text elements might be better recalled because they are better learned. In other words, the effect might be attributable to a process at work when a passage is read. An attractive possibility is that the schema provides the device by which a reader allocates attention. Extra attention might be devoted to important text elements, whereas insignificant elements might be skimmed or processed less deeply. A second possibility on the encoding side is that a schema provides 'ideational scaffolding', to use Ausubel's (1963) apt term, for selected categories of text information. A schema will contain slots for important information, but may contain no slots, or only optional slots, for unimportant information. According to this view, information gets encoded precisely because there is a niche for it in the structure. This is an interesting idea, but as yet I have been unable to think of any implication of the ideational scaffolding hypothesis that might permit it to be distinguished from the regulation-of-attention notion.

The fact that people recall more important that unimportant text elements might be due to processes at work when information is retrieved and used instead of, or in addition to, processes acting when the information was initially encoded. There are several possible retrieval mechanisms that fall out of a schema-theoretic orientation, which might account for the primacy of important text information in recall.

The first can be called the 'retrieval plan' hypothesis. The idea is that the schema provides the structure for searching memory. Consider for illustration the burglar perspective on the story about two boys playing 'hooky' from school. The rememberer will possess the generic knowledge that burglars need to have a way of entering a premise; that they are interested in finding valuable, portable objects that can be 'fenced' easily; that they are concerned about avoiding detection; and that they aim to make clean 'getaways'. Memory search is presumed to start with the generic concerns of a burglar. Generic concerns implicate selected categories of text information. For instance, the fact that all burglars need to enter the place to be robbed is assumed to provide a mental pathway or implicit cue for the specific proposition that the side door was kept unlocked. On the other hand, information in a text that may have been encoded, but does not connect with the schema guiding memory search, should be relatively inaccessible. For example, the passage about the boys playing hookey from school asserts that the house has new stone siding. Presumably, there are no pointers in a burglary schema to information of this type and, thus, this information is unlikely to be retrieved even if it were stored.

We have named another possible retrieval explanation of the 'output editing' hypothesis. The assumption is that the schema contains within itself an index of importance. The rememberer establishes a response criterion based jointly on this index, motivation, and demand characteristics. There are several variants on how output editing might work. In crudest form, the subject simply might not write down information that occurred to him or her because it falls below the response criterion.

I will consider, finally, the possibility that people may remember more important than unimportant information because of a process of 'inferential reconstruction' (Spiro, 1977). There may be information missing from memory, either because the information was not stored, or because it was forgotten. The conceptual machinery of the schema and the information that can be recalled may permit the rememberer to fill gaps by inference. Anderson, Spiro, and Anderson (1977) have illustrated how the process might work as follows. Suppose that a person is trying to recall a story about a meal at a fine restaurant (see the preceding section). The beverage served with the meal cannot be recalled, but since there is a slot in a restaurant schema for such an item, the rememberer is led to try to reconstruct one. If the information that beef was served for the main course can be recalled, then red wine may be generated as a candidate beverage. There are a couple of possible scenarios at this point. Red wine might be produced simply as a plausible guess. A good guess and an element actually remembered often will be indistinguishable to a judge, particularly one applying lenient, gist-scoring criteria. Or, it might be that once a candidate element, such as red wine, has been produced, it is checked against an otherwise inaccessible memory trace. To say this another way, the process might be one of generation, followed by recognition and verification (Kintsch, 1974). In any event, the foregoing gives an account of the primacy of important text information, for the schema is more likely to contain the concepts for reconstructing important than unimportant elements.

Evidence for encoding and retrieval benefits

We have completed several experiments to determine whether schemata have independent effects on the encoding and retrieval of text information and, if so, to begin to pin down the specific mechanisms that are responsible. My student, James Pichert, and I (Anderson and Pichert, 1977) asked undergraduates to read the story about two boys playing hookey from school, from the perspective of either a burglar or a homebuyer. The story was recalled once from the same perspective from which it had been read. Then everyone recalled the story for a second time. Half of the subjects did so again from the same perspective. The other half changed perspectives. Based on previously obtained ratings, a cluster of information important to a burglar but unimportant to a homebuyer (eg a collection of rare coins) and another cluster important to a homebuyer but unimportant to a burglar (eg a fireplace) were identified. As expected, subjects produced on the second recall a significant amount of new information — that is, information that had not been recalled the first time — that was important in the light of the new perspective, but that was unimportant in terms of the perspective operative when the passage was read and recalled the first time. There does not appear to be any way to explain this finding solely in terms of encoding mechanisms. Thus, it seems to be rather strong evidence for a retrieval mechanism independent of encoding.

In the preceding section, three explanations within schema theory for an influence on retrieval were discussed. To review briefly, the first is the retrieval plan hypothesis: a new schema will furnish implicit cues for different types of text information. The second is the output editing hypothesis: when the schema changes, different types of information are above a response criterion. The third is the inferential reconstruction hypothesis: a new schema will provide the concepts for inferring different categories of important but unavailable information.

In a follow-up study, Pichert and I replicated the retrieval benefit identified in the experiment described above. We also collected subjects' introspective descriptions of the processes of learning and remembering. Most subjects discussed strategies and tactics for remembering in a manner consistent with the retrieval plan hypothesis. A number said, in so many words, that reviewing the concerns of a burglar or homebuyer caused them to think of previously unrecalled information related to these concerns. For example, one subject said, 'I was thinking . . . was there anything wrong with the house? And then I remembered the basement was damp.' Another said, 'I remembered [the colour TV] in the second one, but not the first one. I was thinking about things to steal, things to take and steal . . .'

The self-report protocols generally gave little support to the output editing hypothesis. Most subjects insisted that they wrote down everything they could remember. John Surber, another student of mine, manipulated the incentive for recall. He reasoned that if the increment in recall in the perspective-shift group were due to output editing, then the increment would disappear under conditions of high incentive. What he actually found was a difference in favour of subjects who shifted perspective, regardless of whether a 25 per cent bonus was paid for each new idea. Thus, two strands of evidence weigh against an output editing interpretation of the results of this series of experiments. I do not wish to argue that people never suppress information available

35

to them, only that this probably was not a major factor under the conditions that have prevailed in our research.

Spiro (1977) has obtained convincing evidence for reconstructive processes in memory for discourse. Subjects read a story about a couple engaged to be married. The man is strongly against having children. In one version of the story, the women is elated to find this out because she does not want children either. In the other version, she is horrified because a large family is important to her. Several minutes after reading the story, subjects are told either that the couple did get married or that they broke up. Based on the assumption that people's commonsense psychology of interpersonal relations could be represented in terms of Heider's principle of structural balance, Spiro predicted the particular types of 'reconciling errors' subjects would introduce into their recall protocols when the situation described to them was imbalanced. For instance, when the couple got married despite the serious disagreement about having children, it was argued that subjects would modify the story to reconcile the incongruity by claiming, for instance, that 'the problem was resolved when they found out that Margie couldn't have children anyway.' The expected types of reconciling inferences appeared with increasing frequency over a retention interval of six weeks. Subjects were more confident their inferences had been part of the story than they were that propositions that had an explicit basis in the text had been present.

The perspective shift studies described earlier in this section all showed a retrieval benefit but, for a couple of reasons, none clearly established that schemata have an encoding influence as well. This was the purpose of another experiment completed by Jim Pichert and me. A story was recalled, just once, from either the same perspective from which it was read, or from a different one. Both the perspective from which the story was read and the perspective from which it was recalled, which were orthogonal factors in the design employed, had a substantial effect on performance. Thus, both encoding and retrieval influences were demonstrated.

When asked how the assigned perspective affected the manner in which the story was read, most subjects described a process of directing attention to important elements. For example, one subject told to take the burglar perspective said, 'I kept in mind all of the critical things a burglar would be looking for, such as getting in and out, the items that it would be easy to move and take from the house itself.' One assigned the homebuyer perspective reported, 'I spent most of the time looking for items to be interested in when buying a house.' A straightforward way to get converging evidence on the regulation-of-attention hypothesis would be to time subjects on chunks of text material whose importance has been manipulated in some way. We have not done experiments of this type yet.

In summary, this section reviewed evidence that a schema operative when a passage is read affects encoding, possibly by directing attention to text elements that are significant in the light of the schema. Evidence was presented that shows that the schema affects remembering later, probably in part by providing the plan for searching memory. Schemata probably also provide the basis for inferential elaboration when a passage is read, and inferential reconstruction when there are gaps or inconsistencies in memory.

Implications of schema theory for education

Text information is interpreted, organized, and retrieved in terms of high-level schemata. It follows that the student who does not possess relevant schemata is going to have trouble learning and remembering the information encountered in stories and textbooks. Consider, for illustration, the description of an unfamiliar nation in a geography text (cf Anderson, Spiro, and Anderson, 1977). The mature student will bring to bear an elaborate Nation schema that incorporates well-formed subschemata for assimilating information about the topography, climate, economy, culture, and political system. It is only a slight over-simplification to say that the task for the advanced student is simply to fill the slots in an already formed schema with the particular information in the text about the unfamiliar nation. The information will be readily acquired and, once acquired, easily retrieved when needed.

How about the young reader who, for the sake of the argument, will be assumed not to possess a refined Nation schema? In the worst case, a description of an unfamiliar nation would be unintelligible to such a reader, like the Bransford and Johnson (1973) passages for mature readers, where a schema-evoking context was not provided. More likely, the young reader will have a partly formed Nation schema sufficient for some level of understanding of the material, but that will not enable a representation of great depth or breadth.

Whether people possess the schemata appropriate for assimilating a text should be an important source of individual differences in reading comprehension. Smiley *et al* (1977) have obtained some evidence suggesting that this may be the case. Good and poor readers drawn from seventh-grade classes read one folktale and listened to another. Following each story, they were tested for comprehension and recall. Under both reading and listening conditions, good readers recalled a greater proportion of the stories, and the likelihood of their recalling a particular element was an increasing function of the element's structural importance. Poor readers not only recalled less of the stories, but their recall was not as clearly related to variations in importance. Smiley *et al* went on to show that it was necessary to test children as young as first grade before finding another group that showed as little sensitivity to gradations of importance as poor reading seventh graders (see also Brown and Smiley, 1977). On the other hand, Perfetti and Lesgold (in press) have summarized several studies that, by and large, have not revealed substantial differences between good and poor readers in sensitivity to sentence structure or text structure.

Thus, based on evidence already available, it is too early to say whether variations in high-level schemata, or facility in using these schemata, will turn out to be a consistent difference between good and poor readers. I hope only to have shown that this is a very reasonable place to look for differences. If differences are consistently found, there will be implications for diagnosis, design of lesson materials, and approaches to teaching.

Reference notes

1. Schvaneveldt, R W, Meyer, D E and Becker, C A (1974) *Contextual Constraints on Ambiguous Word Recognition.* Paper presented at the meeting of the Psychonomic Society, Boston, November
2. Bower, G H (1977) *On Injecting Life into Deadly Prose: Studies in Explanation Seeking.* Invited address at meeting of Western Psychological Association, Seattle, Washington, April

References

Anderson, R C and Pichert, J W (1977) *Recall of Previously Unrecallable Information Following a Shift of Perspective* (Technical Report 41). Urbana, Ill: University of Illinois, Center for the Study of Reading, April

Anderson, R C, Pichert, J W, Goetz, E T, Schallert, D L, Stevens, K V and Trollip, S R (1976) Instantiation of general terms. *Journal of Verbal Learning and Verbal Behavior* 15: 667-79

Anderson, R C, Reynolds, R E, Schallert, D L and Goetz, E T (1977) Frameworks for comprehending discourse. *American Educational Research Journal* 14 4: 367-81

Anderson, R C, Spiro, R J and Anderson, M C (1977) *Schemata as Scaffolding for the Representation of Information in Connected Discourse* (Technical Report 24). Urbana, Ill: University of Illinois, Center for the Study of Reading, March

Ausubel, D P (1963) *The Psychology of Meaningful Verbal Learning.* New York: Grune and Stratton

Bartlett, F C (1932) *Remembering.* Cambridge, England: The Cambridge University Press

Binet, A and Henri, V (1894) La mémoire des phrases. *L'année Psychologique* 1: 24-59

Bobrow, D G and Norman, D A (1975) Some principles of memory schemata. In D G Bobrow and A M Collins (eds) *Representation and Understanding: Studies in Cognitive Science.* New York: Academic Press

Bower, G H (1976) Experiments in story understanding and recall. *Quarterly Journal of Experimental Psychology* 28: 511-34

Bransford, J D and Johnson, M K (1973) Considerations of some problems of comprehension. In W G Chase (ed) *Visual Information Processing.* New York: Academic Press

Bransford, J D and McCarrell, N S (1974) A sketch of a cognitive approach to comprehension. In W Weimer and D Palermo (eds) *Cognition and the Symbolic Processes.* Hillsdale, NJ: Erlbaum

Brown, A L and Smiley, S S (1977) Rating the importance of structural units of prose passages: a problem of metacognitive development. *Child Development* 48: 1-8

Gombrich, E H J, Hochberg, J and Black, M (1972) *Art, Perception, and Reality.* Baltimore: Johns Hopkins University Press

Goodman, K S (1976) Reading: a psycholinguistic guessing game. *Journal of the Reading Specialist* 4: 126-35

Kintsch, W (1974) *The Representation of Meaning in Memory.* New York: John Wiley & Sons

Mandler, J M and Johnson, N S (1977) Rememberance of things passed: story structure and recall. *Cognitive Psychology* 9: 111-51

Meyer, B J F (1975) *The Organization of Prose and Its Effects on Memory.*
Amsterdam: North Holland Publishing Company

Minsky, M (1975) A framework for representing knowledge. In P H Winston (ed)
The Psychology of Computer Vision. New York: McGraw-Hill

Palmer, S E (1975) Visual perception and world knowledge: notes on a model
of sensory-cognitive interaction. In D A Norman, D E Rumelhart and the
LNR Research Group *Explorations in Cognition.* San Francisco: Freeman

Perfetti, C A and Lesgold, A M (1977) Discourse comprehension and sources
of individual differences. In M Just and P Carpenter (eds) *Cognitive Processes
in Comprehension.* Hillsdale, NJ: Erlbaum

Piaget, J (1926) *The Language and Thought of the Child.* New York: Harcourt,
Brace

Pichert, J W and Anderson, R C (1977) Taking different perspectives on a story.
Journal of Educational Psychology 69: 309-15

Rumelhart, D E (1975) Notes on a schema for stories. In D G Bobrow and
A M Collins (eds) *Representation and Understanding: Studies in Cognitive
Science.* New York: Academic Press

Rumelhart, D E (1976) Toward an interactive model of reading. In S Dornic (ed)
Attention and Performance VI. London: Academic Press

Rumelhart, D E and Ortony, A (1977) The representation of knowledge in
memory. In R C Anderson, R J Spiro and W E Montague (eds) *Schooling
and the Acquisition of Knowledge.* Hillsdale, NJ: Erlbaum

Schallert, D L (1976) Improving memory for prose: the relationship between
depth of processing and context. *Journal of Verbal Learning and Verbal
Behavior* 15: 621-32

Schank, R and Abelson, R P (1975) Scripts, plans, and knowledge. *Proceedings
of the Fourth International Joint Conference on Artificial Intelligence.*
Tbilisi, Georgia: USSR

Smiley, S S, Oakley, D D, Worthen, D, Campione, J C and Brown, A L (1977)
*Recall of Thematically Relevant Material by Adolescent Good and Poor
Readers as a Function of Written versus Oral Presentation* (Technical Report
23). Urbana, Ill: University of Illinois, Center for the Study of Reading, March

Spiro, R J (1977) Remembering information from text: theoretical and empirical
issues concerning the 'State of Schema' reconstruction hypothesis. In
R C Anderson, R J Spiro and W E Montague (eds) *Schooling and the
Acquisition of Knowledge.* Hillsdale, NJ: Erlbaum

Swinney, D A and Hakes, D T (1976) Effects of prior context upon lexical access
during sentence comprehension. *Journal of Verbal Learning and Verbal
Behavior* 15: 681-9

Thieman, T J and Brewer, W J (in press) Alfred Binet on memory for ideas.
Genetic Psychology Monographs

1.3 Some methods for representing structure of concepts in prose material

RICHARD J SHAVELSON AND CATHLEEN STASZ

(Paper presented to the Annual Meeting of the American Psychological Association, San Francisco, California, August 1977. Reproduced with permission of the authors.)

Our research on curriculum and instruction has focused on methods for effectively and efficiently communicating a subject-matter structure to students of differing aptitudes. We have, then, theoretical and applied interests in representing structure. Our theoretical interests are both curricular and psychological. As educators, we are interested in concepts and their interrelation in a subject matter as they convey knowledge and skills. As psychologists, we are interested in how psychological models of information-processing and problem-solving might help in communicating a subject-matter structure. Our interests are also applied in that solving instructional problems cannot await a resolution of some of the thorny problems we and other psychologists have in representing a subject-matter structure. We must make some compromises in order to get on with our applied work. In broad terms, then, the compromises that need to be made in representing a subject-matter structure are the focus of this paper.

Specifically, we will argue that problems with psycholinguistic and logical models for examining subject-matter structure have not been sufficiently resolved to permit us to *apply* these methods to an analysis of a curriculum. Moreover, we will argue that, at present, these sophisticated methods are subjective, in spite of their 'scientific clothing'. Our conclusion will be that we have too readily discarded expert judgement as a formal method for representing a subject-matter structure because of its lack of scientific respectability. And yet we may know more about this method for representing structure than the formal methods currently in vogue. Finally, we wish to point out that human judgement is involved in all methods currently used to map subject-matter structure. The methods differ in the degree to which the *rules* for arriving at a representation are known explicitly. When curriculum experts make judgements, their policy underlying these judgements is not well known. When more formal logical and linguistic systems are applied, the policies become clearer and the role of judgement decreases. We view formal systems for representing structure as a long-term goal and judgements of experts or mature readers as an interim resolution for applied research.

Limitations of some methods for representing subject-matter structure

SIMILARITY STRUCTURE OF A SUBJECT MATTER

In discussing limitations of current methods for representing subject-matter structure, it seems appropriate that we start with the digraph method developed by the first author some nine years ago. With this method, subject-matter structure is defined as the relationship between key terms and the similarity between these terms is the focus of the analysis. First, key terms are identified by curriculum experts. Then, sentences with two or more of these terms are examined syntactically, using a traditional parsing procedure (eg Warriner and Griffiths, 1957). Using rules for mapping each parsed sentence (Shavelson and Geeslin, 1973) on to a directed graph, key terms and their relationships are translated on to a digraph and a digraph distance matrix is formed. This matrix gives the shortest distances between each pair of terms. Finally, this distance matrix is scaled using multidimensional scaling or cluster analysis and the resulting geometric representation of key terms is interpreted as a representation of subject-matter structure. Analyses of data from curriculum on physics, probability and mathematics produced interpretable representations of the abstract, similarity structures of the subject matters (eg Shavelson and Geeslin, 1973; Shavelson and Stanton, 1975).

Clearly, there are a number of problems with this approach. The major limitation is that distinction between the different ways key terms might be related in a subject matter are not made. Thus, for example, the terms mass and gravity are related by similarity and by equation. However, the digraph representation of subject-matter structure ignores these different relations and produces a vague similarity representation. This criticism is supported by our data; we find only a weak link between the degree to which subjects have learned a similarity structure of subject matter and their achievement-test scores.

MICRO AND MACROSTRUCTURE REPRESENTATIONS OF A SUBJECT MATTER

Psycholinguistic and logical methods have avoided some of these problems by carefully distinguishing between different kinds of relationships between key terms and ideas. Within-sentence relationships specify the meaning of connected discourse at a 'microstructure' or content level. (See for example Crothers, 1972; Fredericksen, 1975; Kintsch, 1974; Meyer and McConkie, 1974.) Between-sentence, or macrostructure relationships for certain types of discourse, such as stories, specify the text 'form' (McConkie, 1977). Some parsing systems attempt to handle both levels of analysis, eg Fredericksen distinguishes between semantic (micro) structures and logical (macro) structures.

Kintsch's work (1972; 1974) stands as a good example of microstructure analyses. He represents the meaning of a text by *text bases*, consisting of lists of propositions. Propositions are n-tuples of word concepts, formed according to a set of rules which are part of a

41

person's semantic memory. The formalisms for constructing propositions come from linguistic theory, and need not concern us here. The important point is that the construction of propositions allows for specification of linguistic components and relationships in prose material which are absent in the first method for determining content structure. In addition, Kintsch (1974) has conducted a series of experiments which tend to confirm the psychological reality of the propositional representation and delimit the precise nature of propositions.

Our reading of the work in this area suggests that, from a practical point of view, several limitations can be identified: 1. The time and energy needed to obtain a microstructure representation of a paragraph, let alone a chapter or entire curriculum, is enormous. 2. The methods seem to do well with specially constructed prose passages but they are often problematic when used to examine material written by an unwitting author. 3. The representation that is obtained is an extremely complicated, informal graph or tree structure which defies application to studies of curriculum and instruction. (If you have not seen these results, picture a platter of spaghetti and you will not be too far afield.) And 4. these representations have been tested with data from free or cued recall tests. However, achievement tests have not been used to examine students' applications of the subject-matter structure to more or less familiar situations or problems. In educational settings, achievement is often the major indicator of the extent to which a subject matter has been learned.

In contrast to the microstructure analyses, studies of story structure intentionally bypass a detailed analysis of propositional content (Mandler, Johnson and DeForest, 1976; Mandler and Johnson, 1977; Rumelhart, 1975; Thorndyke, 1977). They focus on identifying the elements of the more abstract organizational structures which are common to simple stories regardless of their specific content (Thorndyke, 1977). These elements — eg episodes, plot, attempts, events — are combined hierarchically by rules of story grammar into a general structure or schema. The research attempts to demonstrate what was observed by Bartlett (1932): an abstract structural schema aids memory for discourse by guiding comprehension processes during encoding and acting as a retrieval mechanism during recall. To the extent that an individual is able to identify a particular story as an example of a general, previously learned structure, his or her memory for the story should be enhanced.

Subject-matter structure, in this case story structure, is found by parsing the story according to the rules of the grammar. As is the case with microstructure analyses of discourse, the parsing system is not always straightforward. Mandler *et al* (1976) reported that their attempts to apply Rumelhart's analyses to new stories frequently failed. This prompted them to modify the system somewhat, in order to describe adequately a larger range of stories. Likewise, Thorndyke (1977) has simplified Rumelhart's system by deleting some of the structural components. The trick, of course, is not to simplify the grammar so much that structure may be indeterminately specified and propositions may be misrepresented.

The results of these studies of macrostructure look promising for psychological theory. And they look tempting for curriculum analysis, especially as researchers apply their analyses to school-related topics (see Thorndyke, 1977; Greeno, 1976; Kintsch, 1976). But there are a number of issues that worry us: 1. Most important, systematic methodological studies which compare the various versions of story grammar have not, to our knowledge, been carried out. Perhaps different grammars produce different structures for the same story and make different predictions about recall. 2. Although knowledge of macrostructure may promote story recall, it may or may not affect achievement-test performance. 3. We do not know to what extent macrostructure analyses can be applied to longer passages of discourse. Finally, 4. researchers typically focus on either micro or macrostructure representations, each claiming that one or the other is of lesser importance depending on the goals of the research. It seems that more work should be done investigating the interface between these levels of representing structure.

PSYCHOLOGICAL MODEL OF SUBJECT-MATTER STRUCTURE

A third method for representing subject-matter structure is to begin with a psychological model and then examine a subject-matter structure in the light of the model. The best known representative of this category with a long and illustrious history in applied settings is Gagné's (1965) task analysis of competencies. Newer approaches have been proposed by Greeno (1973), Scandura (1977), Landa (1976) and others. Task analysis focuses on that aspect of subject-matter structure which specifies operations needed for performing tasks or solving problems with the subject matter. This approach offers some solution to the problems of the two methods discussed above. For example, such representations of structure predict achievement-test performance reasonably well. And it would be possible to apply representations to research on curriculum and instruction.

However, they have a number of limitations. First, the particular representation of subject-matter structure depends on the psychological model used to examine structure. And, in most cases, rules have not been set forth for systematically applying the psychological model to a curriculum in order to obtain a representation of subject-matter structure. In the absence of these rules, different representations may be obtained by different analysts. And the same analyst, changing one or two minor assumptions, may change the representation of structure. Second, curriculum theorists and others have argued that there is more to the structure of a subject matter than just what is represented by the task analysis (eg Schwab, 1962).

Some practical solutions for getting representations of subject-matter structure

While criticism comes easy, clearly some recommendations can be made about methods for getting quick, rough representations of subject-matter structure in order to proceed with research on curriculum and instruction. These methods have provided interpretable representations of structure which have predicted students' performance on achievement tests and other measures. Of course, we recognize that our proposals have their own flaws, but we feel that they deal with some major theoretical and applied problems in a manageable way. By way of introducing these methods, two short scenarios may help. The first scenario comes from research we have been doing. We asked a professor of mathematics education and his graduate student to develop a short piece of curriculum on the topic of mathematical systems. It took them a couple of months of quibbling to produce ten pages which they agreed were a reasonable, short treatment of the topic. Then we asked them to identify the key terms in the material and judge the similarity between them. The representations of subject-matter structure obtained with our lengthy digraph analysis looked just like the scaling solutions based on the experts' similarity judgements. It took us about half an hour to get the judgements using three different measurement methods.

The second scenario is pieced together from our reading of Bonnie Meyer's research with George McConkie. Our information comes from an article published in 1973, an AERA paper presented in 1974, and a symposium presented at AERA in 1977. The accuracy may not be perfect, but the 'gist' ought not to lie.

In her masters thesis, Meyer attempted to determine what aspects of information from prose would be recalled after one or more presentations of a passage. In order to examine the recall data, she had to get a representation of the 'idea units' in the passages themselves. This was done by subjectively examining the passages 'to identify what seemed to be individual ideas stated in the text. These ideas could consist of words or phrases' (Meyer and McConkie, 1973, p 110). Then a judge built a hierarchical tree structure of ideas by selecting 'the most important idea in the first paragraph, then proceeded to select other ideas that described or gave information about this main idea' (p 110). The reliability of this method was demonstrated by showing that two other judges built virtually the same tree structure. Finally, the logical structure was shown to predict performance on the recall task.

However, Meyer was dissatisfied with this judgemental method for representing structure because 'the approach to discourse analysis which was used to obtain the logical structure of the passage was a very subjective one. Second, there was no control for the nature of the content of the passage high and low in the logical structure' (Meyer and McConkie, 1974, p 1). The solution? Of course, add scientific respectability by doing a psycholinguistic graph analysis of the passage similar to that done by Fredericksen (1972; 1975). This linguistic analysis, as we understand it from a distance of 3000 miles, is now the central focus of McConkie's work. And from last report, progress is being made, but the analyses are problematic. Scorers judging recall protocols for their similarity to text structure show different reliabilities with respect to the level of analysis. While reliability for scoring the number of elements was .99, reliability for scoring the *type* of *elements* and *propositions* dropped to .78 and .84 respectively. (McConkie and his group are to be commended for reporting reliabilities since most researchers in the field tend not to report these data.) Also, the output of the tree structures looks increasingly like spaghetti.

The morals of these stories are that: 1. Human judgement underlies all current methods of representing subject-matter structure but methods vary as to the degree the judgements are governed by explicit rules. 2. Human judgement is often a reasonable, if not respected, means of doing behavioural science. But 3. we have tended not to refine our methods of using human judges to tell us about the structure of a passage or a curriculum. Further, 4. as we delve deeper into a problem, we often forget our initial purpose that led us to the problem in the first place, and 5. we sometimes mask human judgement in some other form of scientific analysis. In spite of this, 6. representations of subject-matter structure from human judges, be they curriculum experts, psychologists creating information-processing diagrams, graduate students building tree structures or just mature readers, seem to produce interpretable representations of subject-matter structure and predict students' performance on achievement tests.

Our proposal, then, is to use human judges to obtain representations of subject-matter structure for the purposes of research on curriculum and instruction until we can solve some of the thorny problems of the more formal methods. Further, we propose that knowledge about the use of human judges in getting representations of subject-matter structure be accumulated systematically. What follows, then, are some methods for getting representations of subject-matter structure using experts' judgements.

METHODS FOR REPRESENTING THE SIMILARITY STRUCTURE OF A SUBJECT MATTER

Studies using several different methods for eliciting experts' judgements of the similarity between key terms provide representations that closely match some linguistic, logical or intuitive representation of subject-matter structure. For example, Johnson (Johnson, Cox and Curran, 1970; Johnson, Curran and Cox, 1971) found that experts' judgements of similarity between key terms in Newtonian mechanics closely matched the logical structure of these terms based on the equations in the subject matter. Some of our work with math curriculum theorists suggests that different methods for obtaining their judgements about key terms in a subject matter provide representations of structure which correspond closely to the results of the digraph analysis described above (Shavelson and Stanton, 1975).

Finally, studies by Wainer (Wainer and Berg, 1972; Wainer and Schofer, 1977) suggest how experts' (in some cases, not-so expert) judgements can be used to identify structure underlying short stories and poems. In the 1972 study, advanced French majors read nine short stories by de Maupassant and then judged their pairwise similarity. A scaling of the data indicated that they could be represented by two content dimensions: violence and deception. In the other study, a literature professor (as well as other subjects) judged the similarity

45

between ten poems, selected because they all dealt with 'a man's relationship with his mistress and are all variations on the theme of seduction'. Two dimensions served to represent the professor's judgements: metaphor and emotion.

REPRESENTATION OF THE MICROSTRUCTURE OF A SUBJECT-MATTER STRUCTURE

We do not see a direct link between the psycholinguistic identification of propositions and human judgement. What seems important here but is often overlooked is the reliability of judges' application of linguistic rules to the prose passages.

Nevertheless, we have proposed that experts identify the key terms or 'ideas' in the prose material for both the analysis of similarity structure and the analysis of macrostructure. These units have rough correspondence, at times, with the identification of propositions. It may be that experts may reliably identify the important propositions in a passage and thereby provide a method for bypassing the lengthy microstructure analysis in working with curriculum.

METHODS FOR REPRESENTING THE MACROSTRUCTURE OF A SUBJECT MATTER

In a number of studies, researchers have identified the key terms in a subject matter and then used judges to link them together in order to get a representation of a subject-matter structure. In this way, Meyer and McConkie (1973) were able to predict accurately subjects' recall of stories.

The examination of the macrostructure of stories seems like an attempt to formalize this judgemental approach. Stories are assumed to have certain elements of form — episodes, plots, events — that can be identified and linked hierarchically by a grammar. These elements sound to us a lot like the categories used in our college literature classes to examine stories. Further, the categories changed somewhat for plays and poems. Nevertheless, these categories represented years and years of experts' attempts to specify the form of stories. Since the experts' attempts to identify forms represented a psychological endeavour, it seems reasonable for us to study the way in which experts analyse the macrostructure of stories and to have them make judgements about the organization of the subject matter. Methods for making these judgements are, in some case, well known (eg similarity judgements) and, in other cases, in need of development (eg identifying idea units and linking them together). These judgements could be used until the time that a general grammar for the examination of the macrostructure of stories has been achieved.

REPRESENTATION OF A STRUCTURE OF COMPETENCIES IN A SUBJECT MATTER

The task analysis of a lesson, passage or curriculum is guided by a psychological theory but is, in the end, judgemental. Some research on the reliability of these representations would be helpful. Furthermore, the representation is restricted by the particular theory adopted. Nevertheless, this method seems to represent that aspect of a subject-matter structure measured by achievement tests. We suspect that, in combination with a macrostructure or similarity structure analysis of curriculum, the representation of competencies will continue to provide important information for research on curriculum and instruction (see, for example, Greeno, 1976).

Summary

In summary, we recognize that a curriculum, a lesson or a prose passage is the result of some person or group of people (experts) attempting to communicate what they know and feel. The curriculum, lesson or prose passage, then, represents data on the psychological structure of the author(s). We recognize that there are other ways to obtain representations of the authors' psychological structure, and one important way is by having them make judgements. In fact, we have proposed that a serious attempt be made in developing and accumulating methods for obtaining and representing judgements of experts for the purpose of doing research on curriculum and instruction. Judging from past research, combinations of these judgemental methods have a good chance of detailing what is to be learned from a subject matter and the sequence for learning it. We see this as a temporary solution to the problem of obtaining a representation of the structure of a subject matter until the problems with more formal linguistic and logical systems have been solved.

References

Bartlett, F C (1932) *Remembering.* Cambridge, England: Cambridge University Press

Crothers, E J (1972) Memory and recall of discourse. In J B Carroll and R O Freedle (eds) *Language Comprehension and the Acquisition of Knowledge.* New York: Winston & Sons

Fredericksen, C H (1972) Effect of task induced cognitive operations on comprehension and memory processes. In J B Carroll and R O Freedle (eds) *Language Comprehension and the Acquisition of Knowledge.* New York: Winston & Sons

Fredericksen, C H (1975) Representing logical and semantic structure of knowledge acquired from discourse. *Cognitive Psychology* 7: 371-458

Gagné, R M (1965) *The Conditions of Learning.* New York: Holt, Rinehart & Winston

Greeno, J G (1975) The structure of memory and the process of solving problems. In R L Solso (ed) *Contemporary Issues in Cognitive Psychology.* Washington, DC: Winston

Greeno, J (1976) *Process of Understanding in Studying from Text.* Paper presented at the Annual Meeting of the Americal Educational Research Association, San Francisco, April

Johnson, P E, Cox, D L and Curran, T E (1970) Psychological reality of physical concepts. *Psychonomic Science* 19: 245-7

Johnson, P E, Curran, T E and Cox, D E (1971) A model for knowledge of concepts in science. *Journal of Research in Science Teaching* 8: 91-5

Kintsch, W (1972) Notes on the structure of semantic memory. In E Tulving and W Donaldson (eds) *The Organization of Memory.* New York: Academic Press

Kintsch, W (1974) *The Representation of Meaning in Memory.* New York: Wiley

Kintsch, W (1976) Memory for prose. In C N Cofer (ed) *The Structure of Human Memory.* San Francisco: Freeman

Landa, L N (1976) *Algorithmization in Learning and Instruction.* Englewood Cliffs, NJ: Educational Technology Publications

Mandler, J and Johnson, N (1977) Remembrance of things passed: story structure and recall. *Cognitive Psychology.* 9: 111-51

Mandler, J, Johnson, N and DeForest, M (1976) A structural analysis of stories and their recall: from 'once upon a time' to 'happily ever after'. La Jolla, San Diego, Ca: Center for Human Information Processing, University of California

McConkie, G W (1977) Studying retention from prose: a content structure approach. Paper presented at the Annual Meeting of the American Educational Research Association, San Francisco

Meyer, B J and McConkie, G W (1973) What is recalled after hearing a passage? *Journal of Educational Psychology* 65: 109-17

Meyer, B J and McConkie, G W (1974) Effect of position of information in a passage's organizational structure on recall. Paper presented at the Annual Meeting of the American Educational Research Association, Chicago

Rumelhart, D E (1975) Notes on a schema for stories. In D G Bobrow and A Collins (eds) *Representation and Understanding.* New York: Academic Press

Scandura, J M (1977) Structural approach to instructional problems. *American Psychologist* 32: 33-53

Schwab, J J (1962) The concept of the structure of a discipline. *Educational Record* 43: 197-205

Shavelson, R J and Geeslin, W E (1973) A method for examining subject-matter structure in written material. *Journal of Structural Learning* 4: 101-9

Shavelson, R J and Stanton, G C (1975) Construct validation: methodology and applications to three measures of cognitive structure. *Journal of Educational Measurement* 12: 67-85

Thorndyke, P W (1977) Cognitive structures in comprehension and memory of narrative discourse. *Cognitive Psychology* 9: 77-110

Wainer, H and Berg, W (1972) The dimensions of de Maupassant: a multi-dimensional analysis of students' perception of literature. *American Educational Research Journal* 9: 485-91

Wainer, H and Schofer, P (1977) Measuring the effect of a liberal arts education on the perception of poetry. *American Educational Research Journal* 14: 125-35

Warriner, J E and Griffiths, F (1957) *English Grammar and Composition: Complete Course.* New York: Harcourt

1.4 Analysing eye movements to infer processing styles during learning from text

ERNST Z ROTHKOPF

(Paper, of the same title, from J W Senders *et al* (eds) (1978) *Eye movements and the Higher Psychological Functions.* Hillsdale, NJ: Erlbaum. Reproduced with permission of the author and the publishers.)

The primary aim of our research is to understand how people learn from written material. My associates and I have concentrated on examining the control of processes by which readers extract information from text when they are reading for specific purposes. In this connection we have developed techniques for recording and analysing eye movements during prolonged reading in realistic settings. I will describe these techniques and illustrate their usefulness with results from experiments on goal-guided learning and on text readability.

General nature of research

We have sought a better understanding of basic psychological processes during purposeful reading in the hope that it will help in writing clearly and in fostering effective study of written teaching materials. Much of our work has been focused on factors that influence effective, purposeful reading in realistic settings. We have attempted to identify attributes of the instructional environment that shape and maintain effective processing activities, and to use this information in designing aids for learning from text.

Typically, in our experiments with adjunct aids, we have used instructional passages that ranged in length from 2000 to 9000 words. The subjects read through these passages at their own pace under systematically controlled conditions. Most commonly, the nature of the written material is held constant while instructional contingencies or task demands are systematically manipulated. We then measure what students learn under various conditions. The experimental manipulations may involve, among others, the use of text-embedded questions, interactions with teachers or teacher surrogates, and the use of directions that specify instructional goals to students.

We assume in our research that the students' processing activities are at least as practically important as text characteristics; that processing activities determine the nature of the effective stimulus; and that the effective stimulus, in turn, determines what is learned.

Why record eye movements?

Concern with the role of the learner has led us to postulate a class of activities called mathemagenic activities (eg Rothkopf, 1971; 1972; 1976). *Mathemagenic* is a coined word derived from Greek roots that mean *giving birth to learning.* Mathemagenic activities are those activities that are relevant to the translation of the written stimuli into internal representation. Included here are not only the primary translations of written symbols into usable internal codes, but also the concatenation of dispersed information, inferences, and other construction of mnemotechnic activities during reading.

The mathemagenic activities that are most interesting from a psychological point of view are largely invisible. In our research, inferences about these mathemagenic activities have been made indirectly, usually through measurement of what was learned. It has long been hoped that some other ways of indexing processing activities by readers may become feasible in realistic instructional settings. Two kinds of measurements offered some promise as additional indices of mathemagenic activities. These were the measurement of inspection time and eye movements during reading. Our work on inspection time has produced very interesting results (Rothkopf and Billington 1975a; 1975b; submitted for publication [a]). Two years ago we began to investigate eye movements during the study of written materials in order to obtain a descriptive model of the subjects' activities during purposeful reading.

Methods for observing eye movements

We chose a method that would meet the following requirements. First, we needed a technique that would allow observations of eye movements during 5 to 60 minutes of reading under conditions that resembled reading assignments in realistic instructional settings. We did not want to alter reading conditions in such a way as to interfere with the student's persistence during study or to change the student's usual approach to the study of written material. For example, we judged it unacceptable to restrict unduly the student's head movements or to burden the student with devices that might alter his usual reading style. Second, we needed a technique that would allow study without significant interruptions or other interferences not directly related to the reading demands being made on the student. Third, we needed a method that was clearly within existing technology of eye movement measurements and was both reliable and technically simple. Direct mapping of eye movements on the experimental text was not considered necessary, although we would have been pleased to have that capability if it had been practicable. As it is, we found that an indirect mapping technique, nystamography, suited our purpose well.

The procedure was as follows. The experimental text was prepared on negative 35mm slides and presented by rear projection. Slides were presented in sequence and controlled by the subjects with a switch. A blank slide appeared between text slides. The subject's head was supported by a chin rest 80cm from the rear projection screen. A line of text on the screen subtended a visual angle of approximately 25°.

A 16mm silver chloride skin electrode (Beckman) was placed approximately 2cm laterally from the external canthus of each eye. These electrodes were used to record the corneo-retinal potential relative to an 11mm reference electrode which was fastened to the dorsal surface of the left ear lobe. Only horizontal eye movements were recorded.

Prior to placing the electrodes, the skin surface was cleansed with isopropyl alcohol. The electrodes were filled with *Synapse* electrode cream (Med-Tek Corp) and fastened to the skin with Beckman plastic adhesive collars of appropriate size.

The signal from the electrodes was amplified by AC techniques with a 3-second time constant using an input coupler (Beckman, Type 9859) connected to a Beckman RM Dynograph. The amplified position potential and its derivative (obtained by use of a Beckman, Type 9841, nystagmus velocity coupler) which corresponds to the velocity of the eye motion, was recorded on FM magnetic tape. An Ampex Model 500 recorder/reproducer operating at a speed of 7.5 inches per second was used for that purpose. The operation of the slide changing mechanism was also recorded on tape. The eye movement potentials as well as the slide change record were visualized by a rectilinear pen linkage on paper tape and also on a large-screen (39 x 28cm), multiple trace oscilloscope.

The principle analysis was performed on the velocity signal (first derivative of EOG output). The recorded output of the velocity channel, sampled 100 times per second, was fed into a PDP–11/40 computer for analysis after the completion of the experimental session.

Several analysis programs have been developed. The major relevant programs were based on the principle that within 10 to 12° of ocular movement, angular excursion is approximately linear with velocity of eye movement (Fuchs, 1971, p 346). The computer analysis uses prespecified magnitudes and directions of the eye velocity signal to define (a) left to right saccades, (b) regressions, (c) the duration of fixations that follow these two types of movements, and (d) return sweeps (movements of the eye from the right margin of the page to the left).

The statistical rationale for specifying the upper and lower velocity boundaries that identify the eye movement characteristics listed above has not yet been established in rigorous detail. However, empirical techniques for approximating these boundaries have been developed and provide reliable results. This is achieved by using a sample page, specifying boundary estimates, and then comparing the results against tracings of the positional signal. Marked discrepancies between the results of the velocity analysis and positional data are corrected by revising the velocity boundary parameters. The estimation procedure is repeated until uniformly satisfactory results are obtained for the entire trial page.

Once satisfactory velocity boundaries have been established for the several eye movement characteristics of interest, suitable computer programs provide line-by-line analysis of horizontal eye movements for

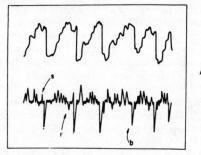

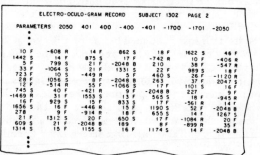

ELECTRO-OCULO-GRAM RECORD   SUBJECT 1302   PAGE 2

PARAMETERS 2050	401	400	-400	-401	-1700	-1701 -2050
10 F	-608 R	14 F	862 S	18 F	1622 S	46 F
1442 S	14 F	875 S	17 F	-742 R	10 F	-406 R
5 F	799 S	21 F	-2048 B	2 10	38 F	-547 R
33 F	-1064 S	21 F	1331 S	22 F	989 S	18 F
723 F	10 S	-449 R	5 F	460 S	26 F	-1120 R
28 F	1056 S	8 F	-2048 B	263	37 F	2047 S
12 F	-514 R	55 F	-1066 S	17 F	1101 S	16 F
745 S	40 F	-421 R	9 F	-2048 B	227	9 F
-1469 R	31 F	1553 S	13 F	565 S	18 F	-945 R
16 F	929 S	15 F	833 S	17 F	-561 R	14 r
1656 S	16 F	-446 R	15 F	1190 S	52 F	-2048 B
278	9 F	-914 R	18 F	655 S	14 F	1267 S
21 F	1312 S	20 F	650 S	17 F	-1084 R	20 F
609 S	21 F	-2048 B	189	8 F	-899 R	35 F
1314 S	15 F	1155 F	16 F	1174 S	14 F	-2048 B

B

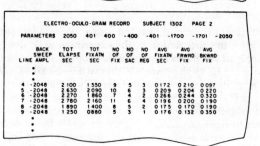

ELECTRO-OCULO-GRAM RECORD   SUBJECT 1302   PAGE 2

PARAMETERS 2050   401   400   -400   -401   -1700   -1701   -2050

LINE	BACK SWEEP AMPL	TOT ELAPSE SEC	TOT FIXATN SEC	NO OF FIX	NO OF SAC	NO OF REG	AVG FIXATN SEC	AVG FRWRD FIX	AVG BKWRD FIX
4	-2048	2 100	1 550	9	5	3	0 172	0 210	0 097
5	-2048	2 630	2 090	10	6	3	0 209	0 204	0 220
6	-2048	2 270	1 860	7	4	2	0 266	0 244	0 320
7	-2048	2 780	2 160	11	6	4	0 196	0 200	0 190
8	-2048	1 890	1 400	8	5	2	0 175	0 170	0 190
9	-2048	1 250	0880	5	3	1	0 176	0 132	0 350

C

Figure 1. *Electronystagmogram and two of the printouts produced by the computer analysis of the velocity signal. The top record in Panel A is the primary positional trace. The bottom of the trace corresponds to the left edge of the text. The bottom record of Panel A is the first derivative of the top record and corresponds to velocity of the eye movement. The features marked s, r, and b are examples of a saccade, regression, and backsweep respectively.*
Panel B shows the features of velocity records from Panel A. The parameters specify from left to right the upper and lower limits for labelling features, as saccades (S), fixations (F), regressions (R), and backsweeps (B), respectively. Records in the printout provide a numerical code corresponding to the maximum velocity occurring within features S, R, and B. For fixations, (F), the numbers correspond to temporal duration (.01 seconds).
Panel C shows the summary of eye movements for approximately the lines shown in Panel A.

each text slide or for any prespecified set of text slides. A sample nystagmogram and two sample printouts resulting from its computer analysis are shown in Figure 1.

Results

Results obtained by our method of analysing eye movements will be illustrated using data from experiments on the effects of descriptions of learning goals on learning achievements, and from experiments on text readability. The use of computer storage and subsequent analysis of large numbers of horizontal eye movements that occur during a substantial period of reading has made it possible to investigate phenomena that were difficult to examine in detail in the past. These include, among other things, the determination of eye movement patterns for selected text segments and the nature of individual readers' reactions to task demands.

Learning prespecified information from text

Providing readers with explicitly described learning goals has a very marked effect on what the readers remember about a text. The number of goal-relevant questions correctly answered on a postreading test has been observed to be two to three times greater than questions about incidental (not goal-relevant) text information (eg Gagné and Rothkopf, 1975; Rothkopf and Billington, 1975b; Rothkopf and Kaplan, 1972). Several studies showed that the amount of incidental information remembered by goal-guided students was somewhat lower than that remembered by a control group who were directed to learn as much about the text as possible and not provided with explicit learning goals (Gagné and Rothkopf, 1975; Rothkopf and Billington, 1975b), although reversals of this effect have also been reported (Kaplan and Rothkopf, 1974; Rothkopf and Kaplan, 1972). The literature on learning prespecified information from text has been reviewed in detail elsewhere (Rothkopf, 1976).

In attempting to examine the effects of prespecified learning goals on reading, eye movements were observed under various experimental conditions. Subjects memorized six learning goals and then studied a 1498-word passage on oceanography presented on 35mm slides, each containing 150 to 200 syllables of text (Rothkopf and Billington, submitted for publication [b]; Rothkopf and Billington, in preparation). Six of the slides in the experimental series contained *no* information relevant to learning goals. These will be called *incidental* slides. Each of the other six slides included exactly one goal-relevant sentence as well as two or more incidental sentences. These will be called *goal-relevant* or *mixed* slides.

Our recording method avoids technical problems that arise in mapping eye movements on the text by direct observation. The following procedure was developed to infer eye movements in goal-relevant text neighbourhoods of mixed text slides. The procedure was based on the assumption that subjects inspecting text slides used *one* of two inspection styles. These were 1. the incidental mode, which included the text for goal-relevant information, and 2. processing aimed at learning goal-relevant information.

Eye movements during processing of a goal-relevant sentence, in slides containing a mixture of incidental and goal-relevant material, can be reconstructed in the following way. The total observed quantity of each of the various classes of eye movement for mixed slides was divided into two components: those eye movements generated during background reading, and those produced during goal-processing. The basis for the division was the number of *objective text* lines that were expected to be read in the background, incidental mode (I). In the Rothkopf and Billington (submitted for publication [b]) experiment, there were on average 12.3 lines of incidental text and 2.2 lines of goal-relevant material on each mixed slide. The number of text lines in a mixed slide that were read in the incidental style (I) was therefore 12.3, plus the portion of the 2.2 goal-relevant lines that was read in the incidental style. The latter quantity was $2.2\,k$, where k is the proportion of the goal-relevant sentence read in the background mode, that is, an estimate of how much of the goal-relevant sentence was read in the incidental style before goal-relevance was detected and the subject switched to the goal-processing mode. According to this conception, the number of objective text lines was:

$$I = 12.3 + 2.2\,k$$

We then calculated, on the basis of data from purely incidental slides, how much of any eye movement characteristic should have been produced by (I) lines of incidental text. This quantity was subtracted from the observed quantity of that eye movement characteristic for mixed slides and the remainder was attributed to goal-processing activities.

The general procedure can be summarized as follows. All quantities, unless otherwise indicated, were those appropriate for mixed slides (ie those which included a goal-relevant sentence).

(1) Number of text lines read in background mode (I)	=	Number of incidental text lines		$+ k \times$	Number of goal-relevant text lines
(2) Eye movement characteristics generated by background mode	=	Number of text lines read in background mode (I)	$\times$		Eye movement characteristics observed on incidental slides ÷ Number of text lines on incidental slides
(3) Eye movement characteristics generated by goal-processing	=	Total eye movement characteristics observed on mixed slides	$-$		Eye movement characteristics generated by background mode

The only quantity used in this procedure, not directly or indirectly based on observation, was the constant of proportionality k. It seemed reasonable to assume $0 < k < 1$. We determined a plausible value for k by asking observers to judge at what word in a goal-relevant sentence they felt certain that the sentence was relevant to a particular goal. The average value of k obtained by this method in Rothkopf and Billington (submitted for publication [b]) experiment was .64.

Using this technique we found that an average sentence composed of 20.7 words and covering 2.2 text lines resulted in the model inspection pattern summarized in Table 1.

	Goal-relevant*	Incidental
Line scans	3.76	2.24
Saccades	19.52	10.10
Regressions	15.71	6.01
Duration of fixation after saccades (in secs)	.233	.216
Duration of fixation after regression (in secs)	.212	.184

* Includes inspection in the incidental mode prior to detection of goal-relevance (k = .64) for all except the duration of fixation entries.

Table 1. *Modal inspection patterns for a 20.7 word sentence (2.2 text lines) when it contained goal-relevant information and when it included only incidental matter*

As can be seen, the inspection of goal-relevant material involved 1.52 more line scans, 9.42 more saccades, and 9.7 more regressions than incidental material. Duration of fixation was 17msec longer after saccades and 28msec longer after regressions with goal-relevant material than with incidental sentences.

Similar results were obtained in two experiments. They suggest a simple descriptive model of subjects' responses to task demands. When a sentence is goal-relevant, the density of fixations is increased, and the durations of fixations are lengthened. It would be but a small leap of the imagination, though one still consistent with the current *Zeitgeist*, to translate density of fixation into the likelihood of appropriate internal representation of text components, and to equate the small increases in the average duration of fixations with greater depth of processing. Both the likelihood of appropriate internal representation (eg Rothkopf, 1976) and increased depth of processing (eg Craik and Lockhart, 1972) have been reported to increase instructional achievement.

Because our method allows us to collect very substantial amounts of eye movement data from each reader, it becomes possible to analyse style differences among individual subjects in their response to reading demands. The results of this kind of stylistic analysis suggest that the kind of modelling described above is inappropriate in certain details. There are two kinds of problem. First of all, the averaged group responses to the demands of learning goals are poor descriptions of the inspection patterns of individual readers. Second, comparison of the eye movement patterns of individual subjects in goal-relevant and incidental text neighbourhoods does not predict relative achievement on goal-relevant and incidental materials well.

Individual responses to task demands

Readers respond to the demands posed by learning goals in several

distinctive individual styles. Some readers change the manner in which
lines are scanned. Others reread lines or vary both rereading and line
scans. Certain subjects have the same inspection patterns for both goal-
relevant and incidental portions of the text. These style characteristics
are not related in any simple way to differential learning of goal-
relevant and incidental information. We analysed individual responses
to task demands in the following way. A measure of each of three eye
movement characteristics on goal-relevant slides was compared with the
corresponding measure on incidental pages for each subject. The eye
movement characteristics were: (a) number of lines scanned, (b) number
of fixations per scanned line, and (c) the average duration of fixations
that followed saccades. Table 2 was obtained by determining, for each
of 32 subjects, whether goal-relevant slides consistently exceeded
incidental slides on measures of these eye movement characteristics
throughout the experimental reading sequence.

Number of subjects	Lines scanned	Fixations per scanned line	$\overline{X}$ Duration. Forward fixations
7	R > I	–	–
2	–	R > I	–
5	–	–	R > I
5	R > I	R > I	–
2	R > I	–	R > I
3	–	R > I	R > I
1	R > I	R > I	R > I
7	–	–	–
Total for each eye movement characteristic	15	11	11
Chance expectation	4.0	4.0	4.0

Table 2. *Number of subjects showing consistently greater
measures on goal-relevant than on incidental text portions
in each of three eye movement characteristics*

The data in Table 2 indicate that the majority of subjects displayed
different eye movement patterns in goal-relevant text neighbourhoods
than in incidental text portions. But there appears to be very substantial
diversity in the style in which inspection patterns are altered by task
demands. Some subjects vary one or more aspects of the way each line
is scanned. For others, the scanning style for each line does not differ
between goal-relevant and incidental text segments, whereas the number
of lines scanned is altered between conditions. Other subjects do not
differentiate between goal-relevant and incidental slides at all. The data
in Table 2 suggest individual styles in response to task demands.
Averaged group data may be useful in indexing passage difficulty or the
influence of a particular task demand on inspection activity. But
averaged group data are not good descriptions of the reactions of
individual readers.

Individual inspection style and learning

Differences in eye movement characteristics between goal-relevant and incidental text are not simple predictors of differences in learning between goal-relevant and incidental information. Rothkopf and Billington (submitted for publication [b]) have found that differentiation in eye movement patterns between goal-relevant and incidental text and differentiation in the relative amount of learning on the two types of material were weakly correlated.

Results for eye movement patterns in the Rothkopf and Billington study (submitted for publication [b]) are summarized in Table 3. It is reasonably clear from an inspection of this table that subjects who showed no differences in inspection patterns between goal-relevant and incidental text neighbourhoods remembered more goal-relevant material than incidental information. Learning achievements on goal-relevant text material were not simply related to inspection activities as indexed by eye movements. Similar results have also been obtained for differences in inspection time between goal-relevant and incidental text slides. The correlation between differential inspection rate in syllables per minute and differential learning on goal-relevant and incidental text was significantly different from chance but small ($r = -.296$).

Preliminary analysis of two additional experiments suggests that the individual style differences observed in goal-guided learning also occur to a somewhat lesser degree in subjects' inspection of text of various difficulty (readability).

Eye movement characteristic in which goal-relevant text exceeds incidental	Proportion correct responses on recall test			
	Goal-relevant information		Incidental information	
	$\overline{X}$	σ	$\overline{X}$	σ
Scanned lines	.73	.28	.34	.15
Fixations per line	.83	.14	.34	.14
Fixation duration	.76	.23	.30	.15
No differences	.83	.29	.26	.04

Table 3. *Differences in eye movement characteristics between goal-relevant and incidental text and the recall of goal-relevant and incidental information*

EYE MOVEMENTS AND READABILITY

The effect of readability on eye inspection patterns was studied using techniques similar to those described above (Rothkopf and Billington, unpublished manuscript). Subjects read 16 passages that varied widely in the Flesch Reading Ease Index. The passages were 93 to 159 words in length. Each passage was photographed on a separate negative slide. The subjects were requested to learn as much about each passage as possible. This request was reinforced by money incentives for high recall test performance. Order of presentation of the passages was randomly varied among subjects.

Averages for various eye movement characteristics were obtained for each of the 16 passages. Means of representative measures for the eight high and the eight low readability passages are shown in Table 4. This table shows significantly more lines scanned with difficult than with easy text. Duration of fixation, both after saccades and after regressions, was longer with less readable material.

Eye movement measure	Readability		
	Low	High	P
Lines scanned per passage	20.80	18.00	$<$.02
Number of saccades per scanned line	5.70	5.83	$>$.05
Number of regressions per scanned line	2.42	2.30	$>$.05
$\overline{X}$ duration, forward fixation	.243	.227	$<$.001
$\overline{X}$ duration, backward fixation	.215	.201	$<$.05

Average Flesch Reading Ease Index was: high = 87.53 (σ = 7.28), low = 29.10 (σ = 15.32).

Table 4. *Eye movements on eight high and and eight low readability passages*

The results of another recent study also support the findings shown in Table 4. Rothkopf and Krudys (unpublished manuscript) using the same 16 passages found that number of fixations per scanned line was relatively unaffected by readability. The correlation between number of fixations per scanned line and the Flesch Reading Ease Index was not significantly above zero (r = − .16). The total number of fixations per unit text, on the other hand, decreased with reading ease (r = − .45). This implies that if group trends are considered, the number of fixations per scanned line remains constant regardless of readability, but that the average reader increases the number of scanned lines when the text becomes more difficult. This interpretation is consistent with the results in Table 4. Rothkopf and Krudys (unpublished manuscript) also confirmed the duration of fixation increases with text difficulty. The correlation between reading ease and average duration of fixation was − .69.

Both the data in Table 4 and the results of the Rothkopf and Krudys study reported above were based on group averages. Just as in the studies of goal-guided learning, individual style analysis of the readability experiments indicated that averaged group results provided a somewhat misleading picture of what individual subjects were doing to cope with text difficulty. These aspects of the eye movement pattern, number of lines scanned, number of fixations per scanned line, and duration of fixations, observed for eight highly readable passages, were compared with those of the eight difficult slides for each individual reader. One-tailed *t*-tests (p $<$ .1) were used for each measure. Among the 27 subjects used in the Rothkopf and Billington (unpublished manuscript) and the Rothkopf and Krudys (unpublished manuscript) subjects, six of these showed no reliable differences between the eye movement patterns observed for difficult and easy text. Fifteen subjects had longer fixations, and six scanned more lines on difficult than on more readable text. The number of subjects who had more fixations per scanned line on difficult than on easy text were about what might be expected by chance.

Our method for analysing nystagmograms by computer appears to be a useful tool for studies of reading. The estimation procedures allow inferences about how particular text neighbourhoods are inspected. The estimation procedure makes it possible to avoid presenting the text one sentence or other small unit at a time. Fragmenting text in this way is one option for investigating inspection of individual sentences when means for mapping eye movements directly on print are not available. Such fragmentation appears to be a suspect research strategy when it is used to investigate persistence in reading, or when selective attention is of interest. The method allows the capture of very substantial eye movement records per subject. This makes it possible to undertake serious investigation of individual reading styles. Such investigations appear to have been somewhat neglected in previous research on eye movements in reading. The findings of Rothkopf and Billington (submitted for publication [b]), Rothkopf and Billington (unpublished manuscript), and Rothkopf and Krudys (unpublished manuscript) indicate that individual readers respond to task demands in markedly different styles. These results raise a number of empirical and theoretical questions that deserve investigation.

There are strong hints in our results that eye movements are not a super highway to the discovery of fundamental psychological processes during reading. The eyes may be the windows to the soul, but they may also provide views of unoccupied rooms. The weak and complex relationship between differential eye movement patterns and differential learning from various text segments suggests that visible inspection patterns include many ineffective and superstitious components. The discriminations necessary for the discovery of goal-relevant information in the text may be sufficient for the marked advantage in the retention of goal-relevant information over the retention of background material. The discovery of goal-relevant information could, in addition, result in a variety of additional inspection activities that add little or nothing to the learned performance of the reader. Substantial portions of the systematic eye movements observed during reading may reflect superstitious inspection activities of that character. Our results indicate the need for caution in interpreting eye movement data as indicators of underlying processing activities during learning from written material.

References

Craik, F I M and Lockhart, R S (1972) Level of processing: a framework for memory research. *Journal of Verbal Learning and Verbal Behavior* 11: 671-84
Fuchs, A F (1971) The Saccadic System. In P Bach-y-Rita and C C Collins (eds) *The Control of Eyemovements.* New York: Academic Press

Gagné, E D and Rothkopf, E Z (1975) Text organization and learning goals. *Journal of Educational Psychology* 67: 445-50

Kaplan, R and Rothkopf, E Z (1974) Instructional objectives as directions to learners: effect of passage length and amount of objective-relevant content. *Journal of Educational Psychology* 66: 448-56

Rothkopf, E Z (1971) Experiments on mathemagenic behavior and the technology of written instruction. In E Z Rothkopf and P E Johnson (eds) (1971) *Verbal Learning Research and the Technology of Written Instruction*, pp 284-303. New York: Columbia University Teachers College Press

Rothkopf, E Z (1972) Structural text features and the control of processes in learning from written material. In R O Freedle and J B Carroll (eds) *Language Comprehension and the Acquisition of Knowledge*, pp 315-35. Washington, DC: V H Winston & Sons

Rothkopf, E Z (1976) Writing to teach and reading to learn: a perspective on the psychology of written instruction. In N L Gage (ed) *The Psychology of Teaching Methods, The Seventy-fifth Yearbook of the National Society for the Study of Education, Part I*, pp 91-129. Chicago: National Society for the Study of Education

Rothkopf, E Z and Billington, M J (1975a) A two-factor model of the effect of goal-descriptive directions on learning from text. *Journal of Educational Psychology* 67: 692-704

Rothkopf, E Z and Billington, M J (1975b) Relevance and similarity of text elements to descriptions of learning goals. *Journal of Educational Psychology* 67: 745-50

Rothkopf, E Z and Billington, M J. Goal-guided learning from written discourse: a descriptive processing model and individual inspection style inferred from time and eye movement measures (submitted for publication) (a)

Rothkopf, E Z and Billington, M J. Effects of task demands on eye movements during goal-directed reading (submitted for publication) (b)

Rothkopf, E Z and Billington, M J. Individual reading style in two learning tasks (in preparation)

Rothkopf, E Z and Kaplan, R (1972) An exploration of the effect of density and specificity of instructional objectives on learning from text. *Journal of Educational Psychology* 63: 295-302

Rothkopf, E Z and Krudys, J. Copying span as a measure of the information burden in written language (in preparation)

Part 2: Writing Skills: Acquisition and Development

2.0 Introduction

In this section of this book the coverage is very broad. Initially it was planned to devote it to the acquisition of writing skills by primary school children. Then it was thought that the whole range of writing skills should be encompassed. Finally, it developed into a set of papers on a rather different theme: all are concerned, in one way or another, with learning to write.

Children's writing

It is difficult to find a short paper on the acquisition of writing skills by primary school children. As can be seen from the edited paper by Ajuriaguerra and Auzias (Paper 2.1) a great many issues can be covered. Psychologists seem to tackle these issues in one of three ways: either they produce a complete book on the topic (eg Markoff, 1976) or they write lengthy chapters of the sort depicted in this text, or they present an observational-descriptive account (of which possibly the best is that of Clay, 1975). It is easier to read the descriptive accounts whose illustrations and examples convey clearly the problems that school teachers face, but such accounts do not have the depth of more scholarly treatments.

Suen (1975) provides a list of publications relevant to the teaching of handwriting. Paper 2.1 complements this list by painting a broader canvas, and by encompassing European research that is not referred to in Suen's bibliography. Currently, at the time of preparing this text, children's writing is becoming the focus of attention of several cognitive psychologists, and it is an area in which we might expect rapid progress to be made. Recent examples of this work are provided in the edited collections of Fredericksen *et al* (1980) and Gregg and Steinberg (1980).

Children's writing is not an easy area in which to do research, but some issues are more amenable than others. In Paper 2.2 for example, Peter Burnhill and his colleagues look at a relatively straightforward but emotive issue. The question being asked is a simple one: is it better for children learning to write to use plain or lined paper? Many teachers seem to think that what matters, as far as children's writing is concerned, is what it is about — not what it looks like. Lines, they argue, hinder creative expression. Paper 2.2 attempts to provide some evidence rather than opinion on this issue.

The role of planning

In Paper 2.3, 'Writing, dictating and speaking letters', we turn to another new area of research. This paper is included to show that office skills (perhaps because of the impetus of new technology) are now beginning to attract the attention of psychologists. Although the central concern of Paper 2.3 is with dictating, the findings are of great interest to writers too. John Gould and Stephen Boies conclude that it is the planning that takes up the time when writing and dictating rather than the execution of the task, even though the dictators themselves — and the general public — do not seem to believe this. The argument is that the skills of dictating can be readily acquired in contrast to the skills of composing, planning, and thinking.

These ideas are developed more fully in a later article by Gould (1980), where he demonstrates that during composition people do not follow a fixed sequence of processes but that they alternate back and forth between generating material, accessing other information, editing and reviewing. A similar viewpoint, based on assessing verbal protocols, is given by Hayes and Flower (1978).

In Paper 2.4 we see the emphasis on planning in a different time scale. In this paper Alan Branthwaite and his colleagues discuss how students cope with the task of meeting the essay requirements of a particular university course. This paper illustrates the varied approaches that different students use to meet a common objective. The students all achieve similar grades, but they get there by different routes. Clearly, too, learning is involved. The students' actions change over time: more students make drafts and discuss their essays in the second year than in the first. What appears to be learned, however, is not how to get better grades, but how to use more socially acceptable strategies of approach.

The ways in which students prepare for and set about writing essays is a topic ripe for research. Despite the fact that most academic psychologists spend a good proportion of their time marking written work, there seems to have been little research on the subject. It is disheartening to have to report that this is also true of research on how students read and use books. (For some notable exceptions, see Mann, 1973; Marton, 1978; Anderson, 1979; and Entwistle *et al*, 1979). When one considers how much academic learning at universities (and elsewhere) takes place through reading and writing, it is really quite remarkable how little we know about how it is achieved.

In some ways it would seem that writing an academic essay is not unlike writing a scientific paper, or indeed, the various introductions to the parts of this text. Upon reflection, though, there are considerable differences. The essays of students are conceived and written in a shorter time scale and with less material to evaluate and synthesize. There is less time for thought and incubation, and the constant assimilation of fresh material.

Writing novels

Writing academic essays — and introductions — allows an author more freedom than does writing to a formal specification — such as that provided by scientific journals (see Part 5), but this freedom in itself poses problems because of the variety it allows. Furthermore, the freedom allowed by an essay is probably less than that allowed by a short story, a novel, or possibly a poem. Clearly works in each of these genres can be prescribed by formulae or recipes, but in most products it is hard to discern such procedures. Few psychologists have written both scientific papers and novels, but there are exceptions (eg Skinner, 1948; Hudson, 1978). Harding (1976) has published both literary criticism and scientific papers. Skinner (1979) has commented on writing an autobiography.

Cowley (1957) in the first of *The Paris Reviews: Writers at Work* argues that there are four main stages in the composition of a novel. First comes the germ of an idea, then a period of more or less conscious meditation, then the first draft, and finally, the revisions. Cowley elaborates on each of these stages with examples of different strategies used by different authors within each stage. To the present writer the descriptions seem so diverse that it is hard to draw any conclusions from them. Indeed, other collections of interviews with writers seem to point more to the contrast between authors than to their similarities (eg see *The Paris Reviews*; Breit, 1956; Jones and Way, 1976).

John Gould, in the paper referred to earlier (Gould, 1980) argues nonetheless — on the basis of the last two volumes of *The Paris Reviews* — that authors have general composition skills as well as specific skills that relate to the domain in which they are writing. Gould suggests that there are areas of communality and areas of difference between successful authors. The communalities he suggests are that the good authors are preoccupied with writing — they like doing it; they practise a great deal — in the sense that they write often; most of them (he claims) revise a great deal; and for most, but not all, writing is a struggle — it does not come easily.

Gould, however, finds many differences between famous authors. Some work rapidly, under pressure. Some work slowly. A few work at night; many only in the mornings. Some plan: some 'just write'. Some emphasize the characters when getting started and some the plot. Some write longhand, some use a typewriter. Some rely heavily on 'environmental idiosyncracies' to help them write (eg Kipling only wrote with the blackest ink that he could find).

In reaching his conclusions, or descriptions, we should note that Gould is relying on brief interviews published in literary journals. The accounts given are not substantial and, indeed, they sometimes conflict — or at least present contrasting pictures to the reader. Thus, for example, Breit (1956) reports finding T S Eliot using diagrams to map out the plot and the characters of the play he was working on at the time of the interview, but no such strategy is mentioned in the interview with Eliot in the 1963 *Paris Review*. Thus, in considering writers at work, it might be better to examine autobiographies than short snippets. Extracts from such material can be found in the edited collections of Ghiselin (1952) and Vernon (1970).

Incidentally, in passing we may note that Gould reports that he has not found a famous author who dictates. If, for a moment we put on one side the works of Barbara Cartland, a more interesting candidate for consideration is Henry James.[1] Between 1895 and 1898 James 'went modern'. He used a bicycle, he installed electric light, he went to one of the first cinema shows, and he bought a new-fangled machine — a typewriter — to help him overcome his writer's cramp. In 1897 he hired an assistant to act as an amanuensis and from that date he dictated his novels which were taken down in type (see Edel, 1977).

It is reported that the later novels of Henry James are more diffuse and abstract than the earlier ones (Chatman, 1972), but it would seem unwise to attribute this solely to dictation. The way in which writers change over time is an interesting topic for research. Psychologists could profitably explore further the techniques of literary criticism used by Chatman. Computer-based counting systems would make this task easier today than in the past.

There appears to have been little detailed research by psychologists into the methods and techniques used by authors in writing books, but there are one or two exceptions. Barron (1968) examined the personality profiles of creative writers; McKellar (1957) devoted several pages to an analysis of Enid Blyton's ways of working, mainly concentrating on her visual imagery; and Pear (1977) commented on Irving Wallace's procedures, casting them firmly in the mould of operant conditioning and behaviour modification. (Wallace keeps regular cumulative records of the number of words written each day, targets to aim at, etc.) Pear points out that not only is Wallace using a self-imposed and self-generated technique of behavioural control but also that such procedures could be taught to or used with profit by other more 'reluctant' authors. Giving oneself a target — and mapping its fulfilment — should be reinforcing!

Concluding remarks

Learning to become a skilful writer is, I think, of extreme importance. In a sense one might argue (somewhat optimistically perhaps) that if teachers focused more on written communication, then the skills of reading might look after themselves. Writing makes speech visible and durable. This allows writers (of whatever age) to reconsider and to rethink what it is that they are trying to say. The act of writing tutors thinking and enhances self-esteem.

In my view it is now time that as much research is devoted to writing as it is to reading. The methods available to psychology in this area are varied. One can quarry in biographies, one can give out questionnaires, one can set up laboratory investigations, one can ask for verbal protocols, and one can introspect and speculate. All of these methods have their advantages and disadvantages, and between them they cover a rich field of enquiry.

[1] I am indebted to Ian Hunter for this information.

References

Anderson, T H (1979) Study skills and learning strategies. Technical Report No 104, Center for the Study of Reading, University of Illinois at Urbana, Champaign.

Barron, F (1968) *Creativity and Personal Freedom.* New York: Van Nostrand

Breit, H (1956) *The Writer Observed.* New York: World Publishing Co

Chatman, S (1972) *The Later Style of Henry James.* Oxford: Basil Blackwell

Clay, M (1975) *What Did I Write?* London: Heinemann

Cowley, M (1957) Introduction. *The Paris Reviews: Writers at Work.* London: Secker and Warburg

Edel, M (1977) *The Life of Henry James (2 Vols).* Harmondsworth: Penguin

Entwistle, N J, Hanley, M and Ratcliffe, G (1979) Approaches to learning and levels of understanding. *British Educational Research Journal* 5 1: 99-114

Fredericksen, C H, Whiteman, M F and Dominic, J F (eds) (1980) *Writing: The Nature, Development and Teaching of Written Communication.* Hillsdale, NJ: Erlbaum (in press)

Ghiselin, B (ed) (1952) *The Creative Process: A Symposium.* California: University of California Press

Gould, J D (1979) Experiments on composing letters: some facts, some myths, some observations. In L W Gregg and E R Steinberg (eds) *Cognitive Processes in Writing.* Hillsdale, NJ: Erlbaum (in press)

Gregg, L W and Steinberg, E R (eds) (1980) *Cognitive Processes in Writing.* Hillsdale, NJ: Erlbaum (in press)

Harding, D W (1976) *Words into Rhythm: English Speech Rhythm in Verse and Prose.* Cambridge: Cambridge University Press

Hayes, J R and Flower, L S (1978) Protocol analysis of writing processes. Paper available from the authors, Dept Psychology, Carnegie-Mellon University, Pittsburgh, Pennsylvania 15213

Hudson, L (1978) *The Nympholepts.* London: Cape

Jones, C and Way, O R (1976) *British Children's Authors.* Chicago: American Library Association

McKellar, P (1957) *Imagination and Thinking.* London: Cohen & West

Mann, P (1973) *Books and Students.* London: National Book League

Markoff, A M (1976) *Teaching Low-Achieving Children Reading, Spelling and Handwriting.* Springfield, Ill: Thomas

Marton, F (1978) What does it take to learn? In J Hartley and I K Davies (eds) *Contributions to an Educational Technology Vol 2.* London: Kogan Page and New York: Nichols

Pear, J J (1977) Self-control techniques of famous novelists. *Journal of Applied Behavior Analysis* 10 3: 515-25

Skinner, B F (1948) *Walden II.* London: Collier-Macmillan (1962)

Skinner, B F (1979) On writing an autobiography. Paper to the American Psychological Society's Annual Convention, New York, September

Suen, C Y (1975) Handwriting education — a bibliography. *Visible Language* IX 2: 145-58

Vernon, P E (ed) (1970) *Creativity.* Harmondsworth: Penguin

Further reading

Fredericksen, C H, Whiteman, M F and Dominic, J F (eds) (1980) *Writing: The Nature, Development and Teaching of Written Communication.* Hillsdale, NJ: Erlbaum (in press)

Gregg, L W and Steinberg, E R (eds) (1980) *Cognitive Processes in Writing.* Hillsdale, NJ: Erlbaum (in press)

2.1 Preconditions for the development of writing in the child

J DE AJURIAGUERRA AND M AUZIAS

(A shortened version of Chapter 18 in E H Lenneberg and
E Lenneberg (eds) (1976) *Foundations of Language Development.*
New York: Academic Press. Reproduced with permission of the
authors and UNESCO.)

In this chapter the conditions for the acquisition and development of
handwriting are discussed in the light of many different aspects: motor
organization, psychomotor and praxic organization required for
writing; speed; hold of the tool; and tonicity. We shall analyse the
'directional conventions' view of the spatial constraints of writing.
Also discussed are stages in mastery of the graphic space by the child;
the most usual tools; methods of learning and handwriting scales;
writing disorders that may develop in some children, their causes, and
relevant re-education methods. Finally, teaching suggestions drawn
from experimental investigations and practice in re-education are given.

The nature of writing

. . . In writing, the hand that speaks gives pleasure to the child, for
whom it is a 'discovery' and a means of representing something within
himself. It is speech and motion. 'The tyranny of letters', as de Saussure
(1916) said? Not necessarily. It is rather mastery of a tool and a new
method of handling language. Although its inert forms may restrict
the liberty of language, to the child they represent mastery of a new
mode of expression. Writing does not become a constraint until certain
school requirements make their appearance. Of all manual skills,
writing allows the child the least liberty, while affording him the greatest
satisfaction, because it can provide an indelible trace of what language
can express. Writing is graphic representation using conventional,
systematic, recognizable signs. It is linear. In Cohen's words (1958), it
consists of a visual and durable representation of language, which makes
it transportable and conservable. The essential requirement of writing is
that it should be transmissible. It is vehicular. In our society, writing is
to be seen and read (although in braille, touch replaces sight). . . .

. . . In the ontogenesis of the child, writing comes after speech. A
conventional, codified activity, writing is an acquired accomplishment.
It is not a gift. It is within our reach once a certain level of intellectual,
motor and affective development has been attained. It is language and
movement, but is restricted by the context in which it takes place, by

its rigorous graphic figuration, and the rules of spelling governing transcription of the language. Serving society in line with certain norms, the modes of graphic expression, despite their variability, remain fairly stable in the overall organization of their planning and as a result of the equivalence of writing instruments. The social framework imposes limits on us to ensure that the signs retain their value as a form of general communication.

Every normal individual, given a certain level of development, has the ability to write. But this potential, which depends on the completeness and maturation of several systems, cannot become effective except by learning. As Leischner (1957) states, the systems in question are not the same for the different levels of writing. In *copying*, sight and perception of the form of the visual symbols are foremost, as are the faculties of motor innervation required for execution. In *dictation*, verbal understanding of the text transmitted orally by another and transcription into graphic symbols are essential. In *spontaneous writing*, it is necessary to set down in symbolic form material formulated by the internal language, and a choice must be made from among the forms of speech and the graphic symbols that society has made available to us. . . .

. . . Writing is not only a permanent method of recording our ideas and memories; in our society it is also a method of exchange, a medium of communication between ourselves and others. For this reason the child must, within the bounds of his personal ability, meet certain requirements imposed by society with regard to legibilty and speed.

Legibility is determined by both the shape of the letters and their ligature, and by the organization of the sequence of letters.

Speed is one of the requirements of the modern world; typists are chosen in accordance with speed scales, and shorthand was invented to compensate for the slowness of handwriting.

Although the aesthetics of writing may have changed with the times and the canons varied with the teachers, one element has been constant: the *layout*, which gives writing its 'verbal melody' and value as an ordered narrative. It is this, rather than the aesthetic qualities, that modulates this silent way of expression.

These three types of requirement are to a certain extent contradictory and cannot be reconciled except by suitable teaching methods. According to the child's ability, these methods will take into account the shape of the letters, the ligatures, the tools. The first steps in learning are decisive, since each child comes to writing with his his own inherent organization, his motor ability, his faculties of structuration, orientation, and verbal representation, writing being an ordered figuration with a meaning.

The motor, psychomotor, and praxic organization in writing

Calling for skilled handling of the writing tool, graphic activity cannot take place without the activation of certain muscles which, first, maintain the writing position with some force, and second, allow flexibility in the sequence of movements on a flat surface. In writing, as in any effector activity, the muscular activity is controlled by the organization of various anatomico-physiological systems. This organization develops with time; it is to a great extent the result of maturation, but it can only be completely understood and studied in *functional performance*. . .

. . .To achieve writing on a small scale, the hand must be capable of fine prehension; furthermore, it must adopt a specific position (in half-supination when a pencil is used), which must be maintained with some force for a fairly extended period of time. Various synergies and co-ordinations must be put into operation to perform the graphic movement; they develop during the pre-writing stage (Lurcat, 1974); the child improves them gradually with practice. The movements, general to start with, have to become precise; the movements of the fingers must gain in refinement and be differentiated from the movements of the wrist and arm, be capable of slight braking while the body learns to keep still to facilitate the complex distal movement. These elementary motor conditions are achieved around the age of six, but at a minimum. The exercise and development of these motor and praxic abilities will enable the movements to become *organized* and gradually to become smooth, quick, supple, economical, and automatic (Ajuriaguerra *et al*, 1964, Vol 1; Freeman, 1954).

To illustrate certain aspects of graphic motor behaviour, we shall consider three problems; the hold on the tool, the speed of writing, the regulation of tonicity.

PREHENSION OF A WRITING INSTRUMENT

The position of the fingers on the tool varies with the tool used (pencil, brush), convention, and more or less conscious imitation. These different factors contribute to an accepted so-called 'standard' hold (for a given tool), while the manner of proceeding of individual adults more or less conforms to this norm, depending on various individual factors.

In children, the position changes with age. For example, a pencil is first gripped by the whole hand before the age of one. Prehension thereafter gradually becomes more distal, until the ends of the thumb and the index finger are opposite one another near the instrument's point. After six years of age, another change occurs: the flexion of the fingers decreases. Sometimes unusual, defective types of prehension occur. They are related either to tension stemming from widely differing origins (too fine a tool, awkwardness, psychic tension about writing), or to gnoso-praxic difficulties: difficulties in awareness, representation, and use of parts of the body, particularly the fingers. Lastly, a particular hold may be the mark of an ostentatious attitude intended to attract attention. From this simple example, it is clear that the graphomotor organization is also psychomotor and praxic.

SPEED OF WRITING

Handwriting scales have been designed to measure children's writing speed (Ajuriaguerra *et al*, 1964, Vol 1; Bang, 1959; Cormeau-Velghe, Destrait, Toussaint and Bidaine, 1970; Harris, 1960, pp 622-4), as well as speed of execution of other activities. They show that speed of movement increases with age and depends on maturation factors, especially in the young child. But other factors influence speed of writing. Daily learning and practice contribute to the *organization of graphic movements*. We have studied the organization of writing gestures when performing a 'horizontal' sequence. Between five and six years of age, the action is *discontinuous*, the hand being almost parallel with the line and the paper held straight. Inscriptive movements alternate with the progression of the hand along the line. During the stages that we were able to describe precisely, this infantile progression is replaced by a well co-ordinated, *continuous*, and economic progression. The elbow tends to remain in one place (between ages 12 and 14), serving as a pivot for the forearm (Callewaert, 1954), while the hand rests below the line and the sheet of paper is tilted, thus liberating the graphic field. Various improvements in graphic action occur simultaneously with this new organization, particularly an increase in speed.

Still other factors influence writing speed. It can be impeded 1. by synkinetic (Ajuriaguerra and Stambak, 1955) and tonic elements, 2. by spelling difficulties, and 3. by specific emotional attitudes toward writing (as at the outset of infantile cramp, to which we shall refer later).

TONIC REGULATION

The writing activity is not related only to brachial and manual mobility. The maintenance of immobility of the central pillar formed by the body axis is all the more necessary as the movements become more delicate and distal. For the forearm to slide easily and smoothly over the table, the body axis must remain motionless, but as Wallon (1928) remarked, in a 'very active state of immobility' with imperceptible compensatory reactions. This function of postural regulation, which develops with acquisition of the walking ability, improves with writing. Between five and seven years of age, the child's torso tends to lean sideways, drawn by the distal movement of the arm and hand advancing along the line. Towards the age of nine, the distal movements are better compensated and are more independent of the trunk, which remains still.

With individual variations that may be considerable, tonicity brings about changes in posture (upright position of the torso between ages five and 14), changes in support (gradual elimination of trunk leaning on the table and lightening of the hand), stability of the hand (the constant position in half-supination is acquired between seven and eight years), and elasticity of the shoulder, wrist, and fingers.

Force and pressure are important tonic factors that affect graphic motor control (Essing, 1965; Harris and Rarick, 1959; Luthe, 1953). It is essential for the child to learn, with practice, to use and distribute his own strength (in accordance with his age and tonic typology) in such a way as to limit his energy output. Sometimes it is necessary to help him do this. Experience gained in re-education has demonstrated that the child can improve his writing skill by learning to make a better use of his strength and by correcting unsuitable tonic reactions (Ajuriaguerra *et al*, 1964, Vol 2).

Tonic regulation in its various aspects governs the entire writing activity and therefore plays an essential role in handwriting. Serious or even slight defects in tonicity and a lack of strength impede motor control, the support function, and prehension of the implement. On the one hand, good tonicity facilitates writing, and, on the other, is evidence of a positive adaptive response to the situation. Any emotional reaction of displeasure can at the physical level produce *paratonic* reactions (exaggerated tonic reactions that impede movements) because of the close relation between tonicity and affectivity — relations that are established in early childhood (Ajuriaguerra, 1970; Wallon, 1949).

Spatial constraints on writing

The writing act is a meaningful graphic movement inscribed on a flat, two-dimensional space. Control over this space, which is always sharply defined, demands of the writer a continuous effort of anticipation. Furthermore, whether writing on a blackboard or on a sheet of paper, one always writes in a *space of representation* that is in relation to the points of reference of the writer's body. The support facing the writer has a top and a bottom, as well as a right and a left side separated by an imaginary median, the vertical projection of the body's axis. For the writer these spatial references to some extent ultimately become qualities inherent in the support, regardless of its position on the table.

Writing takes place in this particular space in accordance with various conventions relating to the shape of the letters and directions to be used, conventions that vary from place to place in the world. Here we shall consider the *directional* conventions, since they are a factor common to many forms of writing and make it possible to take a detached view of the infinite variety of characters used in the world.

The directional conventions of writing are related to the following considerations:

1. *The direction of the development of the line:* the first large unit on a written page is broken down into smaller units consisting of graphic signs (words in phonographic scripts using consonantal or alphabetical representation; ideographs or groups of ideographs in ideographic forms of writing).
2. *The sequential production of minimum units of words:* letters in an alphabetical system, groups of strokes in the elements of an ideogram in an ideographic system (letters and strokes do not serve the same purpose) (Alarcos Llorach, 1968; Alleton, 1970).

Regardless of which method of graphic representation of language is adopted, the hand has to delineate the minimum units in accordance with certain codified directions and in a given order; these units, juxtaposed or connected, are grouped in words, which are aligned according to certain directions that are also codified.

Most types of writing follow a horizontal development of the line (or a horizontal progression of the line), the first line being parallel to the upper edge of the paper, each of the following lines being situated below the preceding line (progression on the page thus being vertical, from top to bottom). Horizontal development is characterized by the fact that the characters are placed side by side, as, for example, the personages in the well-known pictograms of the Cuna Indians of Panama (Cohen, 1958). Horizontal development can be done systematically from left to right, as in Roman script (Western Europe, North and South America, etc), in modern Greek writing, Cyrillic script, Indian writing, and so forth; or from right to left, as in Hebrew and Arabic script. There are also boustrophedon inscriptions, as in ancient Greek writing, in which the lines run alternately from right to left and from left to right, and there is the particular arrangement of signs varying from line to line in the ancient writing discovered on the Easter Island tablets (Centre International de Synthèse, 1963; Cohen, 1958). In Arabic, as in Hebrew script, written from right to left, numbers (Arabic numerals) are written from left to right, in the opposite direction to the writing. Children must therefore learn to allow the necessary space to write down a number in mid-sentence. After the number is set down, the writing continues from right to left. In Hebrew script, two systems of numerical notation exist simultaneously and are learned by children: Arabic numerals and the ancient Hebrew system using certain letters of the alphabet (direction R–L), of which the principle is analogous to that used in upper case Roman numerals.

In the types of writing used in China, Japan, and Korea, the development of the line (or rather column) was until recently vertical, from top to bottom. Progression on the page was from right to left, each column being placed to the left of the preceding one. In vertical Chinese writing, the characters are placed one below the other (like figures standing one below the other), an arrangement followed in ancient Egypt for monumental hieroglyphics (Centre International de Synthèse, 1963).

At the present time in China, as in Japan, horizontal development, starting in the top left-hand corner of the page, is tending to become institutionalized (Alleton, 1970), which does not change the orientation of the characters; they are placed side by side instead of one under the other. This new arrangement is used in printed publications and is taught at school, while the traditional (vertical) system continues to be used, for example for any type of monumental writing (posters) or for some personal uses (wishes, dedications). Vertical writing, and use of the brush and Indian ink, lend the text a certain emphasis derived from the cultural and sentimental value attached to them.

The study of the genesis of writing (Gobineau and Perron, 1954) shows that the child first writes discontinuously; gradually he learns to connect several letters; later he transforms the calligraphy learned into a personal style of writing with new ligatures adapted to it. Some forms of writing are separate by tradition (Arabic and particularly Hebrew), but adult writers also introduce personal ligatures here and there.

Similarly, in cursive Chinese writing, some strokes are connected (Alleton, 1970). It should be remembered that in this writing the various strokes in one ideograph must not only follow certain directions; they must also follow a strict order of succession (they are numbered in the school children's exercise books). Learning the order of succession is facilitated by certain general rules. This order and the ductus of strokes must therefore be carried out by the children for each character they learn (some of which have been simplified since 1958) — in other words, 1000 to 2000 of the most common characters. This way of writing may seem extraordinarily difficult to users of alphabetic scripts, which all in all have about 30 forms of letters to learn (60 including capital letters). But, in fact, although it takes longer to learn Chinese writing than alphabetic script (Gray, 1958), there is no doubt that the children do finally master this system of writing, and even the still more complicated Japanese system.

But are alphabetic scripts really easier to write? Actually, the intellectual and perceptomotor activity of the alphabetic writer is, if we think about it, just as complex. Any form of writing calls for *anticipation* of the spatiotemporal development of small units in accordance with the development of the narrative and the method of representing language. A sequence of graphemes must correspond to a sequence of phonemes, which is achieved through a graphomotor rhythm and internal formulation of narrative proper to writing, a medium of expression that ultimately acquires a certain autonomy in relation to the spoken language (Alarcos Llorach, 1968).

Matters are still relatively simple — in phonographic systems — when the laws of correspondence between graphemes and phonemes are themselves fairly simple. But the difficulty of certain written languages can be considerably increased by the polyvalence of graphemes and the polygraphy of phonemes, as in French and even more so in English, where the writing system is quasi-semiographic (Alarcos Llorach, 1968, p 562). One could even go so far as to say that these scripts are at least as complex as ideographic or semiographic writing, because they continue to be taught as phonographic writings — which they basically are, according to the system of representation of language adopted — and because continuous reference to the *signatum* is as necessary as it is in Chinese writing to transcribe the correct sign and correct spelling.

Difficulties inherent in various scripts do not therefore stem exclusively from their particular spatial constraints. However, the child must pass certain stages, on the level of representation of space, to arrange the layout and development on the page of the writing he has to learn. . . .

The tools

. . . The graphic tools used in the course of history have been many and have played an important role in the evolution of forms of writing (Centre International de Synthèse, 1963).

Here we shall deal with a few aspects of the graphic tools most commonly used at the present time (Alleton, 1970): pencil and ballpoint pen the most common, fountain pen, felt pen, chalk, and still occasionally a brush or quill dipped in ink.

The instrument used by each individual may be determined by tradition, by changes in technique, by personal or national economic requirements, by teaching conventions, and lastly by personal needs and tastes. Quite frequently, several tools are variously used as much for the interest and visual pleasure afforded by variety of colour and thickness of line as for the need to adapt the tool to the type of writing required or to its recipient.

Modern teaching methods call for instruments that facilitate the learning of writing and avoid contraction of muscles (Auzias, 1970; Dottrens, 1966; Gray, 1958). Soft chalk (for writing on the board) and soft lead pencil, of necessity used by developing countries, are, in the opinion of many, the instruments best suited to the hand of the young child (Gray, 1958). It is recommended that the pencil be fairly thick, particularly in infant schools (to facilitate the grasp) and that it should also be used at the beginning of primary school, as for example in certain English-speaking countries; the pen with a metal nib is considered particularly unsuitable (Dottrens, 1966; Gray, 1958).

When the time comes to write in ink, which gives writing some relief and makes it more lasting, a ballpoint pen is usually preferred, sometimes a fountain pen. In some countries, a pen dipped in ink is still used (Gray, 1958), because of its 'magic' qualities; these are derived from the cultural, moral, and aesthetic values associated with the art of the calligrapher who used to produce the beautiful lettering in poetic and occasionally sacred texts. The gifts of men have been 'projected' into the tool. They are still: if writing is poor and the hand contracted, it is hoped that frequent changes of tool will bring about a cure, a significant act in one who has developed 'writer's cramp'.

Depending on the country, the price of a fountain pen is quite high, or moderate, or inexpensive, as in the People's Republic of China where it has replaced the brush in school and in daily life (Alleton, 1970), although the brush is still frequently used for posters and announcements In Japan, children learn at the same time to write with a brush and a ballpoint pen. Dedications and wishes are produced with the brush in vertical columns, the brush technique being frequently combined with vertical writing.

The typewriter, more and more used by adults, is also made available to children, especially handicapped children (with motor defects, and the blind). Various facilities have been developed for these children (Brachold, 1966a; Tardieu, 1972). We were able to observe that the multiple techniques for transmission and recording (handwriting, braille, typewriting, tape-recording) used by the same child (very near-sighted) provide an opening on the word, a means of adaptation, and therefore of balance.

But the machine cannot solve all problems for handicapped children, any more than it can for anyone else. It has freed man from the effort of achieving legibility and to some extent from planning layout, but not from the need to formulate the text to be written (a major difficulty for some children with language problems) or from the intervention of the hand, whether handling a tool or tapping the keys. A sound recording dictated by one person can be transcribed by another, who is an extension of that person and on whom that person depends. Furthermore, the more elaborate the machine, the less it is available to the great number; also, as a rule the more elaborate it is, the more cumbersome — there is not yet a pocket computer. Moreover, the real problem of the survival of literature — or its decline, predicted at various times — does not reside in its instruments, which are nevertheless essential. The continuance or disappearance of writing, whether handwriting or some quite other form, will depend on the requirements of society.

Methods of learning to write

Every normal individual, after reaching a certain stage of development, has the capacity to write. But this potential, which depends on the completeness and the maturation of various systems, cannot become effective without apprenticeship.

We do not intend to review the learning methods used today. For this we refer the reader to various works (Ajuriaguerra and Auzias, 1960; Bang, 1959; Gray, 1958; Rudolf, 1973) and to current UNESCO publications relating to functional literacy programmes for adults.

We would merely say that the methods of teaching writing vary greatly and are based on a certain conception of it. For synthetic methods that tend to emphasize penmanship (the oldest), writing is an art of exact imitation of set forms. These methods have been criticized on various grounds. In particular for being tedious, requiring complicated forms that are slow to execute, with the down and up strokes made by pressure exerted on a metal pen (and not by traction, as was the case with the reed pen or the goose quill, a more functional method). All the same, the synthetic methods have certain positive aspects: forms learned one by one, with their particular ductus (direction of stroke), and the simultaneous learning of reading and writing.

Subsequent methods have tended to adapt writing to the child (simplified forms, ligatures adapted to these forms, tools easy to handle, uniform thickness of strokes), and above all, to restore to writing all its value as language, while stressing its meaning (global methods), its role of expression, and of communication (Freeman, 1954; Freinet, 1955). Still other methods have stressed motor and linguistic preparation for writing (in kindergarten), and writing as motion, or its dynamic and cursive aspects (American and Canadian methods).

But some of these, the global methods, for example, of which the positive feature was to emphasize the content of writing with the help of illustration by drawing, had a tendency to reduce the grapheme-phoneme correspondence of written signs (although they dealt with writing as a form of phonographic representation) and did not teach the ductus of letters — which does facilitate the production of precise forms and the cursive movement. Although a child who has no impediments can easily adapt himself to global methods, there is a danger for those who confuse certain phonemes, ill-distinguish the parts of a sentence, or have difficulty in relating to the graphic space.

At the present time, mixed methods are frequently used (Gray, 1958). They tend to retain the positive aspects of earlier methods: learning the letters separately with their phonic value, letters that are soon connected into meaningful words that are deciphered during the reading lesson. As soon as possible, the child himself constructs a short sentence that he writes (whereas in calligraphic writing methods the text was given) and illustrates with a drawing or painting. This dynamic aspect of the method, which provokes a positive attitude to learning in the child, is the most outstanding feature of modern methods compared with earlier ones. They eliminate passivity and boredom and develop in the child a liking for expression, which is the best stimulus to writing. The most valid methods of functional literacy also seek to integrate learning of the written language with the needs and interests of the learners and attempt to make literacy an instrument of genuine education and not of 'domestication'.

In most countries, writing is taught at six years of age, sometimes seven (*Statistical Yearbook*, 1970), which corresponds to the necessary level of maturation for learning the written language. But the maturity of some children can vary quite sharply from the average. A minority of countries introduce writing at the age of five (in kindergarten), but such early learning is not suitable for most children (Auzias, 1970).

The letters used vary with the method. Sometimes connected cursive letters are taught from the beginning, sometimes separate script is preferred (similar to the letters in primers) (Gray, 1958), the translation to cursive writing being introduced latter (Harris, 1960). The advantages and disadvantages of both systems have led to much discussion. Findings of an experiment (Bang, 1959) show that retention of separate script throughout the school years impedes speed.

Writing scales

Many authors have made a point of building up handwriting scales (Ajuriaguerra *et al*, 1964, Vol 1; Bang, 1959; Fernandez-Huerta, 1950; Freeman, 1954; Gobineau and Perron, 1954; Gray, 1958). These make it possible to identify the growth levels of forms of writing and of graphic motor processes. All these studies on the genesis of writing and stages in its development have made it possible to discern more clearly the child's capability at each age: a child of six does not write like a child of nine or 12 years of age. These works have therefore provided the teacher with points of reference. They have also made it possible to study writing disabilities more precisely (Ajuriaguerra *et al*, 1964; Auzias, 1970) and have contributed to the development of re-education methods. These methods have also influenced the teaching of writing in school since the longitudinal method of observing dysgraphia in children has furthered understanding of the mechanics of writing disabilities and led to the institution of techniques that make it possible to prevent them.

Writing scales are therefore reflections of the child's writing,

supported by experimental research. Historically, they constitute a
new phenomenon in the evolution of writing.

Handwriting difficulties

Learning to write can follow a fairly smooth pattern through various
normal stages, including the mastery of difficulties inherent in any
learning process. It can, on the other hand, be impeded either by
defective teaching conditions or inadequate methods, or by the child's
own problems.

Left-handers first attracted the attention of teachers, psychologists,
and doctors (Auzias, 1970, pp 101-10; Clark, 1957). We do not regard
left-handedness as a disorder or an anomaly (with the exception of some
special cases) (Auzias, 1973), but left-handers do pose a problem for
teachers, because their laterality is not always clearly determined and
because of their specific graphic behaviour patterns. In practice, three
types of problem arise with these children: choice of hand
(Ajuriaguerra *et al*, 1964; Freeman, 1954), teaching methods (Cole,
1939; Hildreth, 1947), and sometimes mirror writing (Ajuriaguerra
and Gobineau, 1956; Critchley, 1927).

Nowadays tolerance towards left-handers tends almost everywhere
to replace the former intolerance, but the old anxiety about writing
with the 'wrong' hand still exists. In fact, although the writing
difficulties of left-handed children may be caused by motor disorders
or defects in spatial orientation, most frequently they are the result
of teaching deficiencies. Left-handers' writing problems can be reduced
or even eliminated if parents and teachers are adequately supplied with
information that will limit anxiety reactions and define techniques to
be used to facilitate the learning of writing for these children.

Left-handers are not the only children with writing problems. Some
children, regardless of their laterality, suffer from genuine handicaps
that can be the result of motor, praxic, tensional, or affective
difficulties or the result of ignorance of the language. If these
difficulties are severe, or even slight, they can be aggravated by
unpleasant circumstances (emotional trauma, crowded classes that do
not allow the teacher enough time to pay individual attention to such
and such a child) and lead to genuine troubles in the development of
writing, or dysgraphia. Moreover, functional troubles may develop that
cannot be attributed to a neurological or intellectual defect. Such
troubles are distinguished from simple learning difficulties by the initial
very strong resistance to the teaching efforts of parents and teachers
and the consequent need for strictly therapeutic treatment.

These troubles may take different clinical forms that are defined by
a certain semiology and certain etiology. On the etiological plane, it is
possible to distinguish troubles that derive from (a) disorders of motor
organization (motor debility, slight disturbances of balance and of the
kinesthetic and tonic organization, instability); (b) somatospatial
disorders — disorders in the organization of gesture and space
(difficulties in awareness, representation and use of the body; difficulties
in spatial orientation); (c) difficulties in learning language and reading

that lead to difficulties in graphic expression of the language;
(d) behaviour disorders — anxiety, nervousness, inhibition, and other manifestation of uneasiness that are reflected in one form or another in the writing (Ajuriaguerra *et al*, 1964; Olivaux, 1971).

Sometimes various causes of disturbances are combined in the same child and lead to polymorphic disorders, among them the onset of infantile cramp which is similar to writer's cramp in the adult. Symptoms of this syndrome are more or less intense awkwardness, paratonia, catastrophic reactions when faced with the writing activity, and conflicting attitudes (related to the self-concept), sometimes also associated with problems of laterality and difficulties in handling the written language. The most obvious signs of the onset of cramp are a very severe contraction of the whole arm (particularly in the proximal and distal areas), forced halts in the course of writing, painful and neuroautonomic phenomena (sweating), and a definite dislike of writing.

The semiology of the various writing disabilities (on the level of graphic forms and graphic motor processes: position, kinesthetic development, tonicity, etc) can be related to their origin; for example, there are specific graphic signs of awkwardness, of spatial disorientation, of tension, inhibition, obsessional tendencies, and so forth. Each type of disability has its own unique and particular form related to the factors involved, to the more or less widespread organization of the disorder and its evolution, to the particular coloration given by the child's age (a primary factor), and to the forms of compensation adopted by the child.

Re-education methods have been developed to treat the problems described here, including some of the specific problems of handicapped children (Ajuriaguerra *et al*, 1964, Vol 2; Brachold, 1966a; 1966b; Olivaux, 1971; Tardieu, 1972). Our re-education methods have demonstrated that it is no use dealing with the graphic symptoms as such, writing difficulties being no more than the magnifying glass of various problems. A change must be brought about in the whole complex of which the symptom is part. Although re-education methods and techniques (general relaxation, picto- and scriptographic techniques, etc) must be familiar to the re-educator, he must not apply them rigidly but rather must mould them, vary them, adapt them to the case of each child, while handling the special relationship between the child and the re-educator, which is an integral part of a dynamic re-education process.

Experience of functional disorders of writing and various data described in this article would point to the advisability of instituting pedagogical measures of all kinds, both practical and psychological, at the time of learning the written language, so as to eliminate certain hazards that can hinder the child and to create an open and genuinely educative situation: preparatory exercises, tools easy to handle, simple forms clearly taught, a calm class atmosphere, opportunity for the child to compose the texts he writes, and elimination of improper or punitive exercises in the written language. Writing should be experienced by the child not as an alienating yoke, but as a language and a praxis available to him in order to plan, construct, and create.

References

Ajuriaguerra, J de (1970) *Manuel de Psychiatrie de l'Enfant.* Paris: Masson

Ajuriaguerra, J de and Auzias, M (1960) Méthodes et techniques d'apprentissage de l'écriture. *Psychiatrie de l'Enfant* 3: 609-718

Ajuriaguerra, J de, Auzias, M, Coumes, F, Denner, A, Lavondes, M, Perron, R and Stambak, M (1964) *L'Ecriture de l'Enfant* (2 volumes: Vol 1, *L'Evolution de l'Ecriture et ses Difficultés*, and Vol 2, *La Réeducation de l'Ecriture*). Neuchâtel & Paris: Delachaux & Niestlé

Ajuriaguerra, J de and Gobineau, H de (1956) L'ecriture en miroir. *Semaine des Hopitaux* 32: 80-6

Ajuriaguerra, J de and Gobineau, H (1955) L'évolution des syncinesies chez l'enfant.

Alarcos Llorach, E (1968) Les représentations graphiques du langage. In *Le Langage.* Paris: Editions Gallimard

Alleton, V (1970) *L'Ecriture Chinoise.* Paris: Universitaires de France

Auzias, M (1970) *Les Troubles de l'Ecriture chez l'Enfant.* Neuchâtel: Delachaux & Niestlé

Auzias, M (1973) La vitesse d'écriture chez les enfants qui ecrivent de la main gauche. *Revue de Neuropsychiatric Infantile* 21: 10-11, 667-86

Bang, V (1959) *Evolution de l'Ecriture de l'Enfant a l'Adulte: Etude Expérimentale.* Neuchâtel: Delachaux & Niestlé

Brachold, H (1966a) *Einschulung Schwergeschädigter Armloser. Armbehinderter Kinder.* Stuttgart: Ernst Klett

Brachold, H (1966b) Synthetischer oder ganzheitlicher Schreibunterricht? *Praxis der Kinderpsychologie und Kinderpsychiatrie* 15: 308-15

Callewaert, H (1954) *Graphologie et Physiologie de l'Ecriture.* Louvain: Nauwelaerts

Centre International de Synthèse (1963) *L'Ecriture et la Psychologie des Peuples.* Paris: Armand Colin

Clark, M (1957) *Left-handedness.* University of London Press

Cohen, M (1958) *La Grande Invention de l'Ecriture et son Evolution.* Paris: Imprimerie Nationale

Cole, L (1939) Instruction in penmanship for left-handed children. *Elementary School Journal*, February, 436-48

Cormeau-Velghe, M, Destrait, V, Toussaint, J and Bidaine, E (1970) Normes de vitesse d'écriture: étude statistique de 1844 écoliers belges de 6 à 13 ans. *Psychologica Belgica* X 2: 247-63

Critchley, M (1927) *Mirror Writing.* London: Kegan Paul

Dottrens, R (1966) *Au Seuil de la Culture: Méthode Globale et Ecriture Script.* Paris: Editions Scarabee

Essing, V W (1965) Untersuchungen über Veränderungen der Schreibmotorik im Grundschulalter. *Human Development* 8: 194-221

Fernandez-Huerta, J (1950) *Escritura Didactica y Escala Grafica.* Madrid: Consejo Superior de Investigaciones Cientificas. Inst. San Jose de Calasanz de Pedagogia

Freeman, F N (1954) *Teaching Handwriting.* Washington, DC: American Educational Research Association

Freinet, C (1955) *Méthodes Naturelles dans la Pédagogie Moderne.* Paris: Bourrellier

Gobineau, H de and Perron, R (1954) *Génétique de l'Ecriture et Etude de la Personnalité.* Neuchâtel & Paris: Delachaux & Niestlé

Gray, W S (1958) *The Teaching of Reading and Writing: An International Survey.* Paris: Unesco (Second edition, 1969)

Harris, T L (1960) Handwriting. In C W Harris (ed) *Encyclopedia of Education Research.* New York: Macmillan

Harris, T L and Rarick, G L (1959) The relationship between handwriting pressure and legibility of handwriting in children and adolescents. *Journal of Experimental Education* **28**: 65-84

Hildreth, G (1947) *Learning the Three R's,* Minneapolis: Educ Publ

Houis, M (1971) *Anthropologie Linguistique de l'Afrique Noire.* Paris: Presses Universitaires de France

Leischner, A (1957) *Die Störungen der Schriftsprache.* Stuttgart: Thieme

Lurcat, L (1970-1971) Genèse de l'idéogramme; graphisme et langage. *Bulletin de Psychologie* **16/18**: 932-47

Lurcat, L (1974) *Etude de l'Acte Graphique.* Paris et La Haye: Monton

Luthe, W (1953) Der elektroscriptograph. *Psychologische Forschung* **24**: 194-214

Olivaux, R (1971) *Désordres et Réeducation de l'Ecriture.* Paris: Editions ESF

Rudolf, H (1973) *Schreiberziehung und Schriftpsychologie.* Bielefeld: Pfeffer (preface by O Lockowandt)

Saussure, F de (1916) *Cours de Linguistique Générale.* Lausanne: Payot (Seventeenth edition, 1972). Paris: Payot

Statistical Yearbook. Paris: Unesco (1970)

Tardieu, G (1972) Education thérapeutique de l'habileté. *Les Feuillets de l'Infirmité Motrice Cérébale.* Paris: Ass Nat Infirm Motrice Cérébraux

Wallon, H (1928) La maladresse. *Journal de Psychologie Normale et Pathologique* **25**: 61-78. Also in *Enfance* 3 4: 264-76

Wallon, H (1949) *Les Origines du Caractère.* Paris: Presses Universitaires de France

2.2 Lined paper, legibility and creativity

PETER BURNHILL, JAMES HARTLEY AND LINDSEY DAVIES

(A shortened version of this paper first appeared in *Educational Research* (1978) 14 1: 62.)

Introduction

Despite the extensive literature on teaching handwriting (eg see Paper 2.0) little research appears to have been carried out on the effects of lined or unlined paper on learning to write. In the past, teachers of writing tended to use paper ruled with single or multiple lines and children were taught to regulate the size and shape of their letters by these guidelines. In recent years, however, particularly in the United Kingdom, there has been a move away from these traditional methods towards an approach which concentrates much less on the control of spatial organization. Teachers have been encouraged by writing manuals such as that provided by Inglis and Connell (1964): children, they say, 'welcome emancipation from the restriction of lines and the freedom to set out their work according to their own tastes and abilities. . .' and '. . .not only does the use of unlined paper facilitate the development of fluent and rhythmical writing and early appreciation of correct size and spacing of letters and words, but children using it find pleasure and satisfaction in their work.' Inglis and Connell and the influential Bullock Report (1975) recommend the use of unlined paper for writing on throughout the primary school: 'the paper on which children are to write should always be unlined and of a sufficient size to be unrestricting' (Bullock Report, p 185).

In an earlier study (Burnhill *et al*, 1975) we assessed the effects of lined and unlined paper on the legibility of children's writing. In that particular investigation children from three primary schools, who had been writing for about two years, and who had learned to write on unlined paper, wrote daily in booklets containing alternating pages of lined and unlined paper. These children were not specifically instructed to write on the lines and, indeed, nothing was said to the children about them. The results, in terms of contrasting legibility, were quite startling. The legibility of the writing on the lined paper was obviously so much better that the headmasters of the three schools concerned all reversed their initial policy and ordered lined paper for future use throughout the schools.

It was anticipated, at that time, that this reversal of policy would allow us to carry out a unique investigation. We planned to gather samples of writing from this first group of children, and then to return to the schools two years later to take similar samples. Thus, we hoped, we would be able to compare the writing of the children who had learned to write on unlined paper with those who had learned to write on lined paper. Accordingly, then, each child in the first group of pupils who had learned to write on unlined paper was asked to write two essays — one entitled *My Home* and the other *My School* — one on unlined and one on lined paper and, two years later, we were able to repeat this exercise in two of the original schools.

Our plans for the comparison study unfortunately did not materialize: the schools had experienced difficulty in immediately obtaining lined paper; the teaching personnel had changed; and the children in 1977, it was claimed, were less able than those of 1975. Nonetheless the data we collected in 1977 did enable us to replicate the 1975 study. Furthermore, in this study we were able to examine the view, held by many teachers, that the use of lined paper has a detrimental effect upon the creativity of young children's writing.

These two considerations — legibility and creativity — form the focus of this paper.

1. Lines and legibility

Fifty-six children, 32 girls and 24 boys, with an average age of seven years and two months were asked by their teachers to write an essay on *My Home* one week, and on *My School* a week later. These topics were suggested by the teachers and were, of course, the same as those used in the earlier study. The children from one school wrote the first essay on lined paper and the second essay on unlined paper, and the children in the second school did the reverse. (The paper was A4 size, and the lines faintly ruled in blue, 20mm apart.) The children were allowed 40 minutes to complete the task.

The resulting essays were xerox-copied in order to 'remove' the lines. Each essay was then coded on the reverse side, in terms of the name and sex of the writer, the type of paper used (lined or unlined), and the topic of the essay. (Thus essays coded 1BHL and 1BSU were essays from participant number 1, who was a boy, *My Home* written on lined paper and *My School* written on unlined paper.)

Ten undergraduate certificate of education students (of both sexes, but mainly female) then acted as judges of legibility. Each judge was asked to compare in turn the two essays written by each child and to record on a specially prepared recording sheet the code number of the essay they found to be the more legible: the coding system was not explained to the judges until the task was completed.

RESULTS

The results were quite clearcut: 75 per cent of the essays written on the lined paper were rated as more legible than essays written by the same children on the unlined paper: 20 per cent were rated as not being any different, and 5 per cent were rated as being more legible on the

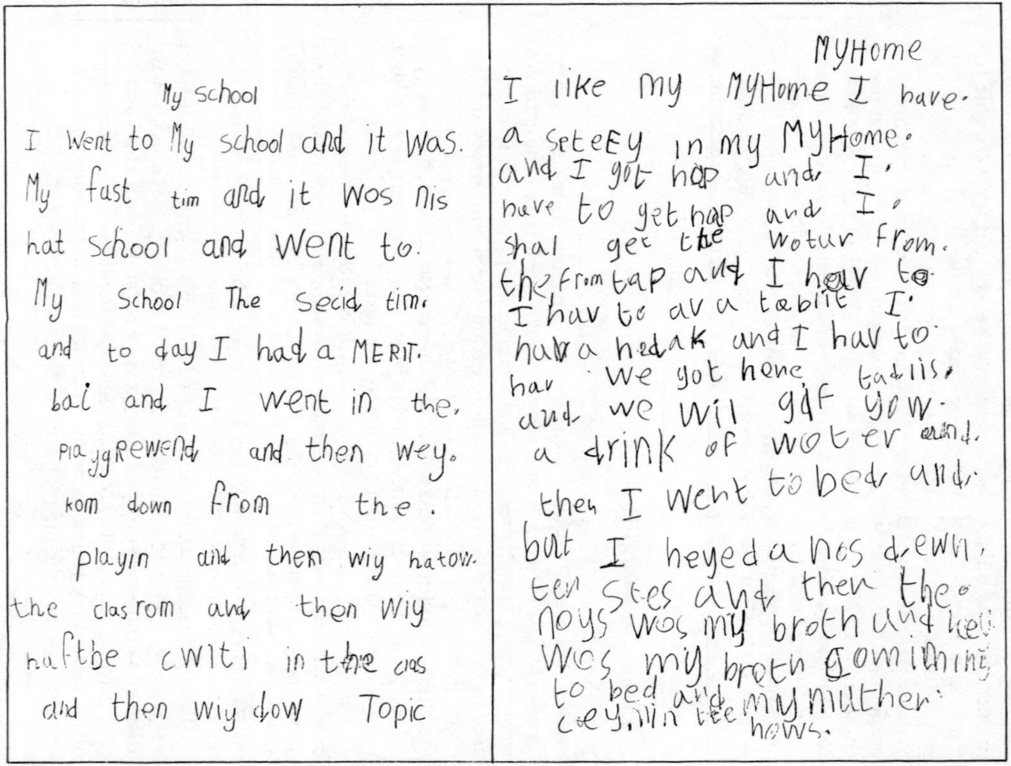

Figure 1. Writing on lined (left) and unlined (right) paper from the same child. (Original size, A4)

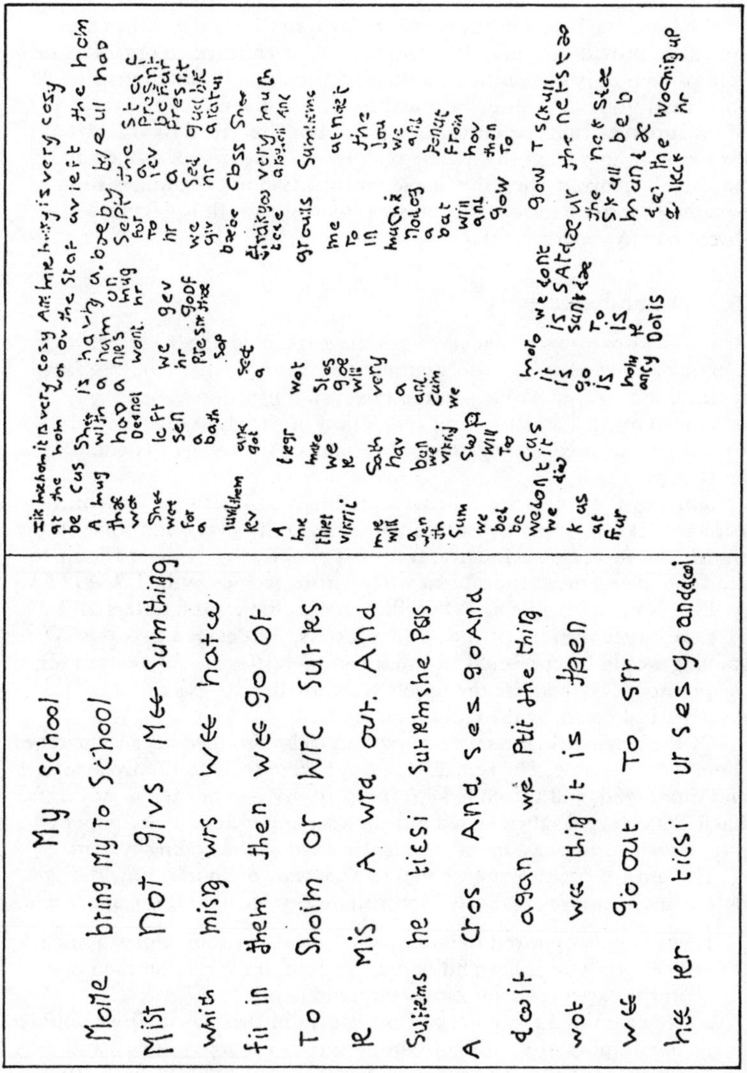

Figure 2. *Writing on lined (left) and unlined (right) paper from another child. (Original size A4)*

unlined paper than on the lined.

These results thus replicated those obtained earlier by Burnhill *et al* (1975). It was again found that the lined pages had a marked effect on the overall organization of the work of most children. The children did not always write on the lines: sometimes they wrote between them, and the spacing between the words seemed more regular. Lines thus appear to provide a framework which enables children to organize the void of an empty page into a number of manageable and dimensionally consistent units of two-dimensional space. On the unlined pages it was often apparent that the only guide a child had received to organize his writing came from the line he had written above and, as a result, if 'slippage' occurred, then the linear organization of the phrases soon became chaotic. Figure 1 provides a typical illustration. Figure 2 shows a more extreme case.

2. Lines and creativity

As noted above, many teachers consider that lined paper hinders creativity of expression. This argument apparently views the supposed restriction imposed by lines in the physical dimension as being paralleled by an accompanying restriction of the child's creative ability. In this part of this investigation we set out to try and gather some data on this issue.

Some of the essays were written originally in the Initial Teaching Alphabet (ITA), some in traditional orthography (TO), and some in the transition stage. Consequently, for most people, they were difficult to read. To overcome this problem we re-wrote each essay in TO. As ITA spelling is not the same as TO spelling and as the capital letters in ITA are larger versions of the smaller letters, we decided that the TO spelling would be corrected and that capital letters would be used for proper nouns. Otherwise the essays were unaltered — so that the grammatical errors of the child remained.

Of the original 112 essays several had to be dropped because parts of them were illegible. The remaining essays were then randomly assorted and numbered, and the code kept privately by one of the investigators. Each TO essay was then typed out on a separate sheet of A4 paper by a typist who was unaware of the significance of the coding system.

The most difficult issue we had to face was, of course, how did one define and measure creativity? In this enquiry we used three approaches.

1. We simply counted the number of words written. Our argument here was that if lines hindered freedom of expression then one might expect shorter essays on lined paper.
2. We examined the syntax of the essays in two ways: (i) we counted the number of words containing three or more syllables; and (ii) we looked for essays in which tenses in addition to the present tense were used.
3. We asked teachers themselves to rate the essays for creativity — using their own assessment of what this meant. Just what this involved is described in more detail below.

RESULTS

In this enquiry, because two schools were involved and because each child contributed two essays, the data from the topics and the schools were combined. The analyses reported are thus concerned with the lined and unlined essays only, and not with the essay topics.

Number of words. The average number of words written for the essays on the lined and on the unlined paper is shown in Table 1.

		Lined paper	Unlined paper
Boys	$\overline{X}$	120	137
(N = 18)	sd	70	88
Girls	$\overline{X}$	135	127
(N = 24)	sd	63	64

Table 1. *The average number of words written for the essays on the lined and the unlined paper*

A two-way analysis of variance (conditions x sex) indicated that there were no significant differences between the amount written by the boys or the girls on the lined or the unlined paper.

Number of syllables. Table 2 shows the average number of words written containing three or more syllables in the essays on the lined and the unlined paper. These differences were not significant.

		Lined paper	Unlined paper
Boys	$\overline{X}$	2.78	2.39
(N = 18)	sd	2.96	2.40
Girls	$\overline{X}$	1.75	1.50
(N = 24)	sd	1.48	1.38

Table 2. *The average number of words written containing three or more syllables on the lined and unlined paper*

Additional tenses. The proportion of essays in which there were changes of tense is shown in Table 3. This difference was significant in favour of the essays written on the lined paper ($p < .05$, two-tail test).

Rating creativity. Stage 1. A two-stage procedure was used in the rating of the creativity of the essays. First of all, 19 education students were asked to sort 50 of the essays into five piles, each pile corresponding to one of five categories — 1. least creative, 2. not very creative, 3. average, 4. fairly creative, 5. most creative. It was stressed that the judgement should be based solely on a consideration of creativity and should not be influenced by factors such as lack of punctuation, but the term 'creativity' was not defined.

This procedure allowed us to assess the frequency with which each of the essays was placed in each category. Accordingly, we were able to select the five essays which occurred most frequently in categories

	Lined paper	Unlined paper
Boys (N = 18)	0.78	0.61
Girls (N = 24)	0.79	0.58

Table 3. *The proportion of essays in which there were changes of tense on the lined and unlined paper*

1. to 5. Table 4 indicates the number of times that each of these five essays was placed in a particular category and the essays themselves are reproduced in Table 5.

Essay number	Category number				
	1	*2*	*3*	*4*	*5*
16	14̲̲	3	1	0	1
28	2	13̲̲	3	1	0
17	0	5	10̲̲	4	0
18	0	1	3	11̲̲	4
47	0	0	3	3	13̲̲

Table 4. *The distribution of the ratings for each of the five selected essays*

Category 1. (least creative)
in my home we have a settee in the sitting room in the sitting room there is a table with some chairs a tellie and sideboard on the sideboard is a model fish upstairs there is bunkbeds

Category 2. (not very creative)
I like my school I like to go on the apparatus because it gives us exercises I like to go on the playground my best friend is called Erica and as soon as we come of the playground we go on the mat and sing song and we have our prayers and then go back to the classrooms and do some work and then have dinner at 12 o'clock

Category 3. (average)
we make things with paper we can make pictures with wool we can do anything with paper we can make things with cotton wool I like my school it is fun in school there are toys in school we say our prayer in the morning when we come to school we go on the playground I like to play batman and Robin it is on tonight we have got a head master we sing in a manger

Category 4. (fairly creative)
my home is big and my home has a chimney I have three rooms and five beds and I have got a canary in my home and I have a bathroom and when I go for a bath there is a spider in the bath and last time I seen a spider come out of a hole and it was in the bathroom and when Brian came in from school I was hiding in the blankets and he could not find me I was in my dads room

Category 5. (most creative)
my daddy has a new car it has got a fan in it to cool the radiator it has
a radio in it so it needs an aerial it has got one it is four doors on it my
daddy is making a tool box on it it has hydra gas the hydra gas has no
gravity my daddys car can go one hundred than twenty miles an hour
I love riding in it would you it is called Austin Allegro 1500 it has a square
steering wheel and headlamps I live at Four Garrick Rise I am going to a
party tonight we are having hot dogs cakes I am also having fireworks
tonight we are letting one off bang crash wallop and now let the rocket
off whizzzzzzzz now the sparklers bang whizzzzzzzzzzzzzzzz pop two
more bang crash bang crash

Table 5. *The most frequently occurring essay in each category*

Rating creativity. Stage 2. We next asked a second set of judges
(13 qualified teachers) to rate the creativity of all the complete pairs
of essays, using the examples shown in Table 5 to help them in the task.
The results were then assembled so that each essay had 13 separate
category ratings (from 1 to 5) and a total creativity score — the sum of
these 13 ratings.

A two-way analysis of variance was conducted with these total scores,
and the overall results, shown in Table 6, indicated that there were no
significant differences between the total creativity scores obtained by
the boys or the girls on essays written on lined or unlined paper.

		Lined paper	Unlined paper
Boys	$\overline{X}$	36.6	36.6
(N = 18)	sd	13.2	16.0
Girls	$\overline{X}$	38.1	39.3
(N = 24)	sd	11.4	11.3

Table 6. *The mean total creativity ratings given to essays on the lined and unlined paper*

Finally, correlation coefficients were calculated between the various
creativity measures used in this investigation, and the overall results are
shown in Table 7. The correlation of 0.25 (between the number of
syllables used, and the tense changes) was significant at the $p < .05$ level
of significance: the remaining coefficients were all significant at the
$p < .01$ level.

One interesting anomaly did arise in these results in that the intercorrelations between the number of syllables, the number of tense
changes, and the creativity ratings differed for the boys and the girls
on the lined and the unlined paper. For the boys the correlations
between syllables and tense changes were 0.33 on lined paper and 0.18
on unlined paper, and between syllables and the creativity ratings they
were 0.75 on both. For the girls, however, the correlations were -0.02
on the lined and +0.48 on the unlined paper and -0.01 and +0.67
respectively. In short, the correlations for the girls were lower on these

measures with the lined paper. In all the conditions, however, (boys, girls, lined, unlined) the correlations between the number of words written and the creativity ratings ranged between 0.89 and 0.91, suggesting that the length of the essay and its overall creativity (as rated by the judges) was closely interrelated.

	Number of words	Number of syllables	Tense changes	Creativity ratings
Number of words	1.00	0.52	0.48	0.89
Number of syllables		1.00	0.25	0.54
Tense changes			1.00	0.51
Creativity ratings				1.00

Table 7. *Intercorrelations between the different creativity measures (N = 84)*

Comments

To summarize this section on creativity: none of the measures used showed any differences between the essays written on lined and the essays written on unlined paper, with the exception of the use of tenses in addition to the present one. Here there was a greater proportion of essays with additional tenses written on the lined paper. Whether using additional tenses reflects creativity is, of course, an open question, although this was in fact one of the criteria used by the judges in rating the essays. (The judges were asked, when they had completed the rating task, to indicate what criteria they had used. The main ones given are listed in Table 8.)

Criteria	Frequency
Story line with linkage and time sequence	6
Use of imagination	5
Ability to share experience	5
Descriptive ability	5
Quality of content and vocabulary	4
Use of future tense	3
Relevance to subject	2
Novelty in approach to subject	2

Table 8. *Examples of judges' criteria for rating creativity (N = 13)*

One other observation may be made here, and this is that the essays themselves were not very creative (see Table 5). This may have resulted partly from the topic chosen, which might indeed be considered rather mundane. (This choice, of course, was a consequence of our original intention to carry out a comparison study between children who had experienced different methods of learning to write.) Nonetheless, it can be argued that the children could write freely on these topics and, therefore, that any creativity in them would stand out well. This argument is supported by the example provided in category 5 in Table 5.

Concluding remarks

The results of the investigations reported in this paper allow us to report one thing with certainty and one thing with rather less confidence. There seems to be no doubt that lined paper helps children to write more legibly than unlined paper. It is not quite so clear, however, whether or not lined paper hinders creativity. In our view, the results suggest not — and indeed point to a contrary view.

Because of the clear effects of lines on legibility we feel it wise to advocate that teachers of handwriting use lined paper with their children. We are not saying that lines should dominate the teaching of writing but, more simply, that lines provide helpful guidance for the novice. We believe that the appearance of written work and the way it is set out deserves specific attention. Children should grow up accustomed to taking care in the way they present their work and to regard its appearance as an important aspect of the whole production. This means that when their handwriting is being developed there needs to be attention not only to the shape of individual letters and words but to the spacing of words and lines, the relative height of letters, the paragraph indentations, the form and the style of the headings, and the width and the depth of the surrounds. Practice in these matters should not take the form of drill, in which the child copies material of no other value. It should derive from activities where the task carries a purpose for the child.

The paragraph above (apart from the first two sentences) was taken from the Bullock Report. We agree with its sentiments but we disagree with how best to achieve them. In our view lined paper is a factor in achieving these desirable goals: unlined paper is not.

Acknowledgements

We are indebted to the headmasters, staff and children from Nursery Field School, and Pear Tree School, Rugeley, who took part in this experiment, and to Miss Lynn Townsend and Miss Mary Chaloner who collected the data on creativity.

References

Burnhill, P, Hartley, J, Fraser, S and Young, M (1975) Writing lines: an exploratory study. *Programmed Learning & Educational Technology* 11: 84-7
Great Britain (1975) *A Language for Life.* Report of the Committee of Enquiry. Chairman Sir A Bullock. London: HMSO
Inglis, A and Connell, A (1964) *The Teaching of Handwriting.* London: Nelson

2.3 Writing, dictating and speaking letters

JOHN D GOULD AND STEPHEN J BOIES

(Gould, J D and Boies, S J (1978) *Science* 201: 1145-7. Reproduced with permission of the authors and the American Association for the Advancement of Science © 1978 American Association for the Advancement of Science.)

The composition of letters, memos, essays, and technical reports is widespread, time-consuming, and often difficult (1). Although most people write their compositions by hand, alternatives such as dictating and typewriting are used by some. Differences in the process of composition and in its resulting quality and speed made by these different methods have been speculative. We now summarize key findings from ongoing research that provide some understanding of these issues (2). Our experimental approach is to vary the tasks assigned to authors and the methods they are to use and to videotape them while they compose. The assigned tasks were varied by requiring each participant to compose 16 different letters. The methods they used were to write, dictate, or speak letters or to compose in 'invisible writing'. For invisible writing, participants wrote with a wooden stylus on paper with carbon paper underneath.

Dictating is potentially five times faster than writing, on the basis of estimates of maximum writing and speaking rates when composition is not required (3). Dictating may also be qualitatively superior: potentially faster transfer of ideas from limited capacity working memory to a permanent record may reduce forgetting attributable to interference or decay.

Speaking may be more 'natural' than dictating because authors assume that a recipient will listen to what they say rather than read it. This allows a phraseology appropriate for listening but not necessarily for reading. Speaking may also be more natural because authors do not give typing instructions, which is a potentially disruptive secondary task.

Participants were generally college graduates, 25 to 45 years old. Eight had never dictated before. On a single day of training, they (i) learned the basic rules of dictation and how to use a dictation machine (IBM Executary) (45 minutes) and then (ii) dictated and subsequently proof-edited 16 fairly simple business letters (four to five hours). They returned the next day for the experiments reported here. Eight other participants were experienced dictators, business executives who had dictated regularly for years and preferred dictating to writing. They did not go through the training day.

Each participant composed eight 'routine' business letters, two each by writing, invisible writing, dictating, and speaking. These were replies to information requests. Each then composed eight more 'complex', one-page letters, two each with each method. Topics included the author's feelings on capital punishment, the US Bicentennial, and a letter of recommendation. The orders of the four composition methods and the eight specific letter-assignments, and the combinations of letter-assignments and methods, were counterbalanced across participants within a group with a modified 8 by 8 Greco-Latin square design.

Composition times were recorded from a participant's receipt of a letter-assignment until he or she indicated completion by stopping a clock. The videotapes were used to analyse composition times into three subtimes: pausing; generating (actual writing, dictating, or speaking); and reviewing. Written, dictated, and invisibly written letters were typed by a secretary and returned after one hour for participants to proof-edit. There was only one proof-editing cycle. The quality of the retyped letters was rated afterwards by several independent judges on various attributes, for example, syntax and substance. Judges listened to and rated spoken letters on the same attributes (2).

Participants' experience, the type of letter (routine or complex), methods, and the combination of letter-assignments and methods were factors in the 2 x 2 x 4 x 2 analysis of variance for each measure, with the last three factors as the within-subjects sources of variance. Separate analyses of variance were carried out for each measure shown in Table 1.

Means for composition time and its component generation and pause times were longer for complex letters than for routine letters $[F (1,14) = 99.28, 70.84, 25.07,$ respectively; all $P < .001]$. In general, this was true in all methods and for both groups. Composition time depended upon method $[F (3, 42) = 26.95; P < .001]$. Speaking (6.5 minutes) was faster than dictating (7.7 minutes), and both were faster than writing (9.4 minutes) and invisible writing (8.9 minutes); Duncan's multiple range test, $P < .01$. The main reason for this was that participants' generation times were faster in dictation (3.7 minutes) and speech (3.1 minutes) than in writing (7.0 minutes) and invisible writing (6.6 minutes); Duncan's multiple range test $p < .01$. On the other hand, pause times were longer in dictation (3.0 minutes) and speaking (2.9 minutes) than in writing (2.4 minutes) and invisible writing (2.3 minutes); Duncan's multiple range test, $P < .01$. These longer pause times in dictation and speech were caused entirely by the novice dictators [experience-by-method interaction, $F (3, 42) = 9.10; P < .001]$. Review times were brief in all methods (Table 1). They are not reported for writing because the videotapes rarely showed with certainty whether participants were reviewing. Reading time is included in pause times for all methods. Novice dictators wrote a little faster and dictated a little slower than the experienced dictators [experience-by-method interaction, $F (3, 42) = 2.88; P < .05]$.

The speed advantage of speaking over dictating (6.5 versus 7.7 minutes; $P < .01$) may have arisen because composing an oral letter to be read rather than to be heard may require extra time. Alternatively, a person may just talk more slowly when the listener must type what is said.

Quality of letters, on the average, was about the same for both groups, all methods, and both types of letter. For example, on letters composed by novices, rated on a 5-point scale, where 1 = unacceptable, 3 = acceptable, and 5 = excellent, the scores were writing, 3.2; invisible writing, 3.1; dictating, 3.0; and speaking, 3.1 $[F (3, 21), P > .10]$. The quality of letters composed by the experienced group was similar (2, 4).

Does dictating take a long time to learn? Composition time for novice dictators was the same in writing and dictating (Table 1), both on routine letters $[F (1, 7) = 1.39; P > .20]$ and on complex letters $[F (1, 7) = 1.54; P > .20]$. Quality scores were 3.2 and 2.9 for writing and dictating, respectively $(P > .10)$, on the routine letters, and 3.2 and 3.1 $(P > .20)$ on complex letters. Proof-editing changes were usually minor on both written and dictated letters.

How much faster does one become with years of practice at dictating? Those with experience dictated routine letters about 20 per cent faster than the novices [but $F (1,14) = 2.48; P > .10$], and they dictated the complex letters in the same time as the novice did. Compared with themselves, experienced dictators dictated routine letters about 35 per cent faster than they wrote them and they dictated complex letters about 20 per cent faster than they wrote them (Table 1). Clearly, they did not dictate five times faster than they wrote.

Writing is easier to review than dictating. Does this difference affect performance? To test this hypothesis, invisible writing was compared with writing and with dictating. For novice dictators, composition times, quality, and number of subsequent proof-editing changes (few) were the same in invisible writing (where review is impossible) as in writing and dictating [all $F (2, 14)$; all $P > .10$]. Results were similar for experienced dictators, except that dictating was faster than writing and invisible writing on routine letters and faster than writing on complex letters (Duncan's multiple range test, $P < .05$).

The limiting factor in composition is evidently not output modality. As shown by words per minute (WPM) during generation (5)(Table 1), participants wrote at roughly half their maximum possible writing rate (40 WPM) and, regardless of experience, dictated at roughly one-fourth their maximum possible speaking rate (200 WMP). During generation, WPM were at least twice as great in dictating and speaking as in writing. This speed advantage had a small effect on total composition time, however, because generation time was only a small fraction of total composition time; planning time was about two-thirds of total composition time. Facial expressions, lip movements, and participants' comments indicated that planning occurred during pauses. Planning time was estimated from pause time plus a fraction of generation time, which was [generation time – (number of words/maximum possible WPM)]. The important finding that planning time is about two-thirds of composition time, regardless of method or experience, suggests that planning and generating are not independent processes. An alternative hypothesis had been that planning is independent of method of

Measure	Letter complexity	Novice dictators				Experienced dictators				Critical values*
		W	IW	D	S	W	IW	D	S	
Composition time (minutes)	R	6.4	6.8	5.7	3.6	7.1	7.0	4.6	3.5	1.7 to 1.9
	C	11.2	9.8	10.2	8.8	12.9	12.1	10.2	10.0	2.9 to 3.3
Generation time (minutes)	R	4.9	4.9	2.7	1.7	5.2	5.1	2.9	2.0	1.1 to 1.3
	C	8.4	7.7	3.9	3.2	9.5	8.5	5.4	5.6	2.0 to 2.3
Pause time (minutes)	R	1.5	1.7	2.1	1.7	1.8	1.9	1.4	1.3	NS†
	C	2.8	2.0	5.0	5.1	3.4	3.6	3.3	3.5	2.0 to 2.2
Review time (minutes)	R			0.8	0.2			0.3	0.3	
	C			1.0	0.4			1.1	0.9	
Generation periods (No)	R	5.8	4.8	6.7	3.6	4.8	4.7	4.8	3.7	2.0 to 2.2
	C	9.2	6.3	11.6	10.0	6.9	5.8	12.0	10.6	3.3 to 3.8
Pauses (No)	R	5.9	4.6	5.5	3.2	4.8	4.7	3.8	3.1	1.9 to 2.1
	C	9.0	6.5	10.9	9.9	6.9	5.8	8.4	7.3	3.0 to 3.5
Reviews (No)	R			2.6	0.4			1.9	1.7	
	C			2.4	1.0			6.6	5.5	
Words (No)	R	87.5	83.8	95.6	95.1	80.6	82.8	91.6	95.1	NS
	C	166	154	208	219	180	165	241	287	66 to 75
Words per minute	R	14.1	13.0	17.4	29.2	12.1	12.0	20.9	29.3	5.4 to 6.7
	C	15.1	16.3	22.5	29.3	14.3	14.5	25.2	30.5	7.4 to 8.4
Words per minute of generation time	R	18.6	17.3	36.5	61.6	16.2	16.3	33.9	49.9	9.8 to 11
	C	20.3	20.3	59.5	78.1	23.9	20.5	46.0	55.0	15 to 17
Sentence length (words)	R**									
	C	17.9	16.5	19.2	19.4	18.1	16.7	19.3	19.7	NS

* Duncan's multiple range test (9) with α = .01 and 98 degrees of freedom. To interpret, first rank order means within a row. The smaller critical value must be exceeded if adjacent means are to be significantly different; the larger value must be exceeded if the two extreme means are to be significantly different. Critical values for pairs of means separated by more than two but fewer than seven means can be approximated by linear interpolation.

NS† Not significant.

** Routine letters did not lend themselves to this measure. The component times do not always sum exactly to total composition times because of rounding errors and occasional difficulty in analysing a videotape record.

Table 1. *Means of measures for composing routine (R) and complex (C) letters by novice and experienced participants in writing (W), invisible writing (IW), dictating (D), and speaking (S)*

95

composition; that is, planning time is constant regardless of method, although it may be affected by experience. This hypothesis receives some support from the data on complex letters, where planning time was about the same for all four methods and two groups (7.1 to 8.0 minutes). On routine letters, this constant relationship did not hold, however. More generally, we doubt the validity of any simple cognitive-stage hypothesis that does not include feedback.

Novice dictators dictated about as well as they wrote. However, we hypothesized that they may not believe it. To test this, eight more participants, similar to the original novice group, were trained to dictate. The next day they rated their compositions on a 7-point scale (4): (i) just after composing each letter; (ii) about 30 to 60 minutes later, after receiving a typed version of their written or dictated letter and incorporating any proof-editing changes; and (iii) two weeks later. As predicted, novice dictators, just after composing, rated their two dictated letters as significantly poorer (3.8) than their two written letters (4.4) $[F (1, 7) = 35.17; P < .01]$. Subsequently they rated them as equivalent (stage 2: dictated = 4.6, written = 4.5, $P > .20$; stage 3: dictated = 4.1, written = 3.9, $P > .20$), as did outside judges (dictated = 3.6, written = 3.6). Experienced dictators, on the other hand, rated their written and dictated letters as equivalent at all stages. Written and dictated letters were similar in style. Judges performed only slightly better than chance when required to distinguish typed versions of dictated and written letters.

While dictation may fulfil some characteristics of a skill (6), it does not fulfil the most observable ones. Novices learned rapidly (in a few hours); problem-solving behaviours related to dictation *per se* were nearly absent after one training day; differences between the novice and experienced dictators were small; and differences between good and poor composers were larger than differences among composition methods. Composition, acquired with difficulty over years, appears to be the fundamental skill.

Our present understanding of composition includes more than a performance view. Performance theory (7) seeks to understand human behaviour by identifying the skills, abilities, capacities, conditions, and cognitive mechanisms that limit and determine human behaviour. This approach, while useful, is incomplete as a guide to understanding composition because it does not consider attitudes, tastes, motives, and feelings of authors. Our results suggest that both actual performance and perceived performance probably affect one's choice of method of composition in everyday life. A third class of reasons, which include secretarial variables and the sociology and organization of one's environment, need to be studied for a further understanding of compositional methods.

These results make several theoretical contributions. For example, the finding that planning time is two-thirds of composition time identifies the key process in composition, regardless of method or complexity. The conclusion that composition is the fundamental skill, and method of composition is secondary to it, contributes to the recent surge of interest in studying how experts do skilled tasks. The results demonstrate that composition can be studied successfully in the laboratory. They provide a context for investigating more specific cognitive issues in composition (8). At the same time, it is important to extend the present approach to longer documents, typewriting, use of computer text-editing terminals, interrupted environments (as offices are), discretionary tasks, and informal communications.

References and notes

1. E T Klemmer and F W Snyder (*J Commun* 22: 142 [1972]) reported that industrial laboratory personnel actually spend 14 per cent of their day writing and believe that they spend 22 per cent.
2. J D Gould in *Attention and Performance*, J Requin (ed) (Erlbaum, Hillsdale, NJ, 1978), vol 7; *J Exp Psychol*, 1978, 4: 648-61; J D Gould and S J Boies, *Hum Factors*, 1978, 20: 495-505
3. People can write memorized material or transcribe printed material as fast as 40 WPM, and they can speak memorized material or read aloud printed material as fast as 200 WPM.
4. Experienced dictators, studied several months later, were rated on a 7-point scale: 1 = unacceptable; 3 = acceptable(−); 5 = acceptable(+); and 7 = excellent. Outside judges rated written letters 4.0 and dictated ones 4.5. An interim study suggested the value of using a 7-point scale.
5. Words per minute during generation were estimated by (i) dividing total composition time into 6-second intervals, (ii) classifying a 6-second interval as generation time if a participant wrote or spoke during it, and (iii) dividing the number of words in the composition by total generation time. We are now measuring generation time to 0.1 second accuracy, which gives about the same results.
6. For discussion of skill, see F Bartlett, *Thinking: An Experimental and Social Study* (Basic Books, New York, 1958); D LaBerge and S Samuels, *Cognitive Psychol* 6: 293 (1974); S Card, T Moran, A Newell, *Xerox Rep SSL 76-8* (1976); G Miller and P Johnson-Laird, *Language and Perception* (Harvard Univ Press, Cambridge, Mass, 1976).
7. P M Fitts and M I Posner, *Human Performance* (Brooks/Cole, Belmont, Calif, 1969).
8. See S Rosenberg (ed) *Sentence Production* (Erlbaum, Hillsdale, NJ, 1977) for examples of this in speech production.
9. D B Duncan, *Biometrics* 11: 1 (1955).
10. We thank M Chodorow for his helpful discussions of this work.

2.4 Writing essays: the actions and strategies of students

ALAN BRANTHWAITE, MARK TRUEMAN AND JAMES HARTLEY

(This paper has not previously been published.)

Introduction

There are considerable variations in the approaches of students to their courses. This is a complex matter involving differences in perception of goals and objectives; different values and priorities; the operation of different skills; and the use of different strategies to organize and guide behaviour in relation to the demands and pressures of the situation. Broad typologies have been identified which contrast the approaches of students (Entwistle, 1976). In many cases these differences in students' approaches have been studied in connection with attitudes and ideas about examinations.

In previous research we have noted how students appear to adopt particular strategies for dealing with course assessment (Hartley and Branthwaite, 1976). Initially, a subsidiary psychology course at Keele had been divided into three sections, and the overall assessment had been based on two essay examinations at the end of the year. Later this assessment procedure was changed. The two end-of-year examination papers were taken as before, only this time they constituted two-thirds of the total assessment. The other third came from three essays that the students had written during the year — one for each section of the course. The findings indicated that this change made very little difference to the overall end-of-year marks achieved by the students: the examination performance declined slightly but the essay marks raised the overall mark a little (a mere 2 per cent). However, if the assessment had been based on the examination results alone, then twice as many students as before would have failed with the new system. It was clear that our students had adopted different strategies of approach to deal with the new system. Some had worked less hard for the examination because they knew they had three good essay marks already; others had worked harder for the exam to recover from deficiencies which had already been made apparent.

This paper describes students' approaches to writing essays in the same subsidiary course. The study examined the actions which resulted from students' strategies to meet the course requirements. In particular the research focused on 1. what students perceived to be the desirable attributes of an essay; 2. how they set about producing these; and

3. whether or not they changed their strategies in the light of experience. Because the students studying subsidiary psychology at Keele may be in their first, second or third year at university, we were able to examine differences in strategies between students in these three years.

Method

A questionnaire was given to the students (see Appendix 1) before they handed in their essays and before the essays were marked. The questionnaire listed a wide range of actions related to essay writing and asked students to indicate which ones they had used. The questionnaire could not be anonymous because we wanted to relate the answers on the questionnaire to the marks that were actually given to the essays. However, confidentiality was assured, and the questionnaires were returned in sealed envelopes to a research assistant. These were not opened until the essays had been marked and returned. This procedure yielded a total of 110 questionnaires (ie a return rate of over 80 per cent).

	Original sample						Control sample		
	First essay			Second essay			Second essay		
	M	F	Total	M	F	Total	M	F	Total
First year	13	6	19	6	4	10	12	4	16
Second year	13	10	23	8	7	15	9	8	17
Third year	2	3	5	1	2	3	1	1	2
Total	28	19	47	15	13	28	22	13	35

Table 1. *Sample structure and size*

Table 1 provides a breakdown of this return. Information was obtained from 47 students about their first essay, and 28 of these were also asked about their second essay. This procedure allowed us to compare approaches to writing the first and second essays by the same students. A further control group (N = 35), who had not participated in the study before, also gave information about their second essay. This allowed us to check that any reported differences between writing the first and second essays did not result from participating in the study itself.

Results

1. CRITERIA FOR GAINING ESSAY MARKS

Table 2 presents a list of criteria which students believed tutors used in assessing essays. In addition to those given by the students, we have included those given by the seven tutors who were involved in the setting and marking of the essays.

The table indicates that there is a mismatch between the criteria of the students and those of the tutors. The most striking factor is the position of 'originality' which was the most frequent item mentioned by the students (40 per cent of them), but was not mentioned at all by the tutors! Similarly, students rate 'understanding' and the 'use of their own opinions' higher than do the tutors. 'Evidence' comes high in both lists, but the tutors place more weight on relevance, organization, indications of reading and effort than do the students.

Things tutors are believed to look for in assessing essays		Tutors' criteria in assessing essays	
	% mentioning (N = 82)		% mentioning (N = 7)
Originality	40	Evidence	57
Evidence	39	Reading	57
Structure/organization	35	Relevance	57
English	35	Structure/ organization	57
Understanding	29	English	57
Argument	22	Effort	43
Relevance	17	Critical interpretation	43
Reading	17	Argument	29
Appearance/ presentation	12	Appearance/ presentation	14
Critical interpretation	12	Understanding	14
Own opinions	11		

Table 2. *Criteria for the assessment of essays*

Not only do the students appear to have little appreciation of the criteria on which they are judged by the staff but they also seem somewhat pessimistic about how the system works. Table 3 shows what, on average, students thought their essays were worth, what they thought they would get, and what in fact they actually did get. The students who participated in this study thought that their essays were worth 59 per cent (on average), but that they would only get 56 per cent. In fact, the actual marks given to the essays by the tutors averaged 61 per cent which was above the students' estimates. It seemed that the standards applied were not as hard as students imagined, although social desirability probably also had an influence in making students cautious in their predictions.

There were some differences between the first, second and third year students in their evaluation of the essays (see Table 3). Feelings about what the essays would get were significantly different across the years, the second year students expecting higher marks than either the first or the third years (f = 4.5; df = 2,88 p < .01). The marks given by the tutors were not significantly different between the years, although there was a trend (significant at 10 per cent level) for the more experienced students to get higher marks.

There were no significant sex differences in the estimates of the marks to be given or, in fact, in the actual marks given. There was, however, a tendency for women to give their own work lower marks than did the men. This finding is in line with other research (Nicholson, 1979).

Finally, in this section, we may note that the correlation between

	Average marks out of 100						
	1st year		2nd year		3rd year		Total sample
	M	F	M	F	M	F	
What their essay is worth	58.8	55.6	61.3	59.2	55.0	57.6	58.9
What their essay will get	54.2	53.1	59.2	55.7	50.8	55.0	55.6
Predicted average for all students	57.5	55.1	56.3	58.4	56.3	58.0	57.0
Tutors' actual marks	58.0	60.6	62.1	62.7	65.0	65.2	61.2

Table 3. *Students' and tutors' assessment of essays*

what an essay was expected to get with what it was thought to be worth was 0.63 (p $<$ .01); between what it was thought to be worth and what it actually got was 0.28 (p $<$ .01); and between what it was expected to get and what it actually did get was 0.38 (p $<$ .01). These correlations are small in absolute terms (despite their statistical significance). They too indicate that the students' evaluations of their own essays do not correspond at all well with those of their tutors. While the correlations are no worse than the interreliability of different markers (Cox, 1967) this hardly mitigates this conclusion.

2. THE WAYS IN WHICH STUDENTS PRODUCE ESSAYS

From the responses to the questionnaire, we can build up a general picture of the way in which these students set about writing the essays:

(i) Three-quarters of the sample (78 per cent) worked on one essay at a time. Half the students (52 per cent) allocated time in advance to do the work. On average, work for the essay was started four to seven days before handing it in but a quarter (23 per cent) started work less than three days before handing it in. Almost no one (4 per cent) drew up a timetable on paper for doing their work.

(ii) Three-quarters of the sample (72 per cent) used lecture notes in preparing the essay. In addition, three-quarters (74 per cent) used books and articles other than those recommended by the tutors or the course programme. On average, just over three books were read (at least in part) but only half a journal article. Six per cent of the sample used six or more books, whilst another 6 per cent used only one book. Almost a quarter (22 per cent) of the students looked around for existing essays on the same topic.

(iii) Half the students (52 per cent) claimed that they left some time for reflection between finishing the reading and starting to write the essay.

(iv) Just over two-thirds (69 per cent) made a written plan of the essay structure, and just over half (57 per cent) made at least one draft before writing up the essay. One quarter of the sample (25 per cent) discussed plans for the essay with someone else, usually a student rather than a tutor. (These were not the same students who looked around for existing essays on the topic.) Only 5 per cent discussed the essay with a tutor (on an individual basis).

(v) Well over three-quarters (85 per cent) said that they tried to present their own ideas and draw their own conclusions in the essay. Only 12 per cent found it necessary to fill out the essay in order to make it longer. About 10 per cent gave the essay to someone else to read before handing it in.

3. CHANGES IN STRATEGY WITH EXPERIENCE: COMPARISONS BETWEEN THE FIRST AND SECOND ESSAYS

When we examined the results of the 28 students who completed the questionnaire for both their first and second essays we found a high degree of consistency. In short, there were very few differences which were significant. Three-quarters of the sample were consistent on 12 or more of the 15 behaviours that we asked about. Thus it would appear that these students did not alter their approach or learn much about writing essays from their first attempt. However, changes that approached significance were:

(i) making written plans for the essay structure declined from 81 per cent for the first essay to 60 per cent for the second;

(ii) discussing plans for the essay declined from 32 per cent for the first essay to 14 per cent for the second.

Interestingly enough, there were no significant differences between the average marks given to the first and second essays (61.2 per cent compared with 61.7 per cent).

All the results from the control group (who only gave information about their second essay) were closely comparable to those obtained with the initial sample — thus indicating that these findings were not an artefact of the research procedure.

Comparisons between years. Table 4 presents in summary form the responses on a year-by-year basis for the main categories presented in section 2. It can be seen that there are certain trends in the data according to the length of experience of these students at university. Often the third year students are closer to the first years than the second years. If one takes the individual questions, one at a time, the results across the years are not significant. However, if one takes the data all together and uses a multivariate technique of analysis, then clear differences emerge.

Discriminant function analysis was applied to all the data obtained from the questionnaire. This analysis attempts to distinguish between the groups of students in the three years on the basis of their responses. Using the direct method, all the variables were combined into linear functions which were used to predict the classification of the respondents. In this case it was possible to allocate correctly 96 per cent of the students as first, second or third year students on the basis of two functions.

Table 5 indicates the characteristics of these two functions. The interpretation of the functions has been based on variables which have

		Overall	1st year	2nd year	3rd year
		N %	N %	N %	N %
Work on one essay	Yes	85 (78)	37 (84)	41 (73)	7 (78)
at a time	No	24 (22)	7 (16)	15 (27)	2 (22)
Allocate time	Yes	57 (52)	27 (61)	25 (45)	5 (56)
in advance	No	52 (48)	17 (39)	31 (55)	4 (44)
Draw up a timetable	Yes	4 (4)	2 (5)	2 (4)	0 (0)
on paper	No	105 (96)	42 (95)	54 (96)	9 (100)
Use books not	Yes	81 (74)	29 (66)	45 (79)	7 (78)
recommended	No	29 (26)	15 (34)	12 (21)	2 (22)
Look for existing	Yes	24 (22)	4 (9)	18 (32)	2 (22)
essays on topic*	No	86 (78)	40 (91)	39 (68)	7 (78)
Make drafts	Yes	63 (57)	22 (50)	37 (65)	4 (44)
	No	47 (43)	22 (50)	20 (35)	5 (56)
Discuss plans	Yes	28 (25)	8 (18)	18 (32)	2 (22)
with others	No	82 (75)	36 (82)	39 (68)	7 (78)
Fill out	Yes	13 (12)	7 (16)	6 (11)	0 (0)
the essay	No	96 (88)	36 (84)	51 (90)	9 (100)

(* statistically significant at the 5 per cent level)

Table 4. *Approaches to writing essays according to experience*

	Function 1	Function 2
High scorers:	— expect high marks for the essay — make some drafts but not many — discuss plans with other students and tutors — attend to more than one essay at a time — believe accuracy is looked for by tutors — look around for existing essays on same topic	— make a lot of drafts — read a lot of books — start work for the essay near the deadline — do not discuss plans with others
Low scorers:	— expect low marks — do not make drafts — do not discuss plans — only work on one essay at a time — try to write essays that reflect tutors' opinions	— make few or no drafts — read few or no books — start work early — discuss plans with students

Table 5. *Characteristics of high and low scorers on the discriminant functions*

coefficients of 0.65 or above. Function 1 appears to be a dimension involving confidence, self-assertiveness, and being in control, as opposed to being pessimistic, unenterprising, and being externally constrained. Function 2 is characterized by the presence (or absence) of concentrated, individual hard work.

In our sample, the first year students emerge as intermediate on the first function, and high on the second. That is, they were individual hard workers but they were not very confident or enterprising.

The second year students were high on the first function, and intermediate on the second. That is, they were confident, self-assertive, and in control. They worked only a moderate amount and they were more inclined to discuss what they were doing with their friends.

The third year students were low on both functions. That is, they were pessimistic, unenterprising, and they did not work hard.

In short, the impression is, relatively speaking, that the inexperienced first year students were working individually and following what they thought was a 'proper' progress for writing essays. They were more straightforward and singleminded, they allocated more time in advance to do the essays, they worked on only one essay at a time, they used only the recommended books, and so on.

By comparison the more experienced (second year) students appeared to be more product-orientated, and more aware of the variety of ways in which one could go about essay writing. They were more likely to use books and articles other than those recommended by the tutor, to look for existing essays on the same topic, to discuss their plans with other students or tutors and to give their essays to someone else to read.

The results from the third year students seem curiously out of line. These students we believe are not typical of all third year students at Keele but represent a group making slower progress at the University. At Keele it is usual to take subsidiary subjects in the first or second year. Usually, being a third year subsidiary student implies previous failure at another subsidiary subject, a deliberate choice of slow progress, or perhaps a change of heart (and subject) after a term or two. Our nine third year students were, in fact, all in this latter category. They had not failed a previous subsidiary course, but had all changed their minds from doing two subsidiaries at once to doing them separately, probably − our analysis suggests − because of caution, pessimism, and finding the workload too great.

4. RELATING THE STRATEGIES TO THE MARKS OBTAINED

How do the strategies that students adopt, and the beliefs that they hold, affect the marks they obtain? To answer these questions we carried out some fairly basic analyses. We compared the marks obtained by all the students who used a particular strategy or belief with the marks obtained by all the others who did not use this particular strategy. This procedure produced very little in terms of significant differences. Students did better if they allowed themselves time for reflection between reading and starting to write ($p < .01$), and second year students did marginally better if they made a draft of the essay ($p < .05$). Generally students did marginally better (but not significantly) if they 'made a written plan', and they did marginally worse (but not significantly) if they filled out the essay to make it longer. Students who believed in the value of presenting 'evidence' did

better than those who did not ($p < .1$), whereas those who believed
in presenting their own opinions or (surprisingly) a critical interpretation
did worse ($p < .1$, $p < .05$ respectively).

A further analysis was carried out along the lines of seeing whether
'any strategy was better than no strategy', that is whether students who
used more strategies achieved better marks than those who used only
a few. Students were divided into four groups according to the number
of strategies they had used in writing their essays, but there was no
statistically significant difference in the marks obtained. An attempt
was made to weight each strategy according to its individual
importance in discriminating performance. The weighted number of
strategies used by each student was then totalled, but again there was
no significant relationship with the marks given to the essays.

Discussion

The results described in this paper seem to suggest that in writing
essays for a particular course:

(i) students try to fulfil requirements which they do not clearly
comprehend;
(ii) initial feedback during the first term seems to have little effect on
their actions;
(iii) over a longer period of time there are changes in strategy; but
(iv) few strategies seem to affect directly the outcome in terms of
actual marks.

The most interesting results in this paper come from the discriminant
function analysis. The two empirically derived functions seem to cut
across the various distinctions drawn by other workers. The hard
working student reflects the importance given by Entwistle and Wilson
(1977) to motivation. The notion of being in control oneself, or being
controlled by others, reflects Rotter's (1966) work on locus of control,
Parlett's (1969) work on syllabus-bound and syllabus-free students,
and Witkin *et al*'s work on field independence (Witkin *et al*, 1977).

Similarly in the responses of students who attempt to manage the
system (eg by borrowing other essays) we can detect parallels with
cue-seeking and cue-conscious students (Miller and Parlett, 1974), the
value-motive-strategy dimensions of reproducing, internalizing and
organizing (Biggs, 1978) and the notion of Machiavellianism (Christie
et al, 1970). Rather similar basic concepts seem to underlie these
different formulations and labels, although each has its own peculiar
emphasis and the exact correspondence between them has not been
tested. The parallels between them are interesting because they have
been arrived at in a wide range of contexts using different methods.
Our functions were derived from questionnaire responses systematically
analysed by means of multivariate techniques. They are based on the
students' reported behaviours in writing essays (whereas most previous
research has been concerned with strategies for doing examinations and
has often applied standard personality tests).

The two functions characterize differences in approach between students and correspond to familiar impressions of students in different years: the freshers, cautious, somewhat overwhelmed, unsure of what is expected or how to go about their work but relying on a lot of hard work; and the second years, more confident and assertive, having come to terms with the system. Our small group of third year students is a special group making slower progress through the University course. What was remarkable about this group was their pessimism and inactivity — although in terms of actual marks they were successful. This group seemed to express an inappropriate and unnecessarily defeatist approach to work.

We believe that the change in strategies between the first and second year students reflects experience, but we have no evidence from this research of how or when these changes are brought about. One view is that the accumulated pressure from course-work and examinations which occurs at the end of the year may prompt changes in the mode of working. In this view the re-evaluation of strategies by students would be deliberate and with a degree of insight as a means to solve the problem of workloads. An alternative view, prompted by the nature of the changes in the strategies themselves, suggests that the transition may reflect differences in the social relations of first and second year students. The change in strategy may be produced by the movement from being an individual who is new to an institution, to becoming more integrated, through gaining friends particularly among more experienced students. Perhaps the first year student learns what are the fashionable and socially accepted ways of working from more experienced students as he comes to know them over the course of the first year. The reasons for these ways of working, and their benefits in terms of personal effort, may only be appreciated after adopting them. The changes in strategy may not produce any greater benefits in terms of marks (as was found in this research) but confidence is derived from knowing that you are doing what everybody else does, not from results. The confidence and assertiveness characteristic of the second years' strategy is thus the product of social comparison and social support.

In such a social system, student modes of working and beliefs about assessment are perpetuated with little or no influence from tutors. This may also be an effect of the social relationships that are involved. At the point of assessment, both staff and students come face to face with the needs and expectations of the other, but assessment procedures place a considerable strain on staff-student relationships. At this point education becomes less co-operative and more competitive, and the power relationships produce their own morality and social groupings which can hinder the exchange of ideas. In the vacuum that is created, students have to devise their own strategies and approaches, which do not necessarily correspond with those of tutors.

To improve on this situation we need more openness and more discussion between students and staff about the requirements and the many possible approaches to work. It is indeed remarkable how little formal instruction is given in universities — or indeed elsewhere — about the skills of acquiring knowledge, evaluating information and communicating findings. We are not asserting here that there is or ever will be one correct approach to writing essays. What we are saying is that providing more information would encourage staff and students to find out more about what strategies are available and which ones might suit them best.

References

Biggs, J B (1978) Individual and group differences in study processes. *British Journal of Educational Psychology* 48 3: 266-79

Christie, R and Geis, F L (eds) (1970) *Studies in Machiavellianism.* New York: Academic Press

Cox, R (1967) Examinations and higher education. *Universities Quarterly.* June, pp 292-340

Entwistle, N (ed) (1976) *Strategies for Research and Development in Higher Education.* Amsterdam: Swets & Zeitlinger

Entwistle, N J and Wilson, J (1977) *Degrees of Excellence: The Academic Achievement Game.* London: Hodder & Stoughton

Hartley, J and Branthwaite, A (1976) All this for two per cent: the contribution of course-work assessment to the final grade. *The Durham Research Review* 8 37: 14-20

Miller, C and Parlett, M (1974) *Up to the Mark: A Study of the Examination Game.* Research monograph No 21, Society for Research into Higher Education

Nicholson, J (1979) *A Question of Sex.* London: Fontana

Parlett, M (1969) The syllabus-bound student. In L Hudson (ed) (1970) *The Ecology of Human Intelligence.* Harmondsworth: Penguin

Rotter, J B (1966) Generalised expectancies for internal control of reinforcement. *Psychological Monographs* 80, No 1, Whole No 609

Witkin, H A, Moore, C A, Goodenough, D R and Cox, P W (1977) Field-dependent and field-independent cognitive styles and their educational implications. *Review of Educational Research* 47 1: 1-64

Appendix 1

Name ....

Year   1st   2nd   3rd   *(Please circle)*

How long before handing it in did you start doing work for the essay?

1 day   ....   *(Please tick the appropriate one)*
2 − 3 days   ....
4 − 7 days   ....
1 − 2 weeks   ....
2 − 3 weeks   ....
more than 3 weeks   ....

In preparing and writing this essay, did you: *(Please circle as appropriate)*

— allocate in advance certain times for this work?   **Yes / No**

— read books, articles (not necessarily all the way through)?   **Yes / No**
   If so, roughly how many   (i) books?   ....
                      (ii) articles?   ....

— use lecture notes and handouts?   **Yes / No**

— use books/articles other than those recommended by tutors in the course programme?   **Yes / No**

— draw up a timetable on paper for the work?   **Yes / No**

— leave time for reflection between finishing the reading for the essay and starting writing the essay?   **Yes / No**

— make a written plan of the essay structure?   **Yes / No**

— make a draft of the essay and then write up the essay. *If so,* how many drafts did you make? ......

— discuss your plans for the essay with someone else?   **Yes / No**
   If so, was it (i) another student?   ....
             (ii) a tutor or lecturer?   ....

— give the essay to someone else to read before handing it in?   **Yes / No**

— re-write and re-organize notes made from lectures, books and articles before writing them into the essay?   **Yes / No**

— try to draw your own conclusions and present your own ideas?   **Yes / No**

— find it necessary to fill out the essay to make it longer?   **Yes / No**

— only work on one essay at a time?   **Yes / No**

— look around for existing essays on the same topic?   **Yes / No**

(please turn over)

In subsidiary psychology, essays are marked in percentages.

What mark do you think your essay is worth?   ....%

What mark do you think your essay will get?   ....%

How do you think the mark you will get will compare with other students' essay marks?

Among the best 10% of essays   ....

Among the best 25% of essays   ....   *(Please tick which you think*

Among the top half of essays   ....   *is most appropriate)*

Below average   ....

What do you think will be the average of the essay marks this term in subsidiary psychology?   ....%

Have you participated in this study before by filling in a questionnaire like this for your previous subsidiary essay?   **Yes / No**

If No:

What things do you think tutors look for when assessing essays?

Part 3: Information by Design: Selected Illustrations

3.0 Introduction

The term 'information printing' is used by designers to distinguish the printing of information from the printing of prose, or continuous run-on text. What characterizes this kind of material — instructions, leaflets, catalogues, bibliographies, etc — is that its typographical setting is usually more complex than is that required for the setting of prose. This is, of course, a consequence of the fact that the material in itself is not straightforward.

Such material can be considered in terms of its structure, and the uses to which it will be put. The structure of the information may be hierarchical (tree-like), or list-like (flat) or somewhere in between (lists with regular sub-elements). The text may be used occasionally for quick reference (eg using a dictionary); or parts of it may be read in detail at some particular point in time (eg using an instructional manual to diagnose a fault); or it may be used differently by different users (eg filling in a questionnaire is different from analysing the returns). These two issues — the nature of the text and the uses to which it is put — pose formidable problems for typographic designers and psychologists. Most of the psychological research on typography has been carried out with continuous text, and it is not clear how far the findings (often obtained in the laboratory) are relevant to these other areas of expertise.

In this introduction I will look at these problems in terms of (i) the typographical layout of the material, (ii) gaining access to the text and to components within it, and (iii) clarifying the language of the text. For an extended discussion of the relationships between pure and applied psychology with reference to information printing, the reader is referred to the papers by Wright (1978; 1980a).

Typographical layout

Hartley and Burnhill have argued that the nature of complex text — its underlying structure — can often be indicated to the reader by the way it is displayed on the page. The details of this argument are given in Hartley (1978) and in Paper 3.1, and will not be repeated here. The essentials to observe are the importance attached to (i) the use(s) to

113

which the text will be put, (ii) the decision about what page-size is therefore appropriate, and (iii) how to space systematically the material with that page-size.

ASSIGNMENT PROCEDURES

Conventional assignment procedures are applied when subscriber service is assigned to a spare physical circuit that is providing a working derived circuit. Additional information related to the derived line is entered in the remarks section of the service order (Fig. 3.9). Rearrangement of the cable pairs that include pairs used for single channel carrier circuits should be avoided where possible. Such arrangements require coordination among the engineer of outside plant, assignment office, central office, outside work forces, and repair service bureau to insure that transmission requirements are met. Also, bridge tap restrictions for single channel carrier application may not permit cable pairs to be half-tapped in the central office and/or field location, and may prohibit use of carrier once the outside plant facilities are reconfigured.

Figure 1a. *The original text in the standard form*

ASSIGNMENT PROCEDURES
Conventional assignment procedures are applied
    when subscriber service is assigned
        to a spare physical circuit
            that is providing
            a working derived circuit.
    Additional information related to the derived line
        is entered in the remarks section
            of the service order (Fig. 3.9).
Rearrangement of the cable pairs that include
    pairs used for
        single channel carrier circuits
should be avoided
    where possible.
    Such arrangements require coordination among the
        engineer of outside plant,
        assignment office,
        central office,
        outside work forces, and
        repair service bureau
    to insure that transmission requirements are met.
Also, bridge tap restrictions
    for single channel carrier application
may not permit
    cable pairs to be half-tapped
        in the central office
        and/or field location,
and may prohibit
    use of carrier
        once the outside plant facilities are reconfigured.

Figure 1b. *The same text 'meaningfully indented' by Frase and Schwartz. (Figures reproduced by courtesy of Bell Telephone Laboratories.)*

There have been, in recent years, a number of other suggestions about
how one might space complex text. Frase and Schwartz (1979) found
that 'meaningfully indented' text was searched more rapidly and was
more easily understood than was the same text typed in the standard
way (see Figures 1a and 1b). In their experiments, Frase and Schwartz
used single pages of technical text taken (mainly) from instructional
manuals in the Bell Telephone Company, USA. A critique of the
methodology of their experiments, their ways of segmenting text, and
their conclusions has been provided by Hartley (1980a).

Another suggestion concerning the spacing of complex text has been
made by Jewett (1972a; 1972b). Jewett divides textbook material into
three kinds: basic arguments; explanations of the main points (possibly
with examples); and incidental materials. He then distinguishes between
these three levels of material by using three levels of indentation.
The basic material is flushed left to the left-hand margin; the
explanations and examples are indented seven letter spaces (in
typescript); and the incidental materials are indented a further seven
letter spaces. In his paper Jewett (1972b) uses three vertical 'rules'
alongside the basic material, two alongside the explanations, and one
alongside the incidental material. The resulting text appears as shown
in Figure 2.

> The following analysis is intended to cover college
> teaching in the sciences and technologies from under-
> graduate to early postgraduate levels (including much of
> MD but not PhD training) in those cases where the
> subject is too extensive to be covered adequately in
> the available time. This type of training is generally
> characterized by a 'lecture-textbook' teaching format.

>> The heavy reliance upon lectures in
>> our educational system is probably not
>> because of the egotism of the lecturers,
>> as some cynics suggest. Most lecturers
>> spend considerable amounts of time deve-
>> loping their lectures, and yet many do not
>> enjoy giving them.

> In a Darwinian sense, the lecture-textbook
> format must have considerable 'survival value'
> considering its widespread use and the multipli-
> city of other techniques that have been tried but
> have not supplanted it. However, the 'success'
> of the format need not imply that we teachers
> know what we are doing! In particular, many if
> not most lecturers consider that it is their job

Figure 2. *An extract from the layout proposed by Jewett (1972b)*

Jewett (1972a) acknowledges that more than three levels may be possible or desirable. The point is, though, that readers can skim through the text noting what is essential and grasping the structure of the document very rapidly. Readers may then return to read as much of the material as they feel they need. At a later date, of course, it is easier to review from such a text than it is from continuous prose.

Jewett has not attempted to evaluate his approach, but he comments (personal communication) that one of the major results of preparing text in this way is that it leads writers to re-think what it is they want to say, and to clarify their text. This is a viewpoint shared by Hartley and Burnhill (1977). They comment that clarity in layout leads to clarity in content because it requires clarity of thought.

Finally, we may note here a little-known study which varied in an interesting way the layout of material to be learned by heart (sections of the Bible). Norman Murray (1976) presented blocks of text in the manner shown schematically in Figure 3. Here the reader has to read the material in the blocks that start at the left-hand margin before reading the indented ones. Murray based his approach on the fact that grouping material into meaningful chunks is a well-known way of aiding recall, and that people can usually remember where on a page they saw a particular item (Rothkopf, 1971; Zechmeister *et al*, 1975).

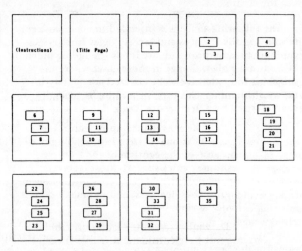

Figure 3. *A schematic representation of the layout used by Murray (1976)*

GAINING ACCESS TO THE TEXT: TYPOGRAPHIC CUES

Typographic cues — italic, bold face, or capital letters, for example — are also often employed by authors and printers to help readers use text more efficiently. The research literature on typographic cueing has been well summarized by Foster (1979). It appears that although it is difficult sometimes to show it experimentally such aids do help the reader, particularly when they are used to clarify important concepts rather than isolated words and when the reader understands their function. (In passing we may note that Foster sees typographic cueing as more economical than adjunct questions as a way of influencing mathemagenic behaviours.)

In my own research I have tended to focus on spatial cues rather than typographical ones, and to argue that spatial cues are more important (eg see Hartley, 1980b; Hartley *et al*, 1979a). However, I readily admit that there are areas where the two may combine, and indeed where a typographic cue may take over the function of a spatial one. For example, a heading in bold-face type does not need as much space to separate it from its related text as does a heading printed in the same type-face as the text. I have emphasized spatial cueing, however, because most authors and printers seem to attach more importance to typographic cues than they do to spatial ones. This may be simply a matter of saving space but to my mind the issues are more complex.

Textbook writers sometimes use multiple cues. Take, for example, the text by John Tukey (Tukey, 1977). Here, seven levels of typographic cueing are employed within three or four pages. Tukey uses words or phrases in capital letters; words or phrases in capital or lower-case italic; words or phrases in capital or lower-case bold; words or phrases isolated in the centre of a line; and words or phrases or sentences in boxes or 'traps'. Tukey maintains (personal communication) that all of these variants have different functions and that these functions are clear to the reader. There is a need, I feel, to see if these cues used by authors and printers, and their multiple combinations are really needed, are confusing, or are even noticed by many readers. Certainly many instructional leaflets, advertisements, forms and lists use a variety of typesizes, weights and faces — with resulting confusion. (See Figure 4.)

GAINING ACCESS TO THE TEXT: COMPONENTS WITHIN THE TEXT

There are, of course, other ways of signalling functions to readers in addition to manipulating typographic cues within the text. There are many devices, or components of text, which can be marshalled in order to improve its clarity. One might consider, for example, the use of contents pages; indexes and glossaries; abstracts and summaries; headings and numbering systems; text directives, and so on. There is some research on the effectiveness of the presence of some of these components (see Hartley, 1978) but much of this research is unhelpful for practitioners. The reasons for this are complex but one particular one noted by Waller (1979) is that most researchers seem to assume — mistakenly — that readers read steadily from start to finish.

The contribution of Waller's 'Notes on transforming' (of which two are contained in Paper 3.2) is to redirect our thinking about much of this research. Waller considers that these textual components are not there to assist comprehension (at least not primarily). The function of these components is to help readers find their way around the text: to make it more accessible.

Waller has so far circulated five sets of 'Notes on transforming' at the Open University and published a related overview article (Waller,

---

Third Priority

ACTION ET PENSEE; 1966 Vol. 42, 1969 Vol. 45, 1970 Vol. 46, 1971 Vol. 47, 1972 Vol. 48, 1973 & 1974. ANNALES MEDICO-PSYCHOLOGIQUES; 1962 Vol. 120 Part I No. 1, 1968 Vol. 126 Part II No 1 & 2. ANNEE PSYCHOLOGIQUE; 1961 Vol. 61. ANNUAL OF ANIMAL PSYCHOLOGY; 1962 Vol. 12 No. 2. ARCHIVIO DI PSICOLOGIA, NEUROLOGIA E PSICHIATRIA; 1961 Vol. 22 Nos. 3-4, 6, 1962 Vol. 23 Nos. 2, 6, 1965 Vol. 26 No. 6, 1966 Vol. 27 No. 6, 1967 Vol. 28 No. 6, 1968 Vol. 29 Nos. 3-6, 1969 Vol. 30 Nos. 1, 6, 1970 Vol. 31 No. 4, 1974 Vol. 35. AUSTRALIAN PSYCHOLOGIST; 1967/68 Vol. 2 No. 2, 1973 Vol. 8 No. 2. BIOMETRIE HUMAINE; 1966 Vol. 1, 1971, 1972, 1973, 1974. BRITISH JOURNAL OF PSYCHIATRIC SOCIAL WORK; Cumulative index to Vols. 1-10, 1960-70. C.E.R.P. BULLETIN; 1964 Vol. 13 No. 1, 1966 Vol. 15 Nos. 3-4, 1967 Vol. 16, 1968 Vol. 17, 1969 Vol. 18 Nos. 1, 3-4, 1970 Vol. 19, 1971 Vol. 20, 1972, 1973, 1974. CRIANCA PORTUGUESA; 1964 Vol. 22 *and all subsequent volumes to date.* EDUCATIONAL RESEARCH; 1962/3 Vol. 5 No. 2. EDUCATIONAL REVIEW; 1961/62 Vol. 14 No. 1. EUGENICS REVIEW; Now journal of biosocial sciences, 1969— HYGIENE MENTALE; 1965 Vol. 54 No. 6, 1966 Vol. 55 Nos. 4-6.

Figure 4. *Typographic cueing without spatial cueing can lead to difficulties for the reader*

1979). Notes on transforming no 1 was concerned with the idea of transforming itself. Waller states that Otto Neurath first used the word 'transformer' in the context of written communication. Neurath founded the Isotype Institution in the inter-war years to develop an international system of pictorial communication (see Neurath, 1974). Neurath found it necessary to include among his staff 'transformers' whose role was to interpret facts and statistics provided by subject-matter experts and to present them in pictorial charts that ordinary people could understand. A transformer in the context of this present book, then, is a person who mediates between the sources of information (the writers, editors, designers, printers, etc) and the public. His speciality is his multidisciplinary understanding of all aspects of written communication.

In Notes on transforming no 2 Waller discusses three functions of text presentation: (i) the enabling function — which provides a clear channel of communication; (ii) the aesthetic function — which provides an attractive reading environment; and (iii) the access function — which identifies and structures particular aspects of the text. In Notes on transforming no 3 the idea of the access function is developed further in connection with the fact that readers can choose what they want to read, when they want to read, and how they want to read.

Notes on transforming nos 4 and 5 (included in this text) differ in their approach and style. No 4 is a close analysis of the use of numbering systems to structure text. No 5 is a broader statement about dimensions of quality in educational texts. Notes 6 and 7 are in preparation.

Two sets of components within text not yet discussed by Waller are (i) illustrations and (ii) statistical tables and related graphic devices.

Illustrations. The role of illustrations in text continues to attract research, but seems to lead to inconclusive wrangling. A main difficulty here, of course, is that it is difficult to operationalize, or to classify, illustrations and their differing roles. Some workers such as Dwyer (1972) classify illustrations in terms of their abstractness (eg from colour photographs through to schematic line drawings), whereas others, such as Duchastel (1978), classify them in terms of their purpose (eg to motivate, to aid explanation, and to sustain long-term recall). Detailed taxonomies of function and purpose have been developed (eg Twyman, 1979).

Good summaries of the research on illustrations can be found in the reviews of Dwyer (1978) and Fleming (1979). Willows (1979) presents a brief but useful introduction to the field. Willows argues, in contrast to Dwyer, that there have been few published studies addressed to the question of 'Does the presence of illustrations contribute to understanding the text?' but agrees that the conclusions reached are far from definitive. Indeed, some workers (eg Samuels, 1977) argue that illustrations in pre-school texts can have a detrimental rather than a beneficial effect on children's learning to read.

Tabular and graphic materials. The voluminous research on the layout of tables and related graphic materials has been cogently discussed by Macdonald-Ross (1977a; 1977b) and by Macdonald-Ross and Smith (1977). These articles are essential reading for anyone interested in the design of graphic materials or their evaluation. Macdonald-Ross (1977b) concludes that no one format is universally superior to all others, but that some are so unsatisfactory that they should no longer be used (eg segmented graphs and three-dimensional forms). Macdonald-Ross states that to choose the optimum format for a particular occasion one has to consider, amongst other things, the kind of data being shown, the teaching points that one is trying to make, and what the learners are required to do with the data presented to them.

One issue, not discussed by Macdonald-Ross, but which is relevant both to graphic materials and to illustrations, is that of their positioning in the text. It is generally acknowledged that such components should be positioned as close to their textual reference as possible, although it is easy to see this rule contravened in practice. Burnhill *et al* (1976) showed that tables which cut across two-column text caused greater reading difficulties for school children than did the same tables in single-column material. They argued that decisions about page size and line lengths should not be made without reference to the size and quantity of other non-textual components in the material.

Andrew Ehrenberg, in Paper 3.3, shows just how thinking carefully about the function and use of statistical material can lead to much clearer presentation methods. (Paper 3.3 is a shortened version of Ehrenberg's earlier (1977) paper which is well worth further study.)

THE LANGUAGE OF TEXT

In a forceful but entertaining paper Alphonse Chapanis (1965) argues that many notices, instructions and directives, although simply expressed, are in fact unintelligible. His example I like best is the notice that reads:

PLEASE
WALK UP ONE FLOOR
WALK DOWN TWO FLOORS
FOR IMPROVED ELEVATOR SERVICE

People interpret this notice as meaning 'to get on the elevator I must either walk up one floor, or go down two floors', or even 'to get on the elevator I must first walk up one floor and then down two floors'! When they have done this, they find the same notice confronting them! What the notice means, in effect, is 'Please, don't use the elevator if you are only going a short distance.' So a suggested revision might read:

PLEASE DON'T USE THE ELEVATOR
if you are only going
UP ONE FLOOR
or
DOWN TWO FLOORS

Several guides have been written about how to present prose clearly (eg Tichy, 1966; Klare, 1975; Hartley and Burnhill, 1978) and there are also some on how to revise text in order to make it easier to understand (eg Hartley *et al*, 1979b). In Paper 3.4 Patricia Wright and Phil Barnard provide a typical example of how research on the use of language can be applied profitably to information printing. (This paper is an earlier version of more detailed ones published elsewhere — Wright, 1977; 1980b).

It has proved relatively easy to measure the difficulty of a piece of text —albeit rather crudely. George Klare (1963; 1974-5) has concisely summarized work using readability formulae, carried out since the 1920s. Readability formulae, despite their limitations, have proved to be useful tools for comparing the relative difficulty of different pieces of text. This is particularly so when one is interested in comparing a revised version with its original. Here there have been some very clear and practical results. It has been shown that more readable texts can have marked effects upon the comprehension of school textbooks (Hartley *et al*, 1980), examination scores (Johnstone and Cassels, 1978), correspondence texts (Klare and Smart, 1973), job aids (Sticht, 1977), car insurance policies (Kincaid and Gamble, 1977), legal jargon (Charrow, 1979) and medical instructions (Ley, 1979). More readable text, it appears, is read for a greater length of time and with better understanding by more people than is less readable text.

The last sentence may appear to be a statement of the obvious. However, it is not necessarily true that more readable text is always better understood. Klare (1976) has skilfully disentangled those factors which are likely to lead to positive findings and those which are not. It appears that if readers are intelligent and/or highly motivated, and if their prior knowledge about the subject matter is high, and if, in these experiments, the testing time is short, then it is unlikely that making the text more readable will have any marked effects. However, if these conditions are reversed, if readers are less able and/or less motivated, if the material is relatively novel, and if the testing time is ample, then the more readable material is likely to lead to improved test scores. Kincaid and Gamble's (1977) experiment indicates this kind of finding. They found that high ability students could understand both the easy and difficult versions of passages from a car insurance policy; that average ability students could understand the easy but not the difficult versions; and that low ability students could understand neither.

Guidelines for clear presentation — such as those presented by Ehrenberg in Paper 3.3 or Wright and Barnard in Paper 3.4 — have to be treated with caution. They have to be considered as ideas to think about rather than as absolute rules to follow. Guidelines make general suggestions, each one of which must be considered on its merits in a specific setting.

In our own work we have written such guidelines (Hartley and Burnhill, 1978) but we personally have treated them as hypotheses to be tested in further research. Thus, of the 50 guidelines that we originally published in 1977 and revised in 1978, four have now been qualified by subsequent experiment. We have shown Hammerton's (1976) results to be in error (Goodwin *et al*, 1977); we have indicated that the link between the role and the position of summaries is more complex than we suggested (Hartley *et al*, 1979); we have found that providing the measure is sensitive enough, teacher-provided underlining in text does affect children's recall (Hartley *et al*, 1980); and we have found in one particular study that sub-headings in text are equally effective in the form of statements or questions, but that less able children appear to benefit more from sub-headings in the form of questions (Hartley *et al*, 1980).

Concluding remarks

Figures 5a and 5b provide an illustration of how notions about layout and readability can be combined. Figure 5a shows the original instructions from a leaflet provided by an international airline. Figure 5b shows a revised version, where both the layout and the text have been changed. Both texts could possibly be improved by the addition of illustrative materials. Neither version, of course, will be any use if the passengers do not read them. How to persuade people to attend to information provided is yet another problem for research.

Putting all of this together then, it seems that to produce

121

IMPORTANT INFORMATION FOR OUR PASSENGERS

Even though you may be an experienced air traveller, there are certain features of this airplane with which you may not be familiar.

AUTOMATIC OXYGEN SYSTEM

The higher altitudes at which this aircraft operates require the prompt use of the automatic oxygen system in case of any sudden change in cabin pressure. Should a decompression occur, oxygen masks will drop down. Take nearest mask and promptly place over nose and mouth. BREATHE NORMALLY (NO SMOKING PLEASE).

SEAT BELTS

Even if the 'SEAT BELT' sign is turned off in flight, it is recommended that you keep your seat belt fastened, whenever you are in your seat.

FLOTATION SEAT CUSHIONS

The cushion on which you are sitting is designed to keep you afloat. In the event of a water landing, grasp the cushion at the rear, pull it forward and take it with you.

EMERGENCY EXITS

There are nine exits provided for your use. The chart below will show you the one closest to your seat. The exits over the wings are removable windows. For easy access to the window, push seat back ahead of the window forward. The two exits at each end of the cabin are doors equipped with fast operating evacuation slides. There is also a door in the rear of passenger cabin. REAR CABIN EXIT (STAIR). (If usable, will be opened by a crew member).

Table 5a. *The original instructions (illustrations omitted)*

IMPORTANT!

This aircraft has special safety features.

Read this card carefully.

AUTOMATIC OXYGEN

If, during the flight, there is a sudden change
in cabin pressure, oxygen masks will drop down
automatically.
If this happens
  — take the nearest mask
  — put it quickly over your nose and mouth
  — breathe normally
  — put out all cigarettes.

EMERGENCY EXITS

There are nine emergency exits.

The chart on the back of this card shows
the exit nearest to your seat.

The two exit doors at the end of the cabin
are fitted with chutes for sliding down.

To get out over the wings you have to
take out the windows.
To make this easier, put the seat-back down
when you are trying to get to the window.

The door at the back of the cabin is labelled
REAR CABIN EXIT (STAIR).
This door will be opened by a crew member.

FLOATING SEAT CUSHIONS

Your seat cushion will keep you afloat if we
make an emergency landing in the sea.
Get hold of the cushion at the back, pull it
forward, and take it with you.

SEAT BELTS

We suggest that you keep your seat belt
fastened when you are seated — even when the
SEAT BELT sign is turned off.

Figure 5b. *A revised version of Figure 5a*
(illustrations omitted)

comprehensible text there are a number of issues to consider. Who is the information for? How is it to be used? How can it be displayed to its best advantage? What access structures are needed to help readers with different aims? How can the text be made easy to understand? What research is available to guide our decision making? There are no straightforward answers to any of these questions.

References

Burnhill, P, Hartley, J and Young, M (1976) Tables in text. *Applied Ergonomics* 7 1: 13-18

Chapanis, A (1965) Words, words, words. *Human Factors* 7 1: 1-17

Charrow, V R (1979) Legal language: policy issues and practical implications. Paper to the Annual Convention of the American Psychological Society, New York. Copies available from the author, American Institutes for Research, Washington, DC

Duchastel, P C (1978) Illustrating instructional texts. *Educational Technology* **XVIII** 11: 36-9

Dwyer, F M (1972) *A Guide for Improving Visualized Instruction.* Learning Services: Box 784, State College, Pennsylvania

Dwyer, F M (1978) *Strategies for Improving Visual Learning.* Learning Services: Box 784, State College, Pennsylvania

Ehrenberg, A S C (1977) Rudiments of numeracy. *Journal of the Royal Statistical Association A* **140** 3: 277-97

Fleming, M (1979) On pictures in educational research. *Instructional Science* 8 3: 235-51

Foster, J J (1979) The use of visual cues in text. In P Kolers, M E Wrolstad and H Bouma (eds) *Processing Visible Language 1.* New York: Plenum

Frase, L and Schwartz, B J (1979) Typographical cues that facilitate comprehension. *Journal of Educational Psychology* 71 2: 197-206

Goodwin, A R, Thomas, S K and Hartley, J (1977) Are some parts larger than others? Quantifying Hammerton's qualifiers. *Applied Ergonomics* 8 2: 93-5

Hammerton, M (1976) How much is a large part? *Applied Ergonomics* 7 1: 10-12

Hartley, J (1978) *Designing Instructional Text.* London: Kogan Page and New York: Nichols

Hartley, J (1980a) Spatial cues in text: some observations on the paper by Frase and Schwartz. (Copies available from the author.)

Hartley, J (1980b) Designing journal contents pages: the role of spatial and typographic cues. *Journal of Communication Studies* (in press)

Hartley, J, Bartlett, S and Branthwaite, J A (1980) Underlining makes a difference — sometimes. (Copies available from the authors.)

Hartley, J and Burnhill, P (1977) Understanding instructional text: typography, layout and design. In M J A Howe (ed) *Adult Learning.* London: Wiley

Hartley, J and Burnhill, P (1978) Fifty guidelines for improving instructional text. In J Hartley and I K Davies (eds) *Contributions to an Educational Technology Vol 2.* London: Kogan Page and New York: Nichols

Hartley, J, Goldie, M and Steen, L (1979) The role and position of summaries: some issues and data. *Educational Review* 31 1: 59-65

Hartley, J, Kenely, J, Owen, G and Trueman, M (1980) The effects of headings on children's recall from prose text. (Paper available from the authors.)

Hartley, J, Trueman, M and Burnhill, P (1979a) The role of spatial and typographic cues in the design of references. *Applied Ergonomics* 10: 165-9

Hartley, J, Trueman, M and Burnhill, P (1979b) Some observations on producing and measuring readable writing. (Paper available from the authors.)

Hartley, J, Williams, C and Trueman, M (1980) Choosing textbooks: the readability factor. *Head Teachers Review* April (in press)

Jewett, D L (1972a) Self instruction and tested multi-level textbooks. *Perspectives in Biology and Medicine* 15 3: 450-9

Jewett, D L (1972b) Query directed lecturing as a means of increasing teacher productivity in science education. *Perspectives in Biology and Medicine* 15 3: 460-72

Johnstone, A and Cassels, J (1978) What's in a word? *New Scientist* 18 May 78: 1103

Kincaid, J P and Gamble, L G (1977) Ease of comprehension of standard and readable automobile insurance policies as a function of reading ability. *Journal of Reading Behavior* 9 1: 85-7

Klare, G R (1963) *The Measurement of Readability*. Ames: Iowa State University Press

Klare, G R (1974-75) Assessing readability. *Reading Research Quarterly* 10: 62-102

Klare, G R (1975) *A Manual for Readable Writing*. Rem Company, 119a Roesler Road, Glen Burie, MD 21061, USA

Klare, G R (1976) A second look at the validity of readability formulas. *Journal of Reading Behavior* 8: 129-52

Klare, G R and Smart, K (1973) Analysis of the readability levels of selected USAF instructional materials. *Journal of Educational Research* 67: 176

Ley, P (1979) Memory for medical information. *British Journal of Social & Clinical Psychology* 18 2: 245-56

Macdonald-Ross, M (1977a) How numbers are shown: a review of research on the presentation of quantitative data in text. *Audio Visual Communication Review* 25: 359-409

Macdonald-Ross, M (1977b) Graphics in text. In L S Schulman (ed) *Review of Research in Education Vol 5*. Itasca, Illinois: Peacock

Macdonald-Ross, M (1979) Language in texts. In L S Schulman (ed) *Review of Research in Education Vol 6*. Itasca, Illinois: Peacock

Macdonald-Ross, M and Smith, E (1977) *Graphics in Text: A Bibliography*. Institute of Educational Technology, Open University

Murray, N B (1976) Design of typographical format and prose recall. Paper available from the author, Brigham Young University, Provo, Utah

Neurath, M (1974) Isotype. *Instructional Science* 3 2: 127-50

Rothkopf, E Z (1971) Incidental memory for location of information in text. *Journal of Verbal Learning and Verbal Behavior* 10: 608-13

Samuels, S J (1977) Can pictures distract readers from the printed word: a rebuttal. *Journal of Reading Behavior* 9 4: 361-4

Sticht, T G (1977) Comprehending reading at work. In M Just and P Carpenter (eds) *Cognitive Processes in Comprehension*. Hillsdale, NJ: Erlbaum

Tichy, H J (1966) *Effective Writing for Engineers, Managers & Scientists*. New York: Wiley

Tukey, J W (1977) *Exploratory Data Analysis*. New York: Addison-Wesley

Twyman, M (1979) A schema for the study of graphic languages. In P Kolers, M E Wrolstad and H Bouma (eds) *Processing Visible Language 1*. New York: Plenum

Waller, R H W (1979) Typographical access structures for educational texts. In P Kolers, M E Wrolstad and H Bouma (eds) *Processing Visible Language 1*. New York: Plenum

Willows, D M (1979) Reading comprehension of illustrated and non-illustrated text. Paper available from the author, Dept of Psychology, University of Waterloo, Ontario, Canada

Wright, P (1977) Presenting technical information: a survey of research findings. *Instructional Science* 6: 93-134

Wright, P (1978) Feeding the information eaters: suggestions for integrating pure and applied research on language comprehension. *Instructional Science* 7: 249-312

Wright, P (1980a) Usability: the criterion for designing written information. In P Kolers, M E Wrolstad and H Bouma (eds) *Processing Visible Language 2.* New York: Plenum (in press)

Wright, P (1980b) Strategies and tactics in designing forms. In R Easterby and H Zwaga (eds) *The Visual Presentation of Information.* London: Wiley (in press)

Zechmeister, E B *et al* (1975) Visual memory for place on the page. *Journal of General Psychology* 92: 43-52

Further reading

Easterby, R and Zwaga, H (eds) (1980) *The Visual Presentation of Information.* London: Wiley (in press)

Kolers, P, Wrolstad, M E and Bouma, H (eds) (1979) *Processing Visible Language 1.* New York: Plenum

Kolers, P, Wrolstad, M E and Bouma, H (eds) (1980) *Processing Visible Language 2.* New York: Plenum (in press)

3.1 Space and structure in instructional text

JAMES HARTLEY

(Paper originally prepared for the NATO Conference on the Visual Presentation of Information, Het Vennenbos, The Netherlands, September 1978.)

This paper (i) describes the underlying rationale of a practical approach to making complex text easier to understand; (ii) presents illustrations of the approach in practice; (iii) considers some of the problems of putting the theory into practice; and (iv) provides three case histories as well as discussing some of the problems of evaluating the effectiveness of such an approach.

Rationale

The history of typographic research is a lengthy one, going back to the 1880s and probably before. The research has been ably summarized by several workers, notably Tinker (1963), Spencer (1969) and Katzen (1977). Yet despite its long history, it is clear that much typographic research seems to have little practical relevance for writers, editors, typographers, publishers and printers. One reason for this, it has been suggested, is that the technical research papers are difficult to understand (Rehe, 1977). In my opinion, although this may be true, this is not the main reason. It seems to me that the early researchers in this field typically concerned themselves with molecular issues (ie with tiny details) rather than with molar ones (ie broad scale issues). Thus these researchers ignored the higher level organizational problems which in practice determine the decisions made at the lower levels. As a result we have a great deal of knowledge concerning the legibility of typefaces, typesizes, line lengths and interline spacing, but much of this knowledge has been gained without reference to the kind of text being printed and little of it has been tested in the context of full pages of meaningful text (Burnhill and Hartley, 1975).

However, when we examine what typographic designers typically do when they are confronted with a typescript, we find that what is of prime importance is how the document is to be used when it is finally printed. So the purpose (or purposes) of the document governs the first major decision — that of determining for it an appropriate page size. A telephone line-man climbing a telephone pole to do repair work does not want to have to hold in his hand a large and weighty instructional manual: he needs small appropriate leaflets which will fit into a convenient pocket.

Today, in Europe, it is likely that the designer will select the page size for his text from one of the standard sizes recommended by the ISO (International Standards Organisation). The dimensions of these sizes in the A and B series are set out in Table 1. The advantages of this system for making basic planning decisions about line lengths, typesizes, etc, are discussed in Hartley (1978)

A series		B series	
Designation	Size (mm)	Designation	Size (mm)
A0	841 x 1189	B0	1000 x 1414
A1	594 x 841	B1	707 x 1000
A2	420 x 594	B2	500 x 707
A3	297 x 420	B3	353 x 500
A4	210 x 297	B4	250 x 353
A5	148 x 210	B5	176 x 250
A6	105 x 148	B6	125 x 176
A7	74 x 105	B7	88 x 125
A8	52 x 74	B8	62 x 88
A9	37 x 52	B9	44 x 62
A10	26 x 37	B10	31 x 44

Table 1. *The ISO series of trimmed paper sizes: ratio* $1:\sqrt{2}$

Once the appropriate page size has been decided on, then the more minor decisions can be made — whether to use one column of print or two, what typefaces and sizes are available and which to use, what interline spacing to employ, and so on. Of course these decisions — which I have called minor — are of considerable importance. Like the major decisions they too are constrained by the nature of the text: the presentation of technical materials containing a large number of tables and diagrams, for instance, suggests a single-column layout (Burnhill *et al*, 1976); retrieval from such materials may be aided by the use of a line space to denote new paragraphs (Hartley *et al*, 1978); and as we shall see below, the effectiveness of such documents can be hampered by an inappropriate use of indentation.

However, the primary argument of this paper is that what affects most the ease of comprehension and retrieval from printed text is the use that is made of the space on a page size of known dimensions — rather than the print. This is, of course, a heads and tails position: one cannot make use of the space without the print — and *vice versa*. But I want to draw attention here to how one can capitalize on the space to convey the structure of instructional text perhaps more easily — and with more effectiveness — than one can capitalize on the print.

Let me remind the reader at this point that in printed text it is space that separates the letters from each other (regularly in typescript); it is space that separates the words from each other (again, regularly in typescript); it is space (and punctuation marks) that separates the phrases, clauses, sentences and paragraphs from each other; and it is space (with headings and subheadings) that separates the subsections and the chapters from each other.

There is some evidence, admittedly equivocal, from eye-movement research which suggests that these spatial cues are important aids to comprehending text. It is argued, for instance, that with increasing maturity and experience, readers come to rely more heavily on such spatial cues to enhance their reading and search efficiency (Fisher, 1976). It has been shown, for example, that the beginning of a line (and not the end) has a marked effect on eye-movement fixations, and that text which starts in an irregular manner (such as poetry, or storybooks) produces more regressive fixations than does regularly spaced text (Carpenter and Just, 1977). The significance of these fixations is, of course, a matter of debate (see Paper 1.4 in this text).

In this paper I maintain that spacing helps the readers to perceive redundancies in the text (and thus read faster); it enables them to perceive more easily the effective from the nominal stimuli (and thus focus on what is personally important); and most important, it aids their perception of the structure of the document as a whole (and thus helps them to comprehend its organization). To do all of this it is important that the space be manipulated in a consistent manner. The next section of this paper illustrates, with some practical examples, how this can be done.

Illustrations

The spacing of a page can be considered both from the vertical and the horizontal point of view. Let us consider vertical spacing first. Peter Burnhill (1970) has argued that the structure of complex text can be demonstrated more clearly to the reader by the consistent and planned use of vertical spacing. Units of space are used in proportion to separate sentences, paragraphs and headings in text. The proportions can be realized by simply doubling the units of line space (eg 1:2:4:8) but other proportional systems can be used.

Let us consider here just three examples: Figure 1a shows the initial version of a piece of text. Figure 1b shows how it is easier for the reader to perceive the structure of the text when there is one unit of space between the sentences, and two units between the paragraphs. Figure 2a shows again an original piece of text. Figure 2b shows how the sense of this text has been clarified first by re-grouping and next by re-spacing the parts in a proportional way. Figure 3a shows a third piece of text. Figure 3b shows how the instructions are easier to follow when some parts of the text are re-written, when each new sentence starts on a new line, when sub-units are separated by half a line space and when the constant 'Go to ...' instruction is re-positioned. These three examples all show how vertical space can be manipulated consistently to group and separate the functionally related parts of a piece of text.

DISPLAY MECHANISM

The 1402 Unit includes an NPN transistor, a display lamp, and a Number 5 relay. When current is applied to the transistor, the transistor activates the Number 5 relay and the display lamp. The 1402 Unit then actuates the paper-tape drive and the display tube.

The paper-tube drive consists of a Number 3 relay, a drive wheel, and the punch mechanism. When the Number 3 relay is activated, the drive wheel rotates and the punch mechanism is released.

The display tube consists of a disinhibit switch, a phosphorescent screen, and a keyboard. When the disinhibit switch is activated, the screen comes on and the keyboard is readied to accept input.

Figure 1a.

DISPLAY MECHANISM

The 1402 Unit includes an NPN transistor, a display lamp, and a Number 5 relay.

When current is applied to the transistor, the transistor activates the Number 5 relay and the display lamp.

The 1402 Unit then actuates the paper-tape drive and the display tube.

The paper-tape drive consists of a Number 3 relay, a drive wheel, and the punch mechanism.

When the Number 3 relay is activated, the drive wheel rotates and the punch mechanism is released.

The display tube consists of a disinhibit switch, a phosphorescent screen, and a keyboard.

When the disinhibit switch is activated, the screen comes on and the keyboard is readied to accept input.

Figure 1b.

... Between Australasia and Africa is the
Indian Ocean.
These are the oceans in the middle parts
of the earth. Round the north of the world,
in the very cold areas, there is the Arctic
Ocean.
It is mostly frozen up, and the North Pole
is in it. Round the southern parts of the
world, around Antarctica, is the Southern
Ocean ...

Figure 2a.

... Between Australasia and Africa is the
Indian Ocean.
These are the oceans in the middle parts of the earth.

Round the north of the world, in the very cold areas,
there is the Arctic Ocean.
It is mostly frozen up, and the North Pole is in it.

Round the southern parts of the world, around Antarctica,
is the Southern Ocean ...

Figure 2b.

STEP 5. Place a call to another person. If you reach the other person, GO TO STEP 6. If you continue to hear dial tone after you dial and the telephone has a rotary dial, GO TO STEP 18. If you continue to hear dial tone after you dial and the telephone has a push button dial, verify that you have TouchTone Service. (You can do this by calling the Telephone Company Business Office.) If you do have TouchTone Service on your line, GO TO STEP 18. If you do not have TouchTone Service, you will only be able to answer calls with this telephone.

Figure 3a.

5. Place a call to another person.
   If you reach the other person   Go to Step 6

   If you continue to hear the dial
   tone, and your phone has a
   circling dial   Go to Step 18

   If you continue to hear the dial
   tone, and your phone has a
   push-button dial, find out
   if you have TouchTone Service.
   (You can do this by calling
   the Telephone Company Business
   Office with another phone.)
   If you have TouchTone Service   Go to Step 18

   If you do not have TouchTone
   Service this phone can only
   receive calls.

Figure 3b.

Likewise, horizontal spacing can be used consistently to group functionally related parts together. Figure 4a shows the original layout of a section of text. Figure 4b presents a re-designed version where the designer's concern has been more with the sense of the content than with forcing the text to fit a particular line length. Figure 4b shows that when the text is printed ranged from the left with equal word spacing, then it is possible to avoid word breaks (hyphens) and starting a new sentence with the last word on a line.

Finally, Figures 5a and 5b show how these two approaches (vertical and horizontal) can be combined. In preparing these figures for this paper it was interesting to observe that I discovered something else: not until I worked on the re-design did I realize that the content in the original layout was not in an alphabetical or numerical sequence. This small detail illustrates again a point we have made before (Hartley and Burnhill, 1977a): clarity in layout leads to clarity in content because it requires clarity of thought.

The figures presented in this paper, of course, have been especially chosen to demonstrate the arguments that we are making. Thus most of them are short, and most can be set in typescript. Longer examples taken from printed materials — with detailed 'before and after' analyses — are provided in Hartley (1978).

... type-face does not specify the actual
size of the printed image (Hartley *et al*, 1975). In
general, however, a good all purpose size is 10-
point type on a 12-point line to line feed: 8-point
on 10-point is possibly about as small as one
would want to go in the design of instructional
materials.

Figure 4a.

... type-face does not specify the actual
size of the printed image (Hartley *et al*, 1975).
In general, however, a good all purpose size is
10-point on a 12-point line to line feed:
8-point on 10-point is possibly about as small as
one would want to go in the design of instructional
materials.

Figure 4b.

June 30, 1975, by Weintraub, Robinson, Smith, Plessas, Roser, and Rowls (579).

1-2 Mass communication

How the challenge of television news affects the prosperity of daily newspapers, by Bogart (50).

Media coverage of children and childhood: calculated indifference or neglect? by Dennis and Sadoff (125).

Television and reading in the seventies, by Feeley (168).

Czechoslovakia's press law, 1967-68: decontrolling the mass media, by Kaplan (282).

Attitudinal change with special reference to the mass media, by Klineberg (303).

The New York City press and anti-Canadianism: a new perspective on the Civil War years, by Kendall (289).

The teaching of reading — a crisis? by Latham (329).

Reading and television in the United States, by Lamb (323).

Literacy training in West Germany and the United States, by Orlow (426).

Changes in inter-ethnic 'attitudes' and the influence of the mass media as shown by research in French-speaking countries, by Guillaumin (221).

Mass media violence and society, by Howitt and Cumberbatch (263).

The media in America, by Tebbel (537).

1-3 Literacy

Adult illiteracy in England and Wales, by Bentovim and Stevens (44)

Literacy in developing countries, by Golub (200).

Towards an assessable definition of literacy, by Hillerich (255).

Reading skills — what reading skills? by Smith (509).

The experimental world literacy programme: a critical assessment, by Unesco Press (554).

Figure 5a.

| Summary of investigations relating to reading July 1, 1974 to June 30, 1975 | 579 | Weintraub *et al* |

1-2 Mass communication

How the challenge of television news affects the prosperity of daily newspapers.	50	Bogart
Media coverage of children and childhood: calculated indifference or neglect?	125	Dennis and Sadoff
Television and reading in the seventies.	168	Feeley
Changes in inter-ethnic 'attitudes' and the influence of the mass media as shown by research in French-speaking countries.	221	Guillaumin
Mass media violence and society.	263	Howitt and Cumberbatch
Czechoslovakia's press law, 1967-68: decontrolling the mass media.	282	Kaplan
The New York city press and anti-Canadianism: a new perspective on the Civil War years.	289	Kendall
Attitudinal change with special reference to the mass media.	303	Klineberg
Reading and television in the United States.	323	Lamb
The teaching of reading – a crisis?	329	Latham
Literacy training in West Germany and the United States.	426	Orlow
The media in America.	537	Tebbel

Figure 5b.

(Note: Normally I would prefer the reference to Weintraub to be placed on the previous page. It is kept here to show how spacing can be used to separate out parts, and also how this entry had to be re-written to fit this format.)

To summarize: as a general rule the procedures adopted by Hartley and Burnhill are as follows:

- ☐ We determine for each piece of instructional text how it is to be used, and what therefore seems to be an appropriate page size for it (from the ISO range).
- ☐ We determine how the text is made up — what are its component parts, and how they are related hierarchically.
- ☐ We examine the original sequence of the document to decide whether or not it is sensible.
- ☐ We use, in proportion, multiples of line feed to separate out the functionally related parts.
- ☐ We use horizontal spacing in addition to vertical spacing for text which is complex and which may contain several levels of importance or detail (see Hartley and Burnhill, 1976).
- ☐ We examine the wording of the opened-up text to see if it can be improved.
- ☐ We consider where to end each line of our revised text.
- ☐ We finally consider the use of typographic cues (eg use of lower case bold for headings) to see if they will further assist the reader.

Our prime contention, however, is that legibility is a function of clearly defined structural relations, and that this is most easily achieved by the consistent manipulation of space.

Theory into practice

The implementation of a systematic use of vertical and horizontal space seems to cause difficulties for most printers and users of word-processing systems. It seems almost impossible to persuade printers to use a 'floating base-line' on each page which will permit them to group functionally related statements. Sometimes, for example, one finds the last line of a paragraph on the first line of the next page; line spacing opened up or compressed; or even tables split in two so that the base-line remains in a constant position on every page. (See here, for example, what the printers did to one of our articles: Hartley and Burnhill, 1977a, pp 242-3.)

It seems to be a little easier to persuade printers to use standard word spacing (unjustified text), largely because unjustified text is cheaper to correct at proof stage and —with metal typesetting — cheaper to set. Few printers, however, are prepared for their operators to consider the meaning of each line of text in order to determine its stopping point.

To achieve this requires careful preparation by the author and a sympathetic printer. It can be done either by typing the text in such a way that the actual number of characters per line corresponds to the line length to be used by the printer in the setting of the text, or by using a grid specification system (eg see Rehe, 1977; Hartley, 1978). A typographic grid specifies the information area of the page in terms of horizontal units (eg characters per line of a certain typesize) and vertical units (eg the line-feed measure). Both procedures were used by Hartley (1978). The grid specification system was used to set the limits of the text, and the manuscript was typed with a maximum of 75 characters to the line. This was equivalent to a column width of 27 ems (10 point type) in the printed text: all the printer had to do was to copy the typescript line for line.

This procedure has additional advantages. If one knows the number of lines of text per page (plus or minus one or two for the floating base-line), then one can specify in advance the position of the illustrations and their depth in terms of line-feed measurements. In this way, the author can determine that illustrations are not divorced from their textual reference. Furthermore, if the printer makes errors in following the specification, one can charge the printer for making corrections, rather than the author.

This particular point — about costs — leads me to comment here on this problem. A constant criticism that we have received in view of our emphasis on space is that it must cost more to produce instructional materials using our methods. We have two replies to this. First, costs can be kept down by using modern printing methods, and by simplifying the typographic procedures. (We showed this in our re-design of a college prospectus — Burnhill *et al*, 1975.) Second, the cost-savings of skimping on space may in fact be wasted if the resulting document is difficult to read or comprehend. We have twice obtained evidence that suggested that our re-designed document — although using more paper — would have saved the originator money in the long run (Hartley and Burnhill, 1976; 1977b). It is interesting, of course, to reflect on the fact that it is difficult to measure the costs to the *user* of badly designed documents.

Evaluation

So far all that has been said may appear to be simply opinions — supported, I hope, by interesting examples. In this section of this paper I want to comment on how one might evaluate the opinions I have expressed so far.

To do this I propose to present here three 'case histories' and then to comment further on problems of evaluation in this area of research.

CASE HISTORY 1: REVISING A COMPLEX LEGAL DOCUMENT

Figures 6a and 6b show part of the original and part of our re-designed version of a leaflet distributed by the British Psychological Society. To test the efficiency of the re-design we typed both versions on A4 paper, and then reduced the typescript by xerox copying to A5 (thus simulating printed text). The original document covered four A5 pages, and the revised version five pages. We then asked undergraduate students to carry out a number of search tasks using the two documents. The results (described in detail by Hartley and Burnhill, 1976) were quite conclusive. With the original layout only six out of 23 students (26 per cent) were able to find all the items of business to be discussed at the meeting: with the revised version 18 out of 21 (86 per cent) found them. With the original layout only 12 out of 23 students

THE BRITISH PSYCHOLOGICAL SOCIETY

(Incorporated by Royal Charter)

NOTICE IS HEREBY GIVEN that a Special General Meeting of the Society with be held in the Small Meeting House, Friends House, Euston Road, London NW1 on Saturday 26 October 1974 at 10.30 o'clock in the forenoon, when the following business will be transacted.

(1) To consider, and if thought fit, to approve the following SPECIAL RESOLUTIONS subject to obtaining the formal approval of the Privy Council:

A. That the Statutes of the Society be amended in the manner following, namely, by deleting the existing Statutes 4 and 8 and substituting the following new Statutes:

4. GRADUATE MEMBERS

(1) All persons who were elected Graduate Members of the old Institution and all persons who are elected as hereinafter provided shall be Graduate Members.

(2) A candidate for election as a Graduate Memeber:

    (a) shall satisfy the Council that he has one of the following qualifications and such higher qualifications as may be provided in the Rules: —

        (i) a university degree for which psychology has been taken as a main subject;

        or

        (ii) a postgraduate qualification in psychology awarded by an authority recognised by the Council;

        or

        (iii) such other qualification in psychology as the Council shall accept as not less than the foregoing;

        or

    (b) shall pass to the satisfaction of the Council such of the Society's examinations as may be required by the Rules.

(3) The Council may elect such eligible candidates to be Graduate Members as it thinks fit.

8. SUBSCRIBERS

(1) All persons who were elected Subscribers of the old Institution and who are elected as hereinafter provided shall be Subscribers.

(2) No technical qualification shall be required of a candidate for election as a Subscriber.

(3) A Subscriber shall be proposed in accordance with the provisions of the Rules.

Figure 6a. *The first page of the original pamphlet sent out by the BPS (with its original spelling)*

The British Psychological Society

(Incorporated by Royal Charter)

Notice is hereby given that a Special General Meeting of the Society will be held in the Small Meeting House, Friends House, Euston Road, London NW1 on Saturday 26 October 1974 at 10.30 o'clock in the forenoon, when the following business will be transacted.

1st item of business

To consider, if thought fit, to approve the following Special Resolutions subject to obtaining the formal approval of the Privy Council: (These Special Resolutions are identical with those approved in principle at the Society's Annual General Meeting held in Bangor on 6 April 1974, with the exception of Statute 15 (see below) in which maximum permitted subscriptions have been reduced.)

Resolution A

That the Statutes of the Society be amended in the manner following, namely, by deleting the existing Statutes 4 and 8 and substituting the following new Statutes:

Statute 4: Graduate Members

(1) All persons who were elected Graduate Members of the old Institution and all persons who are elected as hereinafter provided shall be Graduate Members.

(2) A candidate for election as a Graduate Member:

(a) shall satisfy the Council that he has one of the following qualifications and such higher qualifications as may be provided in the rules:-

(i) a university degree for which psychology has been taken as a main subject;

or

(ii) a postgraduate qualification in psychology awarded by an authority recognised by Council;

Figure 6b. *A spaced typescript version of Figure 6a*

(48 per cent) were able to find the four special resolutions which were to be discussed, whereas with the revised version 20 out of 21 (95 per cent) found them. The time taken to retrieve these items was significantly faster for students using the revised version. In this example then, in terms of paper costs, the revised edition of the pamphlet was more expensive. In terms of cost-effectiveness, however, the revised edition was clearly superior.

CASE HISTORY 2: PARAGRAPH DENOTION IN SINGLE AND TWO-COLUMN TEXT

In this study (reported in more detail by Hartley *et al*, 1978) four pages of text were printed in 10 on 12 point type on A4 paper in either a two-column unjustified setting (each column 20 ems) or in a single-column unjustified setting (42 ems). For each setting the start of a new paragraph was denoted in one of four ways:

(i) new line of text after a one-line space, with no indent;
(ii) new line plus indent but no line space (the traditional method);
(iii) new line, but no indent and no line space;
(iv) no indication: ie the text was set as a solid 'slab'.

These different systems — illustrated in Hartley *et al* — produce variations in the amount of horizontal space that is available to cue the reader, and the aim of the study was to see whether or not this would affect the readability of the text.

Approximately 500 school children aged between 12 and 14 years with a wide ability range participated in this enquiry. The children were first asked to read the text as naturally as possible for a period of ten minutes, and then to mark where they had reached. After this they were asked to search the text for particular phrases during a further ten-minute period.

The results of this latter search task indicated:

(i) There was a significant difference ($p < .05$) in favour of the two-column layout — although this difference was small. The average number of phrases retrieved in the two-column versions (in ten minutes) was 17.6 and in the single-column versions it was 16.7.

(ii) There was a significant difference in the number retrieved which reflected the denotation of new paragraphs. The average scores obtained were as follows:
System (i)   18.2   System (iii)   16.2
System (ii)   17.6   System (iv)   16.7
System (i) was significantly superior to System (iii) ($p < .01$) and System (iv) ($p < .05$) (Tukey test), but it was not significantly different from System (ii).

(iii) There was a statistically significant sex difference: girls doing better than boys ($p < .01$). The average score for the girls was 18.2 and for the boys it was 16.2.

(iv) There were no interactions between these three different measures: ie scores on the single-column layouts for the different paragraph systems did not differ significantly from scores obtained on the two-column ones, and boys did not score differently from girls on different paragraph systems.

These results suggest that a two-column layout is probably preferable to a single-column one for the setting of straightforward prose, although the actual data suggest that the differences are very small. In terms of cost-effectiveness, a two-column layout with paragraphs denoted by indentation (the traditional method) seems best because (i) it is possible to get more words on a page with a two-column layout, and (ii) this layout uses less space than one which uses line spacing for denoting paragraphs. Nonetheless, it should be observed here that if the nature of text demands a single-column structure (see Case history 3), then a line length of 42 ems can probably be used without placing an undue strain on the reader.

CASE HISTORY 3: INSERTING TABLES IN SINGLE-
AND TWO-COLUMN TEXT

In this study (reported in more detail by Burnhill *et al*, 1976) tables of information of various sizes were inserted into a four-page article printed in 10 on 12 point type on A4 paper. Approximately 340 school children, aged between 12 and 14 and of a wide ability range, were asked to search for phrases in the *text* which was printed in a two-column or a single-column format. The results, shown in Table 2, indicated that there was a clear effect due to the presence of single or double columns (the tables cutting across the double columns causing greater difficulty), and that sex and ability were important.

			One-column	Two-columns
High ability children	Girls	$\overline{X}$	20.8	18.8
		sd	4.8	6.5
		N	28	28
	Boys	$\overline{X}$	16.9	13.4
		sd	5.0	5.1
		N	22	30
Low ability children	Girls	$\overline{X}$	14.5	11.8
		sd	3.4	4.3
		N	26	21
	Boys	$\overline{X}$	12.1	10.3
		sd	3.5	4.8
		N	20	25

Table 2. *The mean number of phrases correctly retrieved in prose with large tabular insertions by high and low ability children*

The findings of this study suggest (with readers of this age) that a single-column structure for text on an A4 page may be preferable to a double-column one for text containing differing components. The study suggests that decisions concerning the column structure of a page should not be decided by a simple concern for line length alone but should also take into account the structural requirements of the text and its non-textual components.

Further observations on evaluation

In our research we have used a number of different methods. We have made 'before and after' comparisons in terms of:

- ☐ reader preferences
- ☐ speed of retrieval of information
- ☐ comprehension (as measured by cloze tests and factual recall measures)
- ☐ costs and ease of production (eg printing costs, typing speeds).

And, in nearly all cases, we have worked with actual instructional materials.

Some of the measures that we have used have proved more useful than others (see Hartley *et al*, 1975). Subjective preferences, for example, are interesting but they are not always informative. Not only does one man's meat appear to be another man's poison, but also one cannot assume that there will always be a positive relationship between preference, speed of retrieval and ease of use (Hartley *et al*, 1973).

Another issue of interest is that it is not possible to evaluate all of our design decisions. In the act of designing (or re-designing) we examine mentally and in rapid succession the typographical image of a range of possible solutions, each one having the status of a hypothesis to be tested and, if necessary, rejected on logical, technical or economic grounds. For example, I prepared four versions of Figure 5b before further revising the one I have presented in this paper. So, in practice, a selection has to be made, and in evaluation studies only the major variations are compared. (This is partly a function of cost: producing eight versions of four pages of A4 text for an experiment can cost in the region of £300.) In addition, in re-designing, we usually make several changes all at once, so it is not possible — in simple 'before and after' comparison studies — to attribute any effects that are found to any one particular variable.

Furthermore we need to note here that in carrying out comparison studies the process of measurement may actually destroy the very thing we are trying to measure. Psychologists and typographers face a real difficulty here. In order to replace subjective opinion with fact, measurement must take place, yet the need to gain evidence has to be balanced against the possibility that the method of gaining it renders the evidence invalid. In all of our experients, for example, the participants have known that they were taking part in an experiment. Klare (1976) has pointed out — in another context — that in such situations the participants are likely to be highly motivated, and that high motivation, sustained over a short period of time (as in most typographic experiments), is likely to render insignificant any small effects (due in this case to typographic variables).

An alternative view, of course, is that under certain kinds of pressure (eg constant interruptions) some documents might be more difficult to use than others.

Finally, we may observe that the traditional research methods that we use today present some serious difficulties: many seem to be weak (in terms of reliability) and some (such as eye-movement recordings) lack ecological validity. In addition, each method contains its own in-built assumptions about the reading process. Most seem to assume, for instance, that readers start at the beginning of a text and read it once, steadily, straight through to the end. Yet, as we all know, there are many different kinds of reading.

There is a need, therefore, for different styles of evaluation and for different research methods as well as the traditional ones. There is a need for more observation on how long documents are used and/or stored, whether they are written on or torn apart, and so on. (One might, for example, look at how many people drop out of correspondence courses which differ only in their typographic layout.) In short we need to look harder at the advantages of using field studies and 'unobtrusive measures' (Webb *et al*, 1966).

Despite these comments, we have shown — using traditional research procedures — savings in production costs, or savings in ease of use in all of the areas where we have carried out evaluation studies. These have included the design of college prospectuses, academic journals, complex instructional materials, complex (legal-type) prose, questionnaires, forms, indexes, and even lecture handouts. References to and illustrations from these studies are provided in Hartley (1978).

References

Burnhill, P (1970) Typographic education: headings in text. *Journal of Typographic Research* 4: 353-65

Burnhill, P and Hartley, J (1975) The psychology of textbook design: a research critique. In J Baggaley *et al* (eds) *Aspects of Educational Technology VIII*. London: Pitman

Burnhill, P, Hartley, J, Fraser, S and Young, M (1975) The typography of college prospectuses: a critique and a case-history. In L Evans and J Leedham (eds) *Aspects of Educational Technology IX*. London: Kogan Page

Burnhill, P, Hartley, J and Young, M (1976) Tables in text. *Applied Ergonomics* 7 1: 13-18

Carpenter, P A and Just, M A (1977) Reading comprehension as the eyes see it. In M A Just and P A Carpenter (eds) *Cognitive Processes in Comprehension*. Hillsdale, NJ: Erlbaum

Fisher, D (1976) Spatial factors in reading and research: the case for space. In R A Monty and J W Senders (eds) *Eye-Movements and Psychological Processes*. Hillsdale, NJ: Erlbaum

Hartley, J (1978) *Designing Instructional Text*. London: Kogan Page and New York: Nichols

Hartley, J and Burnhill, P (1976) Explorations in space: a critique of the typography of BPS publications. *Bulletin of the British Psychological Society* 29: 97-107

Hartley, J and Burnhill, P (1977a) Understanding instructional text: typography, layout and design. In M J A Howe (ed) *Adult Learning*. London: Wiley

Hartley, J and Burnhill, P (1977b) Space revisited: or the BPS does it again. *Bulletin of the British Psychological Society* 30: 253-6

Hartley, J, Davies, L and Burnhill, P (1978) The effects of line-length and paragraph denotation on the retrieval of information from prose text. *Visible Language* XII, 2: 183-94

Hartley, J, Fraser, S and Burnhill, P (1975) Some observations on the reliability of measures used in reading and typographic research. *Journal of Reading Behavior* 7 3: 283-96

Hartley, J, Timson, S and Burnhill, P (1973) Subjective preference and retrieval of information from reference materials. *Visible Language* **VII** 2: 167-70

Katzen, M (1977) *The Visual Impact of Scholarly Journals.* Leicester University: Primary Communications Research Centre

Klare, G R (1976) A second look at the validity of readability formulas. *Journal of Reading Behavior* **8** 2: 129-52

Rehe, R F (1977) *Typography: How to Make it Most Legible.* Carmel, Indiana: Design Research International

Spencer, H (1969) *The Visible Word.* London: Lund Humphries

Tinker, M A (1963) *The Legibility of Print.* Ames: Iowa State University Press

Webb, E J *et al* (1966) *Unobtrusive Measures: Non-Reactive Research in the Social Sciences.* New York: Rand McNally

Acknowledgements

This paper was written whilst the author was a visiting member of the Accoustical and Behavioral Research Center, Bell Laboratories, Murray Hill, New Jersey, USA. I am indebted to colleagues at Bell Laboratories for constructive comments on earlier drafts and to Bell Labs for their support. I am also indebted to the Social Science Research Council, UK who paid for the preparation of this paper.

3.2 Notes on transforming nos 4 and 5

ROBERT WALLER

(The two papers presented here were first distributed at the Open University between May 1977 and January 1978 but have been slightly revised for this text.)

4 Numbering systems in text

Numbering systems are used to organize information in many different ways. How should they be used and when is it appropriate to use them?

There is actually very little guidance available. None of the major style manuals of graphic design textbooks say very much on the subject.

There's not much advice around

Information scientists have thought about the problems of using numbering systems to classify subject areas but not to organize educational texts. Psychological research on the role of short-term memory in the use of numbers is summarized by Gallagher (1974) and research on the legibility of numbers is discussed by Tinker (1963). They are sources of useful information on the design and readability of numerals but they do not attempt to offer advice on the application of numbering systems.

Perhaps because the problem is hidden

It is very easy to imagine that there is no problem. Firstly, reference books, instructional or service manuals, and rule books — the sort of publications that use numbering systems — are less accessible and visible than other publications. Secondly, one of the frequent effects of a numbering system is to make information look well organized, even when it is not.

But take a look at some OU texts

But there is a problem and we have it at the Open University. Here are some examples.

MST281 (Open University courses are usually referred to by numbers, and rarely by name.)

The correspondence texts for this course are numbered 1, 2, 3, 4, 5, 7, 8, 9, 11, 10, 13, 14, 15, 16. The reason why 14 units are numbered

145

26.1.2   A modern coastal environment

The idea of interpreting the past in terms of the present sounds extremely simple, but there are many practical difficulties. An insight into the extent of these can be gained by considering a present-day environment from a geological point of view.

> **So, you should now read the section in Chapter 13 of** *Understanding the Earth* **entitled 'environmental analysis — the beach' (pp. 180-5).**

When you read this section, examine Figure 14 in Appendix 3 (p. 34), which summarizes information on the sediments and faunas of a modern beach. Plate A and TV programme 26 are about this area. *Make sure you have examined Figure 14 thoroughly and have read pp. 180-5 of* Understanding the Earth *given above before viewing the television programme.* The post-broadcast notes will refer you to Appendix 3 which describes a 'geological model' of this stretch of coast and summarizes the sequence of 'rocks in the making' in this environment.

Either now, or after you have viewed the TV programme, consider what you would measure on a present-day beach in order to describe quantitatively such an environment; pay particular attention to the materials and processes which would be preserved when the sediments became rocks.

You should compile your list under the following headings:

(1) Topography

(2) Climate

(3) Water conditions

(4) Flora and fauna

(5) Sediments

DO NOT READ ON UNTIL YOU HAVE ATTEMPTED TO MAKE A LIST.

Figure 1. *This is page 10 of S100 (the Science Foundation course), unit 26. There are cross references to 6 different numbering systems, not including the 2 systems that identify this page (26.1.2 + p.10): Chapter 13 pp. 180-5 Figure 14 Appendix 3+1 Plate A TV prog. 26.*

from 1 to 16 is that units 6 and 12 are 'rest' periods to allow students to catch up. A unit is not a text, apparently; it is a week's work. Well, usually . . . but no one seems very sure what it is. There is probably also a very good reason why the mathematics faculty has used the interesting numerical sequence 8, 9, 11, 10, 13.

PE261

Some units of this recently replaced course use as many as seven different numbering systems — unconnected in any way. There are separate systems for paragraphs, activities, footnotes, tables, figures, parts, pages.

D203

The main teaching text in Block 11 starts with Part 2. Part 1 is the introduction. Part 2 has its own introduction in addition, as does Section 1 of part 2.

A201

This course uses as many reference systems as it has authors. Unit 1, for instance, is divided into sections with paragraphs numbered separately — thus, section 3 starts with paragraph 19. Units 4, 17, 19 and 28 only have section numbers. Units 8-10 are bound together and number their paragraphs continuously — thus unit 8 starts with para 1, unit 9 with para 118, and unit 10 with para 142. Units 20-27 have yet another system: units 20 and 21 contain sections 10.0-16.2 although the contents are also organized as Topics I-X; units 22 and 23 contain sections 20.0-23.2 and units 24 and 25, sections 30.0-34.10, and so on.

Phew!

What are they used for?

If our numbering systems were the products of careful planning and were as consistent and rational as the term implies, they would surely not defy description in this way. Their chaotic state seems to reflect confusion about their purpose.

Numbering systems are used for two main purposes. Firstly, they provide a means of reference. It is useful to be able to refer to particular parts of texts for several reasons — for cross reference within a text, for course team discussions of drafts, for tutorial discussions of units, and so on. Secondly, numbering systems

For cross reference

*and
to show the
structure of
the text*

are often used to display the relative status of different parts of the text — thus the sequence 1, 1.1, 1.1.1 describes three levels of a hierarchy.

The two uses of numbers are obviously related — something labelled 3 must be preceded by something labelled 2, and order of presentation often implies relative status. Nevertheless the distinction between reference and structural purposes of numbering systems is a useful one. It is useful because it isolates the source of most of the confusions we have found — namely the misuse of structured numbering systems.

*Structured
numbering
systems have
serious defects*

Whereas reference-only systems (like page numbers) are neutral and status-free, structured systems embody all the deep curriculum design and writing problems that authors of educational texts will always have. Although such systems may be entirely appropriate in some publications — Acts of Parliament, for instance, or parts catalogues — they have some rather insidious effects on educational texts.

*The coding
is hard to
understand . . .*

Firstly, they are cryptic. The principles of a structured system are almost never explained and only exceptionally well thought-out and well applied systems are self-explanatory. One difficulty arises from the fact that these systems look like ordinary numbers and yet use mathematical notation in quite different ways. Whereas 1.1 and 1.10 normally represent the same number, in a numbering system they may both be part of the sequence 1.0, 1.1, 1.2 . . . 1.9, 1.10, 1.11. Systems with this many items in a sequence usually go to 1.1.1 for the next level in the hierarchy, while systems that never get as far as 1.9 often use 1.11 to mean the same thing. Even when the notation is clear, numbering systems are still

*and is
visually unclear*

inadequate when used on their own to show the structure of a text: 1.12.3, for instance, does not look very different from 1.12.4 — most of the digits have remained the same. There is a useful rule of thumb that says 'precise construction does not guarantee accurate perception.' Applied here it means that the signalling of a new section of text will need more than a change of one digit in a long marginal number — it may also require extra 'redundant' signals like a line space, or an indent or a subheading.

3	General Rules for Copy Preparation
3.1	General instructions
3.2	Standard page
3.2.1	Size
3.2.2	Typing
3.3	Headings
3.4	Sections, sub-sections
3.5	Footnotes
3.6	Cross references
3.7	Quotations
3.8	Figures and tables
3.8.1	Artwork
3.8.2	Tables
3.8.3	Captions

Figure 2. *This part of the contents list from the Open University House Style shows that numbering systems are not adequate to show the structure of text on their own. These numbers are mistakenly aligned at the right (like a sum). The longest and so most prominent numbers refer to the least important categories.*

Few teaching texts are genuinely hierarchical

Secondly, structured numbering systems are insincere — that is, they purport to aid the reader while in fact they often mislead. Textbooks rarely have the sort of structure that numbering systems display. These systems originate in taxonomies — classifications of things or concepts. They are hierarchical organizations of items that claim to be both complete and discrete — that is, there is nothing outside them that should be in, and there is nothing included that should not be. These are not claims that Open University course units should be making. The concepts, arguments, facts, examples, and so forth that make up an academic discipline are connected not as a hierarchy but more as a network. The nature of written language, though, means that subjects have to be represented in a linear way. It is part of the skill of a good teacher to structure ideas for the purpose of explanation without preventing the student perceiving the network in the way that suits him best. It is not easy to make all the necessary connections and allusions without losing the thread of an argument. It certainly cannot be done without some redundancy — some ideas have to be mentioned more than once. Structured numbering systems, though, imply that the ideas mentioned in paragraph 2.2, for example, are definitely in a different branch of the hierarchy from, say,

149

para 8.6.2. The chaotic state of many of our numbered texts results from the fact that authors find that this is not so. Not only do subjects not fit easily into hierarchical prose, but the systems are unable to cope with the various other kinds of discourse that also appear in teaching texts — questions, study hints, summaries, and so on.

and they
create the
wrong atmosphere

Thirdly, numbering systems are officious — they give Open University texts a rather phoney air of authority. They reinforce the insidious notion that originates from the educational technology of programmed learning and that quietly lives on in many OU courses — the notion that textbooks are static and can only be read in one way. Although course units often are excellent examples of scholarship they must nevertheless remain 'tutorials in print', maintaining the distinction between correspondence texts and set books. Numbering systems contribute to an atmosphere of closedness and precision that is out of place. Some of the original sources for numbering systems are illustrated at the end of this paper. They are all texts whose essential qualities include thoroughness, precise ordering of thought and language, and authority. It is worth mentioning that numbering systems in texts are not the only numbers the Open University uses — we also number everything else in our educational system that is quantifiable — students, tutors, assignments, courses, study centres, regions, weeks of the year, broadcasts, and so on. These all set up a relationship between teacher and learner that is hardly welcoming to the beginning student; they also add considerable poignancy to the term 'distance teaching'.

Numbering
for
cross reference

Besides structuring the text the other main purpose of numbering systems is to provide a means of cross reference. To discuss reference systems, though, brings us back almost immediately to a discussion of the hierarchical numbering systems that we have just left — because the most common sort of cross references in texts are references to concepts. And concepts are what structured systems purport to display. To refer to a concept solely by number, however, is inadequate. A reference like 'see 3.1' is ambiguous on two counts. As an instruction it is too vague — should the reader re-read or just glance at 3.1? As a connector of ideas it also fails. It neither reminds the reader of the content of 3.1 nor tells him why it is significant.

Instead I would suggest that numbering systems should only be used to refer to locations in the text, and to genuinely quantifiable series of items. 'Locations' means pages; series of items include figures, exercises or activities, tables and broader subdivisions of texts such as chapters or parts.

*Page numbers
are fine . . .*

A corollary to the advice 'use page numbers only' is: 'use plenty of subheadings and marginal notes'. These not only restore the specificity of reference that is lost where structured paragraph numbers are left out, but the significance of reference to a subheading is self-explanatory.

*but figures,
tables, etc
cause more
problems . . .*

Page numbers need little comment but the numbering of series is more problematical. The reader finds the right page by flicking through the book looking at all the page numbers until he finds the right one. He is using the context of the series to find the particular page he wants. In most publications page numbers appear on every page and there is no problem; but although tables and figures have to be located in exactly

*especially when
there are only
a few . . .*

the same way, there are often very few of them. In other words, to find Figure 3 means finding Figure 2 or Figure 4 first. If there are only a few diagrams in the whole book, context is of little help to the reader. The alternative, referring to 'Figure 3 on page 32', sounds like an admission of defeat by the editor. One quite promising

*so why not
combine them
with
chapter nos?*

solution to this problem may be to use the division of the book into chapters to narrow down the field of search. Thus Tables 1, 2 and 3 may, instead, be referred to as Table 2/1, Table 2/2 and Table 5/1. Oblique strokes are used instead of points to avoid confusion with decimal systems. It may also be possible to incorporate all numbered items in the same series — eg Table 5/1, Table 5/2, Exercise 5/3, Figure 5/4 etc.

*What numbers
should look
like . . .*

Besides the context of the system, the sensible design and placing of the numbers are also important aids to the reader. Some design issues have been the subject of research. Tinker (1930) found little difference between the legibility of ranging numerals and the non-ranging numerals of old-style typefaces which vary in vertical alignment. Perry (1952) showed conclusively that Arabic numerals are much superior to Roman. The numerals of all conventional printing types would, then, seem to be fine. It is worth noting at this point an interesting idea found in *History of Architecture and Design* (A305). The correspondence texts contain a large number of illustrations and the references to them in the text are printed in bold type. This helps readers who are browsing through the pictures to locate the text which discusses them.

and where to
place them

The placing of the reference numbers has not been the subject of experiment, although a greater variation is found in practice. It often happens, in typographic research, that the issues most often researched empirically are those that are least problematical and thus most easily and uncontroversially defined. The skill is to make the numbers prominent enough to see on scanning, but to ensure that they are not intrusive. In practice, this often means placing them in the margin rather than within the text, using discreet numerals in a prominent position. Instead of placing figure numbers or paragraph numbers (if used) always on, say, the left of the column of type, it will help the scanning reader most to place them consistently nearest the fore edge of the book — thus on right-hand pages they will be on the right and on left-hand pages they will be on the left. Two-column texts present different problems — numbers appearing between the columns require more space than is usually available in order to be clearly visible and unambiguous. Here, it may be best to place the numbers on the outside of the page — on the left of the left-hand column and on the right of the right-hand column. Texts with three or more columns may have to incorporate the numbers within the column of type.

Conclusions

Numbering systems are obviously not a primary problem of our educational system. But every component must be thought through if we are to produce functional and approachable texts.

For most educational texts, then, the 'best buy' system can be summarized as follows.

☐ Use numbers mainly for reference. Chapter, page and figure numbers are almost always perfectly adequate for continuous prose texts.
☐ Consider incorporating figure numbers, exercise numbers, and so on in the chapter numbering system, particularly when there are too few figures for easy location or when too many different systems would cause confusion.

☐ Use Arabic numerals not Roman ones.
☐ Place the numbers near the fore edge of the book so that it is easy to see them when flicking through.
☐ If in-text numbering has to be used, place the numbers in the margin rather than within the column.

References

Gallagher, C C (1974) The human use of numbering systems. *Applied Ergonomics* 5 4: 219-23

Perry, D K (1952) Speed and accuracy of reading Arabic and Roman numerals. *Journal of Applied Psychology* 36: 346-7

Tinker, M A (1930) The relative legibility of modern and old style numerals. *Journal of Experimental Psychology* 13: 453-61

Tinker, M A (1963) *The Legibility of Print.* Ames: Iowa State University Press

5 Dimensions of quality in educational texts

How can authors best approach decisions about the presentation of course texts? This paper sets out and expands on some thoughts on this issue that were put to the Technology Foundation Course team in Autumn 1977, who had perceptively recognized the need to consider presentation and design at the earliest stages of course production — even before the curriculum had been decided and authors assigned. The problems were: how can we co-ordinate decisions that are normally made at different stages in the production process so that earlier decisions do not unduly constrain later ones? How might research inform those decisions?

At the moment there is no general view of what presentation is, how it affects the quality of our courses, or how it can be evaluated and improved — yet we produce course units with sophisticated printing methods even for courses with only 100 or 200 students a year. But although the Open University as an institution is in this sense committed to the view that presentation does matter, in practice few course teams manage to do it in more than a fairly haphazard way. For example, most course teams are organized so that designers only rarely attend course team meetings; courses are developmentally tested in rough typewritten drafts; sometimes strange decisions are reached, as in one course team that was recently asked to use a smaller typesize because it would look more 'scientific'!

The approach taken by course team members to problems of presentation is often coloured by assumptions, prejudices or misunderstandings that have arisen in various ways. They may come from traditional textbooks that make few concessions to the student — it has sometimes been argued that badly organized texts are just one of the hoops that an academic training should make students jump through. Sometimes there is straightforward misinformation — for example, a course team was recently told that the reason it could not use the wide margins for headings was that the cost of the extra two inches of film for the platemaking would be prohibitive. There might have been a good reason but that was almost certainly not it.

Sometimes the course team's approach is the result of a personal hobbyhorse of one particular member. Recently observed examples include behavioural objectives, bias, reading purposes, headings, questions, readability, illustrations, typography or many others. There is an opposite effect too — all of us have gaps in our knowledge and so the advice we give will be biased accordingly.

We would often like a theoretical framework or research data to inform our discussions. There are a number of disciplines or subject areas that we can turn to — psychology (of various kinds), sociology, educational technology, typography, literary criticism, and so on. If we limit our attention to only one of these areas, though, our advice is bound to be biased, because they all have very different suppositions about writers, texts and readers.

For example, typographers sometimes see a text only as printed letters on paper, paying little attention to its content. A specialist in the subject of the text, on the other hand, might only be interested in the accuracy of the content. An educational technologist interested in the sequencing of the concepts lies somewhere between these two extremes. It is possible, in fact, to place the interests of many other specialists in a similar way.

Figure 1 displays this in a diagram. It ranges various different approaches to text on a continuum from 'message' to 'medium', borrowing from McLuhan's familiar catch-phrase. This reflects the fact that in practice, if not in theory, you cannot usefully consider 'what to say' separately from 'how to say it'. The continuum is useful as a framework for course team discussion because it corresponds roughly to the course production process. This is essential if it is to be of use. It is the experience of many colleagues, both in course development and research, that any advice they give, however theoretically neat, must relate to the practical problems being experienced by course teams at any particular time. In fact, it is better that the advice is ready before the problems are met. It is essential that decisions taken at any particular stage take into account problems and opportunities that will be met at a later stage — so there is a need to consider all aspects of quality — whether they be of content or presentation — in a co-ordinated way. Figure 1 tries to do this practically as well as theoretically by relating the 'issues' to the division of tasks in the production system and also to the collection of student feedback for the evaluation and refinement of the text.

The first column lists some of the areas where research literature is available (to varying degrees of quality and quantity) to inform course team discussion, and course team evaluation.

The second column shows the span of responsibility of various roles. They vary, of course, according to individual skills and in different course teams. Just as it is hard to say where 'content' ends and 'presentation' begins on the continuum, so it is hard to say precisely where different roles divide. Some of the tensions that exist at present in our production system are at the borderlines between roles — between

M E S S A G E

Research area	Production system	Text	Reader	Communication problem
Epistemology	Authors	Principles, facts, theories, issues, etc	Prior knowledge, skills	Define teaching objectives, eg what facts? What skills? Define potential readership.
Curriculum theory		Examples, cases, explanation, sequencing, etc	Reading purpose (prior knowledge + context + aptitudes)	Outline options for teaching particular skills/knowledge in context of a range of reading purposes.
Structural or rhetorical analysis	Editor	Rhetoric, argumentation, structural cohesion	Analytic skills	Check for coherence of argument, and of links between different parts of course, etc.
Psycho-linguistics		Vocabulary, syntax, tone, etc	Reading skills	Check for readability level, discuss guidelines for authors.
Educational psychology, typographic research	Designer	Questions, access structure, (summaries, headings, etc)	Reading strategy (purpose + environment + aptitudes)	What to signal (what reading strategies to cater for). How to signal (format, typography).
Perception, typographic research		Print specification and quality	Visual acuity, graphic associations	Choice of typeface and layout; legibility; visual associations, availability of technical symbols, etc.

M E D I U M

Figure 1. *A continuum of factors affecting the quality of educational texts*

author and editor, and editor and designer. In the diagram these points of tension are represented by the overlap of lines. Obviously one person cannot do all the work or be completely familiar with all the problems. It is clear, though, that the various mechanisms for co-operation need careful managing — the course team, the 'handover' system, the house style, even the physical accessibility of individuals. The notion of 'transforming' that this series of papers is exploring does not therefore call for one superhuman intellect so much as a team of people with appropriate skills working within an appropriate management structure, with the appropriate ethos and objectives.

The next three columns show in more practical terms the factors that affect the quality of a text. There are corresponding factors in both the reader and the text. Considered together they form 'research issues' for course teams to discuss, and to direct the collection of feedback from students. Problems of quality arise from a mismatch between the two — for example between the prior knowledge of the reader and the specialist vocabulary used in the text.

'Quality' is a vague word — what is meant by it, and what is it that our careful course unit evaluation and developmental testing is meant to improve? If the mismatch idea is correct, then 'quality' means the effectiveness of the interaction of the student with the text. To evaluate this, then, we must look at both. We know quite a lot about the analysis of text from some of the research areas in the first column of the diagram, but the criteria for quality must ultimately be student-centred; the failure to accept this is a reason why some of these disciplines offer so little to practical communicators. Text cannot be judged from formal criteria, but must only be evaluated in relation to the purposes and achievements of its readers, in terms both of their personal and of institutional goals. So formal analysis of course content will not itself tell us whether it is biased, or pitched at the right educational level, or interesting.

I have deliberately used the rather vague word 'quality' so as not to be misunderstood as assigning particular effects to particular levels on the continuum. Mismatches at any level can affect all aspects of the reader-text interaction. It is a mistake to assume, for example, that 'motivation' is only affected by graphic design, or that graphic design only affects motivation. But when course teams (and, indeed, designers) discuss design it is often almost exclusively in this context. It is not necessarily true that superficial judgements are only made from surface-level features of text, or that more substantial judgements result exclusively from deeper levels of the text content. Instead, a whole range of conditions — from motivation (selection, attention, perseverance, etc) to learning outcomes (recall, comprehension, etc) — may be affected by features of the text placed at any point in the continuum. People rarely select a book to read simply because it is well designed; it is also because that book fills a need — personal or curricular — and it appears to be written at an appropriate level of language, entry knowledge and interest. Conversely, learning is not just affected by clear sequencing and explication of content. Educational psychologists have sometimes looked as far down the continuum as graphic design. Rothkopf (1971) has published a study of the effect of the position on the page of a fact on its ease of recall, and Duchastel (1978) has recently discussed the retentional role of illustrations.

What is the nature of the interaction between reader and text, whose effectiveness we have been discussing? Most models of the reading process are rather restricted in scope, being mainly concerned with the cognitive processes that enable readers to extract meaning from marks on paper. This may be theoretically interesting to some, but at the level of fluency we can expect from our students we are not likely to find many problems there. Instead it would be interesting to have a global model of the reading process, so that we might predict the effect of reader-text mismatches on reading behaviour.

Hatt (1976) presents an interesting framework for the discussion of the reading process which is deceptively simple. It is based on three parts.

1. A reader finds a text.
2. He reads the text.
3. He uses the message (or not, as the case may be).

As we have seen, many theorists confine themselves to the cognitive processes that occur within 2. Most, though, now reject the early information-processing model (transmitter-message-receiver) as casting the reader in an unduly passive role. Instead we now see readers as not simply *receiving* messages but as *seeking and finding* them. Hatt extends this idea by studying patterns of entry and patterns of exit from the reading act.

A problem with Hatt's framework is that it appears to be unduly sequential. It may also be that aspects of all three of his behaviours can occur cyclically or simultaneously. Figure 2 uses column headings loosely based on Hatt's framework. All three parts are 'ongoing' rather than sequential. So reading cannot continue satisfactorily if there is no motivation, no effective strategy, or no outcome perceived by the reader.

The columns are open-ended and different observers may classify some things differently. But compare the factors in Figure 2 with the various levels of the continuum in Figure 1. Figure 1 relates the existing state of the perceived readers (knowledge, aptitudes, etc) to the assumptions made by the text. As we have seen, each level on the continuum may affect the experience of the readers at more than one stage in the process of reading and learning, as it is displayed in Figure 2.

A mismatch, for example, may be found at the level of readability; the syntax and vocabulary may be too difficult for a particular student who has done no full-time study previously, or for whom English is a second language. In terms of his reading behaviour, this will demotivate him (he will not enjoy reading or feel he is achieving enough), it will slow him down (prevent him from skimming, perhaps), and may result in a less satisfactory learning outcome (he may miss subtleties, or not perceive the overall structure of the argument).

A mismatch at the level of the access structure of the text would

Motivation	Strategy	Outcome

Attention
  recommendation
  obligation
  attraction
Selection
  relevance to:
    course objectives
    personal objectives
  flavour
    context
    register
Perseverance
  enjoyment
  achievement
	Reading style
	  browse
	  skim/preview
	  search/scan
	  intense study
	  review
	
	Purpose
	  criticize
	  memorize
	  revise
	  understand
	  assignment
	  make notes
	
	Environment
	  home, library, etc
	  distractions
	  lighting, health,
	  comfort, etc
		Goal achievement
		  personal
		  objectives
		
		  course
		  assessment
		
		Knowledge
		  memory
		  insights
		  skills
		
		Pleasure
		  amusement
		  excitement
		  fascination

Figure 2. *Three aspects of the reading process*

also affect reading behaviour in many ways. It might be hard for the student to see the relevance of the text to his needs, because he cannot overview the content. It will restrict his reading style because it assumes a relatively passive linear strategy. It will restrict the learning outcome because he cannot so easily read for specific purposes, and because the text, having no surface structure, offers him no aids to memory.

In summary, the quality of text presentation is a function of many interconnected factors. At present the discussion and control of these factors is rather arbitrary, being dependent more on the experiences, prejudices and philosophies that particular course team members happen to have, than on anything resembling a systematic approach. In addition, the tacit assumptions and the tensions inherent in a rather conservative production system can make innovation unduly problematic. Text quality is dependent on a match between reader and text, and the research, planning, production and testing of texts should aim to minimize potential mismatches. But the various dimensions of quality in texts (Figure 1) do not necessarily correspond directly with particular stages in the reading process (Figure 2). This is because the component factors of any model of the reading process contain elements largely outside the control of the producers of texts — elements determined by the context, strategy, purposes and achievements of the reader. Nevertheless, they are factors which producers of text should endeavour to understand and predict.

References

Duchastel, P (1978) Illustrating instructional texts. *Educational Technology* XVIII 11: 36-9.

Hatt, F (1976) *The Reading Process.* London: Bingley

Rothkopf, E Z (1971) Incidental memory for location of information in text. *J Verbal Learning and Verbal Behavior* 10: 608-13

3.3 Some rules of data presentation

ANDREW S C EHRENBERG

(This paper was first published in the *Statistical Reporter,* May 1977, and is reproduced here by permission of the author and the editor. The paper is a shortened version of the author's 'Rudiments of Numeracy', *Journal of the Royal Statistical Society A* **140** 3: 277-97.)

Most statistical tables are badly presented, requiring much effort even from sophisticated users. It is as if their producers either did not know what the data were saying or were not letting on. Some precepts for improved data presentation are discussed in this article.

The criterion for a good table is that the patterns and exceptions should be obvious at a glance, at least once one knows what they are, but most tables are not like that.

To illustrate, Table 1 gives an extract of data on US|unemployed from Table 572 in the *Statistical Abstract of the United States* for 1975.

Table 1 may at first appear reasonably well laid out, but in forming this view one has probably looked only at the captions. The numbers themselves are not as easy to take in. What are the main patterns? How can they be summarized? How can one tell someone over the phone? What is one likely to absorb or remember?

Looked at with these questions in mind, Table 1 now appears more like an undigested jumble of numbers. Table 2 gives an improved presentation of the same data.

It is now easier to see the major patterns and exceptions, for example:

(a) The number of unemployed decrease with the size of the population, but Connecticut and DC appear high (though in DC the percentages of the work force imply a different conclusion).

(b) On average the numbers of unemployed varied only by plus or minus 10 per cent over the four years, but increased by 50 per cent or more in Florida, Georgia, Arizona and DC and decreased by 25 per cent in Connecticut.

(c) The *insured* unemployed look high in Connecticut and low in Colorado.

(d) Expressed as a per cent of the work force or those covered by insurance, the figures vary greatly from state to state, but appear uncorrelated with the *size* of the state.

These are the more obvious features of the data, but they do not seem as clear in Table 1 even now that we know what to look for. The original table therefore fails both the strong and the weak versions of

| State | Total unemployed[1] | | | | | | | | Insured unemployed | | | | | |
| | Number (1000) | | | | Per cent[2] | | | | Number (1000) | | | Per cent[3] | | |
	1971	1972	1973	1974	1971	1972	1973	1974	1972	1973	1974	1972	1973	1974
Ala	75.0	62.0	62.0	78.0	5.5	4.5	4.5	5.5	20.7	16.9	26.5	2.9	2.0	2.9
Alaska	12.1	12.9	13.9	14.7	10.5	10.5	10.8	10.5	5.6	5.7	6.1	9.5	8.6	8.6
Ariz	32.8	32.0	34.0	49.2	4.7	4.2	4.1	5.6	9.7	10.1	19.1	2.3	1.9	3.3
Ark	40.1	36.1	33.5	39.8	5.4	4.6	4.1	4.8	12.9	12.0	17.8	3.1	2.5	3.5
Calif	737.0	652.0	615.0	670.0	8.8	7.6	7.0	7.3	242.3	228.0	277.8	4.7	3.9	4.3[1]
Colo	36.7	35.2	36.0	42.8	4.0	3.6	3.4	3.9	7.0	7.6	12.1	1.3	1.2	1.6
Conn	116.0	121.0	89.0	88.0	8.4	8.6	6.3	6.1	48.9	36.3	49.3	4.5	3.2	4.0
Del	13.3	11.4	11.6	15.3	5.7	4.7	4.6	6.1	4.3	4.0	6.8	2.5	2.0	3.1
DC	34.0	44.0	59.0	62.0	2.7	3.3	4.2	4.4	7.0	7.0	8.5	2.0	1.9	2.3
Fla	135.0	127.0	132.0	208.0	4.9	4.5	4.3	6.3	30.7	27.7	55.7	1.9	1.3	2.4
Ga	76.0	83.0	81.0	109.0	3.9	4.1	3.9	5.1	18.3	15.1	31.5	1.6	1.1	2.2
Hawaii	20.6	24.7	23.9	27.2	6.3	7.3	7.0	7.6	11.2	10.5	12.4	4.1	3.8	4.1
Idaho	19.4	19.9	19.1	21.5	6.3	6.2	5.6	6.1	6.7	6.6	8.1	4.2	3.5	4.0
Ill	240.0	245.0	203.0	223.0	5.1	5.1	4.1	4.5	87.3	68.4	90.9	2.8	1.9	2.4
Ind	128.0	103.0	101.0	123.0	5.7	4.5	4.3	5.2	30.0	21.8	41.8	2.2	1.4	2.5

1 Data for years prior to 1974 may not be entirely comparable
2 Total unemployment as per cent of total work force
3 Insured unemployment as per cent of average covered employment

Table 1. *Total and insured unemployed — States: 1971 - 1974*
(The first 15 states from Table No 572 of 'Statistical Abstracts' 1975)

States (in order of 1970 pop)	Total unemployed								Insured unemployed					
	In '000				as % of work force				In '000			as % of covered		
	1971	1972	1973	1974	1971	1972	1973	1974	1972	1973	1974	1972	1973	1974
California	740	650	610	670	9	8	7	7	240	230	280	5	4	4
Illinois	240	250	200	220	5	5	4	5	87	68	91	3	2	2
Florida	130	120	130	210	5	5	4	6	30	28	56	2	2	2
Indiana	130	100	100	120	6	5	4	5	30	22	42	2	1	3
Georgia	76	83	81	110	4	4	4	5	28	15	32	2	1	2
Alabama	75	62	62	78	6	5	5	6	21	17	27	3	2	3
Connect	120	120	90	90	8	9	6	6	49	36	49	5	3	4
Colorado	37	35	36	43	4	4	3	4	7	8	12	1	1	2
Arkansas	40	36	34	40	5	5	4	5	13	12	18	3	3	4
Arizona	33	32	34	49	5	4	4	6	10	10	19	2	2	3
Hawaii	21	25	24	27	6	7	7	8	11	11	12	4	4	4
DC	34	44	59	62	3	3	4	4	7	7	9	2	2	2
Idaho	19	20	19	22	6	6	6	6	7	7	8	4	4	4
Delaware	13	11	12	15	6	5	5	6	4	4	7	3	2	1
Alaska	12	13	14	15	11	11	11	11	6	6	6	10	9	9
Average*	110	110	100	120	6	6	5	6	36	32	44	3	3	3

* For the 15 States

Table 2. *'Improved' version of Table 1*
(States in order of 1970 population, figures rounded, fewer vertical rules, column averages)

the criterion for a good table, while Table 2 certainly passes the weak version even if not entirely the strong one.

The strong criterion for a good table. The patterns and exceptions should be obvious at a glance.

The weak criterion. The patterns and exceptions in a table should be obvious at a glance once one has been told what they are.

The strong criterion may sound fine, but really only says that the naive newcomer should gain instant insight, unaided. The weak version is in fact much the more important one. It applies automatically to all situations which are repetitive, that is, where the probable pattern of the new data is already known beforehand. It applies to the experienced user and it can cover more complex tables if a commentary is given.

A common doubt about trying to improve the layout of tables is whether it should not vary with the particular use that is to be made of the data. An 'improved' version like Table 2 is easier for virtually *any* purpose than the original Table 1. The data might perhaps be displayed in a way even more suited to some specific purpose, but that would merely mean taking the procedures of this paper yet further.

Four basic rules

The table improvement just illustrated involved a combination of factors, but these can be considered separately, and I now discuss four major rules or guidelines. They concern rounding, the use of marginal averages, choosing between rows and columns in a table, and ordering the rows or columns.

To illustrate, I use an example concerning the level of unemployment in Great Britain over four selected years, as reproduced in Table 3 from *Facts in Focus*, a statistical paperback comparable to the *Pocket Data Book, USA.*

(Thousands)	1966	1968	1970	1973
Total unemployed	330.9	549.4	582.2	597.9
Males	259.6	460.7	495.3	499.4
Females	71.3	88.8	86.9	98.5

Table 3. *Unemployment in Great Britain − original table*

The table is small and simple (chosen for conciseness of exposition here), but the numerical details are once more not obvious at a glance. Suppose we look away. What do we remember having seen, *without looking back*? What can we say about the number of unemployed?

RULE 1: ROUNDING TO TWO SIGNIFICANT DIGITS

Understanding any set of numbers involves relating the different numbers to each other. In Table 3 this is not easy. For example, mentally subtracting the 1966 total from the 1973 total and remembering the answer is relatively difficult (330.9 from 597.9 = 267.0). Taking ratios mentally (330.9 *into* 597.9) is virtually impossible. Most of us can do such mental arithmetic only by first rounding the figures to one or two digits in our heads.

In Table 4 this rounding has been done for the reader. The general rule is to round to two variable or significant digits, where 'variable' or 'significant' here means digits which vary in that kind of data. (Final 0's do not matter as the eye can readily filter them out.)

000's	1966	'68	'70	'73
Total unemployed	330	550	580	600
Males	260	460	500	500
Females	71	89	87	99

Table 4. *Unemployed in GB — rounded*

Now we can see that the difference between 330 and 600 for total unemployed is 270, and that 330 *into* 600 is almost 2, that is, an increase of almost 100 per cent. We can also see that the increase for males from 260 to 500 is again nearly 100 per cent, and that the corresponding increase for females from 71 to 99 is about 40 per cent (ie 28 out of 71). Total unemployed up by almost 100 per cent, males up by almost 100 per cent, and females up by less than 50 per cent; that is something one *can* remember. It is also easier to recall that the range for total unemployed is from about 330 to 600 than that it is from 330.9 to 597.9.

The male and female numbers have been reduced to the nearest 10,000 and the nearest 1000 respectively, by being rounded to two significant digits *in their own context*. This avoids overrounding when different groups of figures vary greatly in size. A side effect is that the figures do not add up exactly. This is an undoubted nuisance, but a lesser one than the perceptual difficulties of the unrounded data in Table 3. Anyone who cannot learn to cope with rounding errors will probably not get much out of statistical data anyway.

Any comparable assessment of the figures in Table 3 would in any case require mental rounding. (Pocket calculators are not the answer since knowing that 597.9/330.9 = 1.8069 does not greatly help us to see and absorb the patterns in the table.) For better or for worse, drastic rounding is necessary if we are to see and internalize the data.

Rounding tends, however, to raise heated objections. It is accepted in graphical presentations, and most people would not object much to reducing statistical data to *three or four* significant digits, but they often feel that rounding to only two significant or variable digits is overdoing it.

Unfortunately such rounding is necessary to facilitate mental arithmetic. For example, almost none of us can divide 17.9 per cent into 35.2 per cent in our heads (most percentages are mistakenly reported as 'per mille' rather than as 'per centum'). Of several thousand people asked to do this division over the years only two mathematicians at Purdue have claimed success, but since they got different answers at least one of them was wrong. In contrast, dividing 18 per cent into 35 per cent is obviously about 2. Thus two digits are better.

Instead of asking 'Can these data be rounded to two digits?', we need only to check why they should *not* be rounded. A safeguard is that no information need ever be completely lost by rounding. The more precise data can always be stored in a data bank or filing cabinet just in case somebody somewhere should want them sometime. Will the more precise data in fact ever be used? When would the unemployment figures be needed to the nearest 100 people as in Table 3, rather than rounded to the nearest 1000 or 10,000?

The average error in rounding the female unemployed to two digits is 300. This is trivial compared with the overall increase of almost 30,000 in the female figures and with the contrary drop of about 2000 from 1968 to 1970.

The rounding errors are also trivial in contemplating a fuller analysis of unemployment. This would not mean digging deeper into the eight selected readings in Table 3, but taking account of vastly *more* data: unemployment figures for other years, in different regions of the country, different industries, different age groups (with school leavers and college students treated separately), *plus* figures for employment, reported vacancies, inflation, investment, stockpiling, dumping, gross national product, the money supply, birthrates, immigration, mechanization, business cycles, world trade, unemployment in other countries, and so on, as well as intensive comparisons of figures based on different definitions and measuring procedures.

Each monthly issue of the *Department of Employment Gazette* in the United Kingdom gives about 8000 two-to-four digit numbers on unemployment alone, and each monthly issue of *Employment and Earnings* in the United States gives several thousand more. Most of the figures may be the same as in the previous month, but the need to see the wood for the trees becomes even more urgent than with the eight basic figures in Table 3. Hoping to explain variation to the third digit (ie less than 1 per cent) becomes even more absurd.

People who object to rounding to two significant digits because they feel that 'there may be something there' can have had no experience of *successfully* analysing and understanding statistical data.

RULE 2: ROW AND COLUMN AVERAGES

The second rule concerns the use of row and column averages. These can provide a visual focus and sometimes also a possible summary of the data. Table 5 illustrates this by giving the row averages across the four years. (The column totals already in this table serve almost the same purpose as column averages, but are best separated off with a half space.)

Even with a small table such averages prove useful. Noting that the average male/female ratio is 5 to 1 (ie 430/86) and keeping this one figure in mind, we can see more readily how the ratio varies over the years, from less than 4 to 1 in 1966 to just over 5 to 1 in each of the three later years.

The use of such averages is often misunderstood, especially by those who wrongly fear that 'others' (meaning the statistically less sophisticated) will be misled. In Table 5 it is obvious that the averages are not 'typical' of the figures in each row — the 1966 figures are much

165

lower. In fact, the point of the averages is to make it that much easier to grasp the spread between the below-average and above-average values.

000's	1966	'68	'70	'73	Ave
Total unemployed	330	550	580	600	520
Male	260	460	500	500	430
Female	71	89	87	99	86

Table 5. *With averages*

RULE 3: FIGURES ARE EASIER TO COMPARE IN COLUMNS

Figures generally are easier to follow reading down a column than across a row. Even for our small example here it is easier to see in Table 6 that all the numbers were substantially lower in 1966 than in the three later years.

GB	Unemployed (000's)		
	Total	Male	Female
1966	330	260	71
'68	550	460	89
'70	580	500	87
'73	600	500	99
Average	520	430	86

Table 6. *Rows and columns interchanged*

We also notice minor variations and subpatterns more; for example, that contrary to the total trend, the female figures levelled off only for 1968 and 1970 (in fact dropping slightly in the latter year), the 1973 figure of 99 indeed being markedly high. Compared with Table 5 we are beginning to see more of the data.

The improvement is a perceptual one. To see in Table 5 that the main variation for total unemployed is from roughly 300 to 600, the eye first had to take in and then partially ignore all the symbols and gaps in the sequence 330 550 580 600, average 520, and it had to travel relatively far to do so. In Table 6, however, all the 'hundreds' are one under the other, and hence much easier to scan (preferably starting with the average and keeping that in mind as a norm). The eye can run up and down the first digit in each column and more or less ignore the rest.

A common query about changing rows into columns is, however, whether all users of the table will want to compare the figures in the columns rather than those in the rows. In practice one must always do *both*. The main pattern in the data should be looked at first, and hence in columns because that is easier. Then, having seen the main pattern, one can look at the rows and for any row-and-column interactions.

Another query concerns fitting long row captions into column headings. With repetitive data this can often be done by abbreviation, by spreading the headings over two or three lines, and by relegating detail to footnotes. (People who object to having to look at the footnotes to a table are probably not the sort who would get much out of a complex-looking table anyway.)

RULE 4: ORDERING THE ROWS AND COLUMNS BY SIZE

Ordering the rows and/or columns of a table by some measure of the size of the figures (eg their averages) often helps to bring order out of chaos. It means using the dimensions of the table to enable us to see the structure of the *data*, rather than merely reflecting that of the row or column labels (which is usually already well known, like that Arizona follows Alabama alphabetically).

The unemployment data in Table 6 already have the rows in an effective order of size because the trends happen to coincide with the order of the years. To illustrate the rule, Table 7 gives the data with the rows in another order, A to D. Even with such a small table it is now less easy to see that the figures in Row C (or 1966) are generally the smallest. Interactions are even harder to spot: for example, that the male figures in Rows B and D are identical at 500 while the female ones differ markedly at 87 and 99.

GB	Unemployed (000's)		
	Total	**Male**	**Female**
A	550	460	89
B	580	500	87
C	330	260	71
D	600	500	99
Average	520	430	86

Table 7. *Rows in some other order*

One problem with ordering the rows or columns of a table by some measure of size is that different measures of size can be used, possibly resulting in different orders. Users of a table do not have to accept the chosen order as sacrosanct. One order will show up the conflict with another, and *some* visible ordering is always better than none, as in Table 7 here or in the earlier Table 1. In Table 2 anyone could see that the Connecticut figures were out of step.

A non-alphabetical ordering is often criticized as making it difficult to look up the result for a particular state, but a statistical table is not a telephone directory. To use and interpret an isolated figure, one must understand the context of the surrounding ones and see the general pattern of the data. If there are many such tables and they are large, an alphabetical key will also be worth giving. In any case it is probably easier to find an isolated name in a non-alphabetical listing (especially if the names are given in their visually most recognizable form) than to interpret an isolated number from an unstructured table.

A problem that arises when there are many different tables with the same basic format is that straight application of the rule could lead to different orders for different tables. In such cases the same order must be used in every table, based on some general order criterion (like the last census figures used in Table 2).

A subsidiary question when ordering rows or columns by size is in which *direction* the figures ought to go. People differ in their predilections here. Some like to have figures running from large on the left (as in Table 6), or from large at the top, while others prefer the opposite. With time series some like to have time progress from the left or the top of the tabulations, while others prefer to have the *latest* figures there. These views are usually not held very strongly, nor do they appear to have any marked perceptual consequences when ordering columns.

For the *rows* of a table, showing the larger numbers above the smaller numbers helps because we are used to doing mental subtraction that way. It is more difficult to subtract 380 from 640 in the form

$$380 \qquad \text{than as} \qquad 640$$
$$640 \qquad\qquad\qquad 380$$

Facilitating such mental arithmetic is important, especially when one is scanning large sets of data.

Conclusions

The preceding discussion has illustrated four of the basic rules of data presentation — drastic rounding, the use of averages, putting figures that are to be compared into columns, and ordering rows and columns by size. On the whole, the presentation of numerical data to facilitate its use has been a relatively neglected area. Most statisticians have not realized how unnecessarily incomprehensible their supposedly competent tables usually are.

The practical problems of implementing such rules must, however, not be underestimated. Many of us are still unfamiliar with the techniques, or even with the fundamental notion that most tables can be improved so as to communicate better. There can also be very substantial setup and upset costs in changing from traditional practices, but these will generally be more than balanced by the savings in paper and printing, not to mention the fuller and better use of the data.

3.4 Just fill in this form:
a review for designers

PATRICIA WRIGHT AND PHILIP BARNARD

(From Wright, P and Barnard, P (1975) *Applied Ergonomics* 6 4:
213-20. This article is reproduced with permission of the authors
and the publishers, IPC Science and Technology Press Ltd,
Guildford, Surrey.)

This paper reviews the behavioural research, particularly on language
and comprehension, which can be related to the design of forms. Such
research gives rise to a number of simple rules which can be
implemented by forms' designers. These rules concern the structure,
content and organization of sentences and questions. The paper
illustrates how these rules can be applied to forms currently in use:
research findings which point to exceptions to the general rules are
discussed in an appendix. The paper recognizes that we do not yet
have enough information to design perfect forms, but that there is
enough for many forms to be improved and potential pitfalls avoided.

There are numerous prescriptions for writing well (eg Fowler, 1926;
Gowers, 1954; Graves and Hodge, 1943; Partridge, 1957; Tichy, 1966).
Much of that advice could be applied to the design of forms. Why then
need anything more be said? The answer lies in the authority underlying
the advice. It is no longer necessary for style to be based upon arbitrary
conventions, transient fashions or the traditional links between a
classical education and the canons of Standard Received English.
There are empirical studies of the kind of language which people can
most easily understand. The conclusions from these research findings
are summarized below as general rules which, if followed, will help
people understand what they read — rules which, if followed, will make
it easier for all of us who have from time to time to fill in forms.

All general rules have exceptions. For the sake of clarity, the present
text concentrates on the rules themselves, and particularly those which
can be applied to the design of forms. The exceptions to these rules are
dealt with separately in the Appendix. Commonsense justifies this
division. It is usually apparent when attempts to follow the prescribed
rules lead to clumsy and ambiguous constructions; in such cases the
rules obviously need to be broken. But it is common experience that
many clumsy and ambiguous constructions arise because the rules have
not been heeded. This is why the emphasis in the present review is on
what can be done to make things easier for the form-filler. This in turn
will make things easier for the administrators who must process the
information received via the form, since there will be fewer queries,
unanswered questions and misinterpretations to sort out.

Indeed, good form design is cost-effective. In at least one London borough several local authority staff are employed full-time to call on people, particularly the elderly, in order to encourage and assist them in obtaining the benefits to which they are entitled (Yates, 1975). Add to this the administrative time and postage that accompanies returning incomplete or wrongly completed forms and there is clearly room for a considerable saving in expenditure if forms can be designed which lessen these difficulties.

Administrators sometimes think that mistakes made in completing forms can be attributed to the incompetence of those completing the forms. And it has to be recognized that, by definition, half the general public have below average intelligence. Moreover, the section of the general public who are faced with the barrage of forms associated with welfare benefits, means-tested or otherwise, is the section who are less verbally fluent, less familiar with English prose style and much less familiar with 'the system' than are the designers of forms (Bernstein, 1961). But the very existence of this mismatch between the abilities of the administrators and those of the applicants is one of the reasons why it is difficult for forms' designers to be aware of potential pitfalls in their forms. It is hoped that the following guidelines may lessen this difficulty, although they cannot provide a complete answer because there remain several important areas of form design on which no research evidence is available. But they do provide a means for improving the present lot of all form-fillers. The complete cure of a bad form may not yet be possible, but certainly many of its symptoms can be alleviated.

1. Use short, active, affirmative sentences

Short sentences are more easily understood than long ones. This has been known since the early derivation of readability formulae (eg Flesch, 1948; Klare, 1974). But the critical factor is something more than the total number of words in the sentence. Sentences can be short or long in a variety of different ways. Research has shown that the sentences most easily understood have three main characteristics: (a) they have only one clause, (b) they are in the active rather than the passive voice, (c) they are affirmative rather than negative.

(a) Clauses. Research on sentences with more than one clause has shown that people find it extremely difficult to deal with clauses nested one inside the other (Blumenthal, 1966). This can be illustrated by considering sentences such as those found in the story of The House That Jack Built. Research has shown that university students were unable to answer questions about who did what in a sentence such as *The rat which the cat which the dog bit chased ate the malt.* The students fared better when each clause was completed before the next began, eg *The dog bit the cat which chased the rat which ate the malt.* Now it is clear that this sentence can be sub-divided further, eg *The dog bit the cat. This cat chased the rat which ate the malt.* Although the second of these sentences has two clauses (relating to the verbs *chased* and *ate*), available research suggests that there is no advantage in

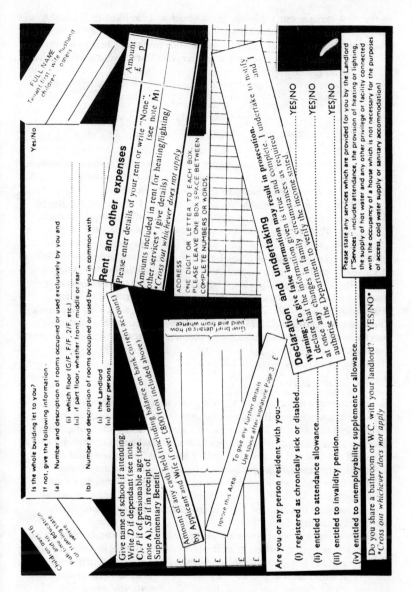

Figure 1.

shortening this sentence further (Bransford and Franks, 1971). Such exceptions are dealt with in Note 1 of the Appendix.

To underline the fact that sentences with multiple clauses are used on forms the following five-verb sentence was found on a Government leaflet issued in the 1970s:

> Your supplementary allowance may be restricted below the amount assessed in the way described above if your income while you are employed or temporarily off work would otherwise be more than you would normally earn in your usual occupation.

In order to implement the general rule about short sentences, writers should scrutinize sentences with more than one verb, looking for alternative ways of expressing information.

(b) Active voice. Research has shown that politicians and scientists are the most frequent users of passive sentences (Goldman-Eisler and Cohen, 1970). Passive constructions rarely occur in the written or spoken language of other people. So it is hardly surprising that in numerous research studies it has been found that active sentences are more easily understood and remembered than the equivalent passive forms (for a review see Herriot, 1970; Greene, 1972). Moreover, there is no need for application forms to say 'The notes should be read' or 'The certificate should be included' when they mean 'Read the notes', 'Include the certificate'. Research has shown that passive questions are particularly prone to difficulties (Barnard, 1974). Passives do have a special use in the language (see Note 2 of the Appendix), but the difficulty of passives when added to other difficulties of comprehension is such that they are best avoided.

(c) Negatives. Negation can be achieved in many ways. Words such as *not, except, unless* all have negative elements. It has generally been found that sentences with negative elements are more difficult to understand than affirmative sentences (see reviews by Herriot, 1970; Greene, 1972). Of course negatives have a special role to play in language (see Note 3 of the Appendix) but they are often used unnecessarily. Two negatives within the same sentence can always be avoided. The form which said *Do not delay returning this form simply because you do not know your National Insurance Number* could as easily have said *Return this form at once, even if you do not know your National Insurance Number.*

Even when single negatives have a clear interpretation, performance will be better if an alternative affirmative can be used (Wason, 1961; Jones, 1966; 1968a). People more easily understand the instruction to *Leave this box blank if you already receive a pension* than the negative version *Do not write in this box if you already receive a pension.*

Similarly, when people are answering Yes/No questions, there is evidence that instructions to tick, underline or circle what does apply are more easily followed than instructions to delete what does not apply. Indeed, the British Post Office recently changed some of its instructions to the general public in order to remove the negative elements. The instructions displayed in public telephone boxes had said *Do not insert money until the number answers*. These instructions now say *Wait until the subscriber answers and then insert your money*. Such changes are seen as cost-effective when considering the consequences of the reader misunderstanding the instructions.

Some words, such as *reduce*, have negative connotations although they lack identifying negative elements (eg un-, dis-, in-, etc). Sentences with such words are more difficult to understand than sentences rephrased so that the positive connotation is used, eg *increase*. Research has shown that this is true for a wide range of comparative terms (Huttenlocker and Higgins, 1971; Clark and Chase, 1972). But probably the studies with the greatest relevance to application forms are those examining the terms *more* and *less* (Palermo, 1973; Wright and Barnard, 1975). These studies have shown that people most easily understand the term *more*. Yet forms tell applicants that they need not declare their interest from savings if the amount is less than £X. Such forms could as easily tell applicants to declare their interest if it is more than £X.

2. Use familiar words

Although it is obvious that people understand familiar words more easily than unfamiliar synonyms, there are still forms referring to *gainful occupation* when they mean paid work, or to *emoluments* when they mean income. One 1975 form had *obtains pecuniary advantage* rather than *gets money*. The notes accompanying a current rate demand have a section dealing with *Mixed hereditaments not connected to the public sewer*. Yet *hereditament* is not even included as a dictionary entry in several pocket editions.

Research has shown that people find it easier to read and to remember familiar words (Solomon and Postman, 1952; Hall, 1954; Loftus, Freedman and Loftus, 1970). People also find it easier to think about and draw inferences from sentences using familiar words (Wason and Johnson-Laird, 1972). The factor of familiarity obviously applies to abbreviations as well. A form used by one local authority in 1975 had the following multiple-choice alternatives, *G/F, F/F, 2/F*, which even when listed as the answer to the question *Which floor?* (do you live on) may not have been worth the paper it saved.

One difficulty with familiar words is that they may not mean the same thing to everyone. The phrase *total income* may mean income before any deductions to some people; to others it may mean after deduction of tax, National Insurance, etc. One of the difficulties with implementing a recent Government scheme for rate rebates was found to be the belief of many rent payers that they did not pay rates at all and so could not apply for a rebate. Even words like *family* and *household* may have different connotations for different members of the public. Does it include Uncle George if he lives next door but comes in to have all his meals with you? Probably the only fail-safe procedure for weeding out difficult words is the *ad hoc* empirical testing of a form before it reaches the general public. By this method one soon discovers whether there is consensus among people over the meaning of the words being used. Testing a large sample is not necessary for this purpose as long as the appropriate target population is selected. If 30 people are asked what is *colour reversal film,* and can give the correct answer there is no need to ask another 300. Similarly, if 28 of the people give the wrong answer there is little point in increasing this to 280 wrong answers. Moreover, since there is usually a desire for very high effectiveness (ie the writer wishes to communicate successfully with almost everyone in the appropriate population), trouble spots in forms and leaflets show up very quickly in such pilot trials. (For a comparative study of five local Government forms see Barnard, Wright and Wilcox, 1975).

3. Ask questions about one thing at a time

Disjunctions and conjunctions are more difficult for people to deal with than simple sentences (Trabasso, Rollins and Shaughnessy, 1971). This is very evident from looking at how easily people answer questions. Questions such as *Are you over 21 and under 65? Yes/No* cause difficulties for many people over 65 who appear to take each part of the question in turn answering Yes to over 21 and No to under 65, so that they then have trouble deciding what to do with the single Yes/No answer at the end of the question. An analysis by one of the present authors of the first 80 electoral roll forms returned in a Cambridgeshire village showed that this question was either incorrectly answered or unanswered on over one third of the forms. The problem is easily solved by making two separate questions, a step which has been taken for this particular question on this particular form. But at least one local authority in 1975 was issuing a form which asked *Do you share a bathroom or WC with your landlord? Yes/No.* Here again, people who do one but not the other may have difficulties answering the question. Worse still, another local authority in 1975 asked for a Yes/No answer to the question *Is the dwelling your normal place of residence? If not, does your spouse live there and pay the rent?*

4. Organize temporal sequences

Research has shown that it aids comprehension when the order in which things are mentioned matches the temporal order in which they have to be carried out (Clark and Clark, 1968). People would therefore find it more helpful to be told *Read the notes on page 4 then fill in the form* rather than the common *Before filling in the form read the notes on page 4.* It is known that having the main verb first also makes things easier for the reader than if the subordinate clause comes first; so people will understand *Read the notes on page 4 before filling in the form* more easily than *After reading the notes on page 4 fill in the form.* However, the verb form is simpler in *Read the notes, then fill in the form* so this is probably the most easily understood version.

5. Beware of ambiguities

Research on language has shown that ambiguities arising from either the sentence structure (eg *Applicants who are visiting immigrants should answer question 10*) or the use of words whose meaning is at first unclear (see Section 2) result in sentences which are more difficult to perceive and to remember (Mackay, 1973; Olson and Mackay, 1974). Retention is a particularly important point in the context of application forms, since often notes are read and then have to be remembered until the appropriate section on the form is reached. Even when it is only the reading of the question which intervenes between the notes and their use, this can be a sufficient interruption to cause errors (Wright, 1969).

Ambiguous words can sometimes be difficult for a reader to detect because he may be aware only of the intended meaning. For example, the question *Sickness benefit from . . .* may elicit the response 'DHSS' whereas the administrator wanted a date. Similarly, an application form issued recently in the Midlands had the instructions *Where man and wife are living together the husband should complete the form.* Tests with Cambridge volunteers showed that the word *husband* was multiply ambiguous in this context (Barnard, Wright and Wilcox, 1975).

On other occasions ambiguous words and phrases assume the role of technical terms that are familiar only to the form designer and administrator. For example, the study by Barnard, Wright and Wilcox indicated that a number of people had difficulty in understanding the phrase 'Widows Industrial Death Benefit'. Not only are such phrases difficult because of their technical connotations, but adjectival modifiers accumulated in this way raise problems analogous to those associated with the use of embedded clauses (see Section 1(a) above).

6. Use headings

Research concerned with the understanding of passages of prose has shown that introducing headings and subheadings can be a great benefit to the reader (Klare, Shuford and Nichols, 1958; Dooling and Lachman, 1971). There is every reason to expect similar benefits from the use of headings within forms. Headings appear to provide a context which assists understanding both at the level of sentences and at the level of words. There are a range of typographic options as to how headings may be distinguished from the remainder of the form, but available research suggests that departures from the horizontal arrangement of words are less easily read (Kolers, 1968); therefore a heading printed sideways, to bracket several rows of questions all relating to the same topic, will be less effective than a heading written horizontally.

7. Consider alternatives to prose

Sometimes sentences become unwieldy because of the content that has to be conveyed. For example, a 1975 local authority form issued by a London borough said:

It should be noted that a rent allowance cannot be granted to
a tenant of a local authority or to a person with a service tenancy

or occupying a dwelling partly used for commercial or business premises but he or she may qualify for a rate rebate.

Ignoring the fact that this was printed in capital letters (see Section 9 below), a 47-word sentence is bound to be difficult to understand. A string of conjunctions such as this might be more easily understood if written as a list:

The following people cannot have a rent allowance but they qualify for a rate rebate:
    tenants of a local authority
    people with a service tenancy.
    people occupying a dwelling partly used for commerce
    or business.

Indeed, this rewritten version avoids the ambiguous pronoun in the final clause of the original, where it was unclear whether the rate rebate applied only to dwellings partly used for commerce and business or to all the other categories as well.

Another alternative to prose is to use a flow-chart (or decision tree, as it is sometimes called). Research has shown that this is a particularly useful format for conveying specific information when there are a great many potentially irrelevant factors (Wright and Reid, 1973; Blaiwes, 1974). Therefore it could be very appropriate in the notes section of forms where different applicants are required to complete different sets of questions.

A modified decision tree, where instructions are given to jump to question X if the answer is Yes or to question Y if the answer is No, has been found quite useful in the educational field (Crowder, 1963). However, it is possible that unfamiliarity with such a format may make it difficult for some members of the general public (but see Jones, 1968b). Very little basic research has been done on how decision trees are best constructed. Certainly there is no *a priori* reason why the tree with the fewest terminal points should be the easiest to use. Because of the lack of empirical guidelines it is always advisable to test algorithms on a small sample from the relevant population of users. Nevertheless, advice on the design and use of algorithms can be found in several places (eg Lewis and Woolfenden, 1969; Wheatley and Unwin, 1972).

8. Provide adequate answer space

Answer spaces need to be adequate with respect to both size and location. That is, they need to be big enough for the applicant to get all the information in, and located relative to the question so that the applicant knows whereabouts he is supposed to write. Let us consider first some problems related to the location of answer spaces. The difficulty people have with embedded constructions was discussed in Section 1(a), and again noted in Section 5. Yet it is possible to find instances where the answers required have been embedded in the middle of the questions. The following question comes from a local authority form being used in 1975:

If the tenant (   ) and/or spouse (   ) is registered under Section 29 (1), National Assistance Act, 1948 (Welfare arrangements for handicapped persons) answer Yes in the appropriate brackets.

Even when a question is complete and is followed by an answer space, there may still be problems. Printers have a tendency to align the questions with the left-hand margin of the page and to put the answer space over on the right-hand side of the page (see Figure 2). For example, analysis of one local authority form containing 14 Yes/No questions showed that the average gap was 62mm between the end of the question and the Yes/No answer. The range of gaps on this form issued by an east coast council was 4 to 111mm. But a south coast city council managed to have a range of 27 to 137mm, with an average of 74mm for a block of six such Yes/No questions. These gaps between questions and answers are likely to lead to errors. Research has shown that even when people are simply copying information across a gap, the bigger the gap the greater the error (Conrad and Hull, 1967).

1. Do you use any part of the dwelling for commercial or business use?	Yes/No
2. Do you pay rates direct to the City Treasury?	Yes/No
3. Are you receiving supplementary benefit from the Dept of Health and Social Security?	Yes/No
4. Is your wife in paid employment?	Yes/No
5. Are you an owner occupier?	Yes/No
6. Are you related to the landlord?	Yes/No
7. Are you a sub-tenant?	Yes/No
8. Is the whole building let to you?	Yes/No
9. Is the landlord responsible for internal repairs and decorations?	Yes/No

Figure 2. *Example of typical layout which introduces large gaps between questions and answers, thereby risking errors when applicants misalign questions and answers*

Although it seems trivial to point out that applicants need enough space to answer the questions, it is very easy to find forms where this exceedingly obvious point seems to have been overlooked. We have a local authority form with only 3mm gaps between successive rows on which people are required to describe certain rooms they occupy. (For comparison, most ruled writing paper gives at least 8mm between successive lines.) Elsewhere on this same form a name has to be fitted into a gap 27mm long. Try writing Reginald Butterworth in this gap (   ). Now imagine doing it if you are elderly, your hand is unsteady and your eyesight is poor.

One other difficulty with answer spaces is the tendency of designers or administrators to sub-divide them. Many forms require the date to be written in three boxes, one box for the day, another for the month and the third for the year. Taken to its extreme it is possible to find writing spaces sub-divided so that names and addresses are written with one letter per space. Research by Barnard and Wright (1976) has shown that this sub-division slows the writer and reduces the legibility of the writing material. They carried out a series of studies which showed that writing one letter per box was worse both for the writer and subsequent reader than writing on blank lines. Writing on lines where the sub-divisions were denoted by small vertical marks (_____ᛁ____ᛁ____ᛁ____ᛁ____ᛁ____ᛁ_____) was even more disruptive for both writers and readers than writing in complete boxes.

9. Choose appropriate print

Although it has long been established that people read lower case more easily than upper case print (Starch, 1914; Tinker and Paterson, 1928; Tinker, 1965; Poulton, 1968), one Midland city council was using a form in 1975 that had all six paragraphs on its front page entirely in capitals. Similarly a London borough has its first three paragraphs and its last paragraph in capitals. A south coast city has a paragraph in capitals at the bottom of each of three pages of a form.

It is also well known that print needs to be at least 8 point (This size) for easy reading: 10 point (This size) would be even better (Tinker, 1965; Poulton, 1969a). Also the interline spacing must be appropriate (Hartley and Burnhill, 1976). Yet some local authority forms being used in 1975 had print as small as 6 point (This size). Few elderly people would be able to read this without great difficulty. Many would be quite unable to read it at all.

Research has also established the minimum reflectance needed between print and background (Poulton, 1969b). If the form is to be processed electronically then the legibility requirements of both man and machine must be considered. But often the requirements of the human form-filler seem to be disregarded. As a result the human reader must try deciphering print that is light blue or pale green because the electronic reader cannot discern these symbols either (!).

10. General layout

The general structure and layout of the form will of course be determined primarily by the contents. However, much can be done to clarify this structure for easy appreciation by the reader. For example, appropriate use of space can often help (see eg Hartley and Burnhill, 1976). The commissioning of a professionally qualified graphic designer should always be considered. Considerable advice about the general design of one particular type of form, the questionnaire, is given in the June 1975 issue of *Applied Ergonomics*. The advice about graphic design by Gray (1975) is relevant to forms in general as discussed here.

11. Areas where further research is needed

It would be quite wrong if this review gave the impression that all the necessary behavioural research had been done, so that the optimal design of application forms could now be specified precisely. This is far from being the case. In particular, a great deal still needs to be discovered about different kinds of questions. Although there is research on some forms of question (Brown, 1968) no comparisons

have been made with the more common variant found on application
forms, namely imperatives such as Name . . . . Age . . . . There are also
problems surrounding the use of multiple-choice alternatives. Is
performance better when people delete options within an overall
sentence context, or when the options are stated with either the
opportunity to tick as applicable or to respond with Yes/No answers
to each option? (See Figure 3.) Even the sequencing of multiple-choice
options does not appear to have been a topic for research.

---

1. My rent is payable weekly/fortnightly/monthly/quarterly
   (Cross out whichever does not apply)

2. My rent is payable   weekly   (   )   )
                          fortnightly   (   )   )   tick whichever
                          monthly   (   )   )   applies
                          quarterly   (   )   )

3. Is your rent payable weekly?   Yes/No
                        fortnightly?   Yes/No
                        monthly?   Yes/No
                        quarterly?   Yes/No

4. How often is your rent payable?   . . . .

Figure 3. *Examples of different ways of asking for the
same information. Research has not yet established when
each alternative should be used*

12. Postscript

The goals facing the designers of forms are easy to state. Forms need
to be easily understood, need to produce accurate information and
need to be easily processed once they have been completed. Yet it has
to be recognized that sometimes these three objectives may conflict.
For example, the applicant may be better off with answer spaces close
to the questions, whereas the administrator may find it easier if
answers are all grouped together on one part of the page. The present
review has been primarily concerned with ways in which forms could
be made easier for applicants. Nevertheless, any compromise between
the needs of administrators and those of applicants needs to be
evaluated empirically. Without such evaluations, *ad hoc* decisions tend
to be made in favour of the administrators. But such decisions may
in fact result in greater demands on administrative time when the
consequences of wrongly completed forms are taken into account.
There is every reason for thinking that such trade-offs require an
empirical evaluation, rather than an *ad hoc* decision in favour of the
administrators. There can be relatively little point in having forms for
official use only.

Appendix 1: Exceptions to the rule about short sentences

SUBORDINATE CLAUSES REDUCE REPETITION

Research by Bransford and Franks (1971) has shown that people find it
easier to grasp the meaning of closely inter-related ideas when these
ideas are all expressed in the same sentence. If one considers adjectival
modifiers this is self-evidently so: contrast 1. 'The black dog chased the
ginger cat' with 2. 'The dog chased the cat. The dog was black. The cat
was ginger.' Indeed, research showed that people who had been
presented with 2. often later recalled it as 1. This tends also to be true
of subordinate clauses, although both the length of the clause and the
number of such clauses within the sentence are limiting factors. There
is no research evidence available at the moment to indicate precisely
where the trade-off comes between needless repetition using short
sentences, and needless difficulty for the reader when using long
sentences. But a glance at almost any 'Notes' section accompanying
application forms suggests that it is the latter which occurs most
frequently.

RELATIVE PRONOUNS AND OTHER 'FUNCTION WORDS'
ASSIST COMPREHENSION

Research by Blumenthal (1966) and Hakes and Foss (1970) has shown
that sentences with subordinate clauses are more easily understood if
the clauses are introduced by relative pronouns (which, that) than if
these pronouns are omitted. That is to say, people grasp the meaning
of 'The dog which the milkman owned chased the cat' more readily
than 'The dog the milkman owned chased the cat.' The pronoun signals
the internal relation between *dog* and *milkman.* In 'The dog which the
milkman . . .' the occurrence of the relative pronoun has indicated that
dog is the subject of the sentence and *milkman* is some extra information
about the dog. Whereas in 'The dog the milkman . . .' the reader must
supply the missing word between *dog* and *the milkman,* and here the
possibilities include not only a pronoun but a verb (eg 'The dog bit the
milkman') or a conjunction — even a comma (as in the sentence 'The
dog, the milkman and the postman walked down the street.'). So
relative pronouns help to resolve the potential ambiguity in the sentence.
This tends to be true of function words in general and accounts for why
telegraphese is more difficult to understand than fully formed
sentences (Cherry,1961). Similarly it accounts for the ambiguities
found particularly in newspaper headlines, when function words are
omitted as in *A Farmer's Wife is Best Shot* (Parsons, 1965).

Appendix 2: The use of passives

Goldman-Eisler and Cohen (1970) showed that passives were most
frequently used when people wished to avoid mentioning the agent of
the verb. The shortness of such sentences may compensate for the
general difficulty of passive sentences. Indeed, such sentences are
shorter than the equivalent actives which invariably require a specific

agent. (Contrast *Pensions were increased* with *The Government increased pensions.*) But imperatives in the active voice require no agent (eg *Apply for a pension* ....), so there can be little justification for passive imperatives (eg *Pensions should be applied for* . . .).

Another function of the passive voice relates to the change in word order which accompanies its use. This can have advantages in maintaining continuity of theme. Consequently when the passive voice is used and the agent is included (eg *Pensions were increased by the Government*), the items of information within the sentence are receiving different emphasis than when the active voice is used. Current research suggests that the passive focuses attention on the agent (Anisfeld and Klenbort, 1973) whereas actives are relatively neutral showing no strong differentiation between the two nouns. Indeed, the active tends to emphasize either the verb or the total relation between the items of information in the sentence. Only when such neutrality is unwanted does it make sense to consider passive sentences.

Appendix 3: The use of negatives

Negatives obviously play an important role in our use of language. In particular they may carry greater emphasis than an affirmative statement. For this reason research on language has shown that negatives are a useful way of correcting assumptions being held by the reader (Wason, 1965; Greene, 1970; Olson, 1970). For example, the stronger emphasis of the instruction *Do not use pencil when completing this form* may result in appropriate behaviour from more people than the instruction *Complete this form in ink*, since the affirmative may be construed by some readers as indicating merely a preference by the administration rather than a vital requirement of some data-processing hardware. Information about avoiding pencil is retained in the instruction *Use something other than pencil when completing this form*. But such a sentence is much clumsier than that achieved by using an explicit negative.

The emphatic function of negatives may be useful at various points on an application form. For example, in the context of providing information about various sources of income, applicants may more frequently give the appropriate information in response to the instruction *Do not include interest on which tax has already been paid* than in response to the instruction *Include all untaxed interest*. Research has shown that there are occasions when people more accurately follow instructions containing phrases such as *Not more than*, or *at least*, than instructions without these negative qualifications (Wright, 1975). This does not mean that such negatives are easier to understand, simply that they involve a particular kind of emphasis which makes them valuable in certain contexts. Where such emphasis is not needed, neither are negatives.

References

Anisfeld, M and Klenbort, I (1973) On the functions of structural paraphrase: the view from the passive voice. *Psychological Bulletin* 79: 117-26

Barnard, P (1974) Presuppositions in active and passive questions. Paper read to the Experimental Psychology Society. Copies available from the author.

Barnard, P and Wright, P (1976) The effects of spaced character formats on the production and legibility of handwritten names. *Ergonomics* 19: 81-92

Barnard, P, Wright, P and Wilcox, P (1975) A comparison of five local government forms. (In preparation. Copies available from P Wright.)

Bernstein, B B (1961) Social structure, language and learning. *Educational Research* 3: 163-76

Blaiwes, A S (1974) Formats for presenting procedural instructions. *Journal of Applied Psychology* 59: 683-6

Blumenthal, A L (1966) Observations with self embedded sentences. *Psychonomic Science* 6: 453-4

Bransford, J D and Franks, J J (1971) The abstraction of linguistic ideas. *Cognitive Psychology* 2: 331-50

Brown, R (1968) The development of questions in child speech. *Journal of Verbal Learning and Verbal Behavior* 7: 279-90

Cherry, C (1961) *On Human Communication.* New York: John Wiley & Sons Inc, pp 115-20.

Clark, H H and Chase, W G (1972) On the process of comparing sentences against pictures. *Cognitive Psychology* 3: 472-517

Clark, H H and Clark, E V (1968) Semantic distinctions and memory for complex sentences. *Quarterly Journal of Experimental Psychology* 21: 137-47

Conrad, R and Hull, A J (1967) Copying alpha and numeric codes by hand. *Journal of Applied Psychology* 51: 444-8

Crowder, N A (1963) Intrinsic programming: facts, fallacies and failure. In R T Filep (ed) *Prospectives in Programming.* New York: Macmillan, pp 84-115

Dooling, D J and Lachman, R (1971) Effects of comprehension on retention of prose. *Journal of Experimental Psychology* 88: 216-22

Flesch, R F (1948) A new readability yardstick. *Journal of Applied Psychology* 32: 221-33

Fowler, H W (1926) *A Dictionary of Modern English Usage.* Oxford: Oxford University Press

Goldman-Eisler, F and Cohen, M (1970) N, P, and PN difficulty a voted criterion of transformational operations. *Journal of Verbal Learning and Verbal Behavior* 9: 161-6

Gowers, E (1954) *The Complete Plain Words.* London: HMSO

Graves, R and Hodge, A (1943) *The Reader over your Shoulder.* London: Cape

Gray, M (1975) Questionnaire typography and production. *Applied Ergonomics* 6 2: 81-9

Greene, J M (1970) The semantic function of negatives and passives. *British Journal of Psychology* 61: 17-22

Greene, J M (1972) *Psycholinguistics: Chomsky and Psychology.* Harmondsworth: Penguin

Hakes, D T and Foss, D J (1970) Decision processes during sentence comprehension: effects of surface structure reconsidered. *Perception and Psychophysics* 8: 413-16

Hall, J F (1954) Learning as a function of word frequency. *American Journal of Psychology* 67: 138-40

Hartley, J and Burnhill, P (1976) Explorations in space. *Bulletin of the British Psychological Society* 29: 97-107

Herriot, P (1970) *An Introduction to the Psychology of Language.* London: Methuen

Huttenlocker, J and Higgins, E T (1971) Adjectives, comparatives and syllogisms. *Psychological Review* 78: 487-504

Jones, S (1966) Decoding a descriptive instruction. *British Journal of Psychology* 57: 405-11

Jones, S (1968a) Instructions, self instructions and performance. *Quarterly Journal of Experimental Psychology* 20: 74-9

Jones, S (1968b) *Design of Instruction.* Training Paper 1. London: Department of Employment and Productivity, HMSO

Klare, G R (1974) Assessing readability. *Reading Research Quarterly* 10 1: 62-102

Klare, G R, Shuford, E H and Nichols, W H (1958) The relation of format organisation to learning. *Educational Research Bulletin* 37: 39-45

Kolers, P A (1968) Reading temporally and spatially transformed text. In K Goodman (ed) *The Psycholinguistic Nature of the Reading Process.* Detroit: Wayne State University Press

Lewis, B N and Woolfenden, P J (1969) *Algorithms and Logical Trees.* Cambridge: Algorithms Press

Loftus, E F, Freedman, J L and Loftus, G R (1970) Retrieval of words from subordinate and supraordinate categories in semantic hierarchies. *Psychonomic Science* 21: 235-6

Mackay, D G (1973) Aspects of the theory of comprehension memory and attention. *Quarterly Journal of Experimental Psychology* 25: 22-40

Olson, D R (1970) Language and thought: aspects of a cognitive theory of semantics. *Psychological Review* 77: 257-73

Olson, J R and Mackay, D G (1974) Completion and vertification of ambiguous sentences. *Journal of Verbal Learning and Verbal Behavior* 13: 457-70

Palermo, D S (1973) More about less: a study of comprehension. *Journal of Verbal Learning and Verbal Behavior* 12: 211-21

Parsons, D (1965) *Funny Ha Ha and Funny Peculiar.* London: Pan

Partridge, E (1957) *Usage and Abusage: A Guide to Good English.* Harmondsworth: Penguin (revised edition)

Poulton, E C (1968) Rate of comprehension of an existing teleprinter output and of possible alternatives. *Journal of Applied Psychology* 52: 16-21

Poulton, E C (1969a) Skimming lists of food ingredients printed in different sizes. *Journal of Applied Psychology* 53: 55-8

Poulton, E C (1969b) Skimming lists of food ingredients printed in different brightness contrasts. *Journal of Applied Psychology* 53: 489-500

Solomon, R L and Postman, L (1952) Frequency of usage as a determinant of recognition threshold for words. *Journal of Experimental Psychology* 43: 195-201

Starch, D (1914) *Advertising.* Chicago: Scott, Foresman

Tichy, H J (1966) *Effective Writing for Engineers, Managers, Scientists.* New York: John Wiley & Sons Inc

Tinker, M A (1965) *Bases for Effective Reading.* Minneapolis: University of Minnesota Press, pp 136-141

Tinker, M A and Paterson, D G (1928) Influence of type form on speed of reading. *Journal of Applied Psychology* 12: 359-68

Trabasso, T, Rollins, H and Shaughnessy, E (1971) Storage and unfamiliar stages in processing concepts. *Cognitive Psychology* 2: 239-89

Wason, P C (1961) Response to affirmative and negative binary statements. *British Journal of Psychology* 52: 133-42

Wason, P C (1965) The contexts of plausible denial. *Journal of Verbal Learning and Verbal Behavior* 4: 7-11

Wason, P C and Johnson-Laird, P N (1972) *Psychology of Reasoning: Structure and Content.* London: Batsford

Wheatley, D M and Unwin, A W (1972) *The Algorithm Writer's Guide.* London: Longmans

Wright, P (1969) Transformations and the understanding of sentences. *Language and Speech* 12: 156-66

Wright, P (1975) Presenting people with choices: the effect of format on the comprehension of examination rubrics. *Programmed Learning & Educational Technology* 12: 109-14

Wright, P and Barnard, P (1975) A comparison of 'more than' and 'less than' decisions when using numerical tables. *Journal of Applied Psychology* 60: 606-11

Wright, P and Reid, F (1973) Written information: some alternatives to prose for expressing the outcomes of complex contingencies. *Journal of Applied Psychology* 57: 160-6

Yates, D (1975) Minutes of Brunel University/Institute of Housing Managers research project meeting. Available from Rent Rebates and Allowances Project, Brunel Institute of Organisation and Social Studies, Brunel University.

Part 4: Communicating in Print: New Techniques

4.0 Introduction

In a recent television film about the American Library of Congress the commentator, Huw Wheldon, remarked to the Director of the Library, Daniel Boorstin, that it felt much more friendly to rifle through a library card catalogue than it did to use a visual display unit (VDU). Dr Boorstin replied that early readers had said the same of handwritten books as opposed to printed ones . . . In short, what is novel and unfriendly for one generation can be quite natural for the next.

What novel techniques will soon be natural in the field of written communication? The following items can be immediately suggested — and the list is not meant to be exhaustive:

> Photocomposition
> Camera-ready copy
> Microfilm and microfiche
> Visual display units or terminals
> Teletext systems
> Word-processors
> Micro-processors
> Computer-aided printing
> Optical character recognition systems
> Computer-based retrieval systems
> Computer conferencing
> Electronic blackboards
> Electronic journals
> Facsimile transmission
> Laser printing
> Laser holography

One of the aims of presenting such a list is to indicate that I had to select articles for this section of this book from a wide range of possibilities. (Another comprehensive list, with a brief discussion of most of the items I have listed, can be found in the *Scholarly Publishers' Guide*, 1978.)

It is clear that most, if not all, of the items in the list depend in some way or another upon advances in computer processing. Some products of the computer age force our attention to progress in this respect (eg word-processors and video displays like teletext) but some products are hidden, even though their effects are possibly more dramatic (eg computer-typesetting, -editing and -pagination). All of these developments offer intriguing problems for psychologists interested in written communication. Our ways of writing, editing and preparing text for publication and display are caught up in a whirl of change. The papers chosen for inclusion in Part 4 are concerned with evaluating the effects of some of these changes.

Computer output microfilm

Paper 4.1 considers the presentation and readability of computer output microfilm (COM). The paper is in fact an excerpt from a lengthy review and bibliography. In this excerpt Herbert Spencer and Linda Reynolds summarize what research has been done on reading and using microfilm, and make suggestions about needs for the future.

Perhaps at this point it would be useful to have some definitions. A *microform* is any form, either film or paper, which contains images too small to be read with the naked eye. Microforms on paper are now so rare that the term microform has become almost synonymous with *microfilm*. A *microfilm reader* is a device used to magnify the images on the microfilm. Most readers are designed for use with one type of microfilm, eg roll film or *microfiche*. A microfiche consists of a piece of film (usually 6 x 4 inches) that can contain images of over 250 pages of A4 sized text. Microfilms and microfiche were traditionally produced by photographing documents, but in recent years computer output has been put directly on to film to produce *computer output microfilm* (COM).

Spencer and Reynolds report that COM is becoming increasingly popular as a form of computer output for a variety of structured texts, such as customer accounts, stock records, parts lists, price lists, hotel reservations, book lists, library catalogues, etc. Its advantages lie in its compact nature: its disadvantages lie in its use.

In most cases the users of COM are involved in brief search tasks rather than in continuous reading — although browsing may occur. Because of these requirements, the spatial arrangement of the text is very important. Unfortunately, COM layouts are often determined by computer programmers who try to minimize the bulk of their computer output: they do this by making a maximum use of the 132 characters per line and the six lines per inch that are available on most line-printers. Reynolds (1979) provides some horrendous examples.

In 1979, Reynolds and Spencer presented the results of two experiments. These were concerned with evaluating different COM layouts (a) by manipulating the inter-column spacing of tabular materials, and (b) by comparing a single versus a double-column format when the presentation was in a cine-mode (vertical roll) or a comic-strip mode (horizontal roll).

In experiment (a) they found that increases in the column spacing were accompanied by increases in the time taken to search the material. In experiment (b) they found overall that the double-column format was better than the single-column one, and that the cine-mode was better than the comic-mode. However, these results were specific to the user's task. When the test involved a lot of searching *within* individual elements, then the double-column format was better; however, when the text involved much searching *for* the actual elements in the first place, as well as within them, then the single column format was better. These results, then, are not unlike those one might expect from experiments with conventionally printed materials. Spacing is important, but so, too, are the requirements of the user.

Nonetheless, in their discussion, Reynolds and Spencer raise the point that is frequently made by researchers in this new area of written communication. They say that the layout of COM is often inappropriately modelled on the layout of conventional text. Their point is that when you change from one medium to another you might require different layouts to suit the limitations and possibilities of the new technique.

Here then is a serious problem. If the earlier research on typography was correctly criticized on the grounds that it was based firstly on a limited knowledge of production issues, and secondly on untenable assumptions about how readers normally use text, then the little that we know about printed text may not have much relevance to the presentation of text in other media.

Teletext

This issue is taken up again by Linda Reynolds in her article (Paper 4.2) on teletext and Viewdata (the Post Office's teletext system). Because it is important I have drawn up Table 1 below. In this table I have tried to suggest (a) where we might expect findings from print-based research to be relevant to teletext communication; (b) where we might not expect these findings to be relevant; and (c) where more research seems to be needed in the context of teletext. These suggestions are, of course, personal speculations which may not be shared by others. A problem in making such suggestions is that research results can become inapplicable because of new developments in the field.

Teletext has certain advantages and certain disadvantages when compared with print. In my view, it is particularly limited in that the text depicted on a television screen is tied to a matrix of 40 letter spaces by 20 lines of type. This results in a remarkably small page in terms of content. Figures 1a and 1b show how much text one might expect to obtain on a normal teletext page. (In passing we may note that if, as some commentators tell us, our newspapers are to be replaced by home-based, computer-operated VDUs we may expect even greater trivialization of the news than we have at present.)

In concluding this introductory section on teletext we might ponder the fact that almost every home and possibly half the schools in the country are equipped with television. Thus the potential for teaching by television is enormous. One might have thought, therefore, that there would be a good deal of research on how to present text on television. Unfortunately, this does not appear to be the case.

	Printed text	Teletext	1	2	3
Quality of image	varies	varies	—	X	—
Size of image	varies	determined by size of TV receiver	—	X	—
Permanence of copy	permanent	impermanent	—	X	X
Access to contents	unrestricted	restricted	—	X	—
Rate of display	reader-controlled	reader-controlled, or computer-controlled	—	X	X
Sequencing of display	page turning, reader-controlled	page 'turning': reader-controlled, or computer-controlled	—	—	X
			—	—	X
Amount of material per page	varies	restricted in terms of total number of characters	—	X	X
Graphics	any format	restricted format	—	X	X
Letter spacing	equal (in typewritten text)	equal	?	—	—
Word spacing	proportional spacing	equal	X	X	X
	equal (in typewritten and unjustified text)	justified text achieved by manipulation of (i) modules of letter space units (ii) abbreviations (iii) omission of punctuation	—	—	—
	unequal in justified text				
Word breaks (hyphenation)	hyphenation	hyphenation	X	X	—
Line endings	unjustified	unjustified	X	—	—
	justified	justified	X	—	—
Line spacing	proportional or variable	proportional in theory: little room for manoeuvre in practice	X	—	X

	Printed text	Teletext	1	2	3
Spatial cueing	various possibilities, depending on page and print size	restricted by smallness of underlying grid (see text)	X	—	X
Typefaces	great variety	restricted	—	X	X
Typographic cueing	size	size (eg double-height)	—	—	X
	italic				
	bold face				
	capitals	capitals	X	—	X
	underlining	underlining	—	X	X
		flashing	—	—	X
Colour coding	colour (minimal)	colour (over-abundance) (lack of consistent usage)	—	X	X
Use of typographic designer in planning options	possibly	unlikely	—	—	X

Table 1. *A comparison summary of the characteristics of printed text and teletext*

In column 1, X indicates that research from printed text seems applicable;
in column 2, X indicates that research from printed text is unlikely to be applicable;
in column 3, X indicates that more research is needed in teletext variants.

Note: This table is based upon personal observation, the review by Reynolds *et al* (1978), comments from Linda Reynolds, and a discussion document by Bork (1979). Bork's document in fact encompasses the broader issues and problems that will arise when users have greater control over the presentation than they do with the teletext system described here.

191

Reports say Skylab has fallen into the Indian Ocean off Australia....102

US President rejects plea to lift sanctions on Zimbabwe Rhodesia....104

Whaling Commission bans factory ships from hunting sperm whales.109

TUC seeks urgent talks with Chancellor on spending cuts................116

Soviet cosmonauts chase record...105
Boeing crew who refused to fly 106
3 Britons aboard missing plane...107
News Index 190   Finance 120   Sport 140

Figure 1a. *News headlines (from a Ceefax page)*

After six years in orbit, the giant American space station, Skylab, has splashed down in the Indian Ocean off the west coast of Australia.

But fragments from the craft, which broke up as it re-entered the earth's atmosphere, have been sighted by residents of several towns in Western Australia including Perth. There have been no reports of injuries or damage.

Earlier today controllers at NASA headquarters put Skylab into a 'tumble' to prevent it from coming down on the heavily populated centres of the northern US and parts of Canada.

MAP FOLLOWS IN A MOMENT

Figure 1b. *News 'in depth' (from a Ceefax page)*

Word-processors

Papers 4.1 and 4.2 are concerned with the effects of new techniques on the presentation of text to the reader. In Paper 4.3 we turn to a different theme: that of how new techniques might affect the writing process itself. Paper 4.3 contains a simple description of some of the different systems of word-processing. It was written as an Appendix to a discussion document for the US Naval Training and Evaluation Group, and it outlines what kinds of system are available, what each can and cannot do, and how much they cost (in 1977). Readers who are interested in more technical details might like to consult the articles by Phillips (1978a; 1978b) or the text by Seybold (1977).

Word-processors are in effect like tape recorders which, instead of playing back sound, play back type. They are, of course, more complicated than this, but this simile seems best to describe what they look like when they are in operation. Word-processing systems keep a record of the text that has been typed; they enable this record to be played back, stopped at any point, and corrected; they allow for the addition and deletion of material, and for the re-sequencing of words, phrases, sentences and paragraphs; they do all of this without the need to retype anything that has not been changed; and finally, when the changes are completed, they provide a fresh, clean manuscript at the touch of a button.

Such machines can now be found in business offices, government departments and educational institutions. A word-processor of some kind is an asset wherever there is repetitive typing to be done. However, as the requirements are so diverse in the three areas listed, there is great variety in the systems available.

A more homogeneous set of requirements can be found in the newspaper industry, where the current fascination is with editorial systems by which stories are created, revised, routed, sub-edited and finally printed, all on line — and possibly by the journalists themselves. In addition, classified advertisements can be entered straight into the paper by non-technical staff. (Industrial conditions in the UK make the introduction of such systems very difficult; however, the American scene provides a somewhat more optimistic note, as is shown in Figure 2.)

The picture conveyed in Figure 2 suggests what it is like to work with text-edited systems of word-processing of the type discussed in Paper 4.3. My own experience with word-processors has been limited to magnetic tape systems, without VDUs (see 4.3). Nonetheless, even these systems have remarkable advantages for someone like me, for whom the process of writing academic text involves much revision. After writing the introductions in this text in longhand and then seeing the first drafts in typescript, paragraphs have been displaced or even discarded, and words, phrases, and sentences have been changed, re-written, and re-arranged — much to the chagrin of my typist. Figures 3a and 3b provide extreme examples.

The problems of revising the text are multiplied when one asks colleagues for their opinions about the suitability of what has been written. Indeed, if the text is being prepared by a group, or written for a committee, then the writing can become tedious. Ernst Rothkopf

Today's newspaper is thoroughly committed to the use of the video display terminal (or VDT) for initial input of reporters' copy. The reporter sits at his terminal much as he would at a typewriter, cradling the telephone to his ear, and takes notes of interviews, building up a scratch pad of information which he can reference at his convenience. This is filed under his name and can be accessed on the screen in a matter of a split second simply by typing the appropriate command. Then the reporter begins to construct his story. He may revise it as he types, and he can use the terminal to manipulate text by moving paragraphs, searching for key words, or making 'global changes' in terminology if this seems indicated. When he is satisfied with the story he can 'route' it to his supervising editor. This is done 'by the system' — usually by his merely pressing the 'send' key. The name of the story will then appear upon the editor's directory, with an indication of the approximate story length and the name of the writer. By positioning his 'cursor' at that location and pressing the 'get' or 'fetch' key, the story will immediately appear on the editor's screen. He is able to 'scroll' through this 'file' and make whatever changes he desires, even incorporating side comments (to his own superior), and he can then 'send' the story to be hyphenated and justified to whatever measure and point size he wishes. In many systems the story will come back (again almost instantaneously) on his screen so that he can review its precise size and appearance. He can then 'send' off his story to someone else for further review, editing or comment, or he can command that it be typeset. In the latter case, the 'file' will be queued for the on-line typesetter and will very shortly appear as a galley to be stripped into position on the indicated page. As of this writing, systems are also beginning to emerge which would route the story next to a page makeup man who would also work with a video tube on which a diagrammatic representation of a particular newspaper page would be displayed. This page editor can indicate desired locations of stories, and when he is satisfied, command that all stories on the page be composed at the same time, to avoid any hand makeup or stripping. High-speed cathode ray tube typesetters, capable of setting full-width newspaper pages, presently exist and can be commanded to call out the desired type faces — of whatever size or variety — without any manual intervention.

Figure 2. *Extract from Seybold, J W (1977) 'Fundamentals of Modern Composition', p 189. (Extract reproduced with permission.)*

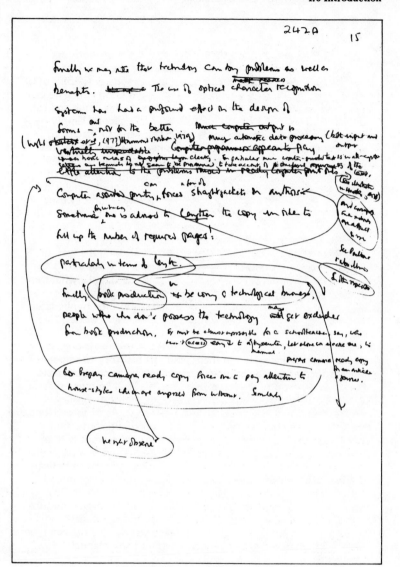

Figure 3a. *The first draft of the conclusions to the introduction. This was re-written (in longhand) before being typed.*

-11-

not for the good (see Wright et al, 1977; Hammond and Wilson, 1979).
Much automatic data processing (both input and output) ignores basic rules
of clarity. Much computer generated text is printed in all-capital letters,
and programmes do not seem to be written to take into account the
structural requirements of text: consequently the resulting mess is
difficult to read (Poulton and Brown, 1968; ← ──── → and see
Hartley 1978 for illustrations). Preparing camera-ready copy provides
new problems for authors and typists, and computer-assisted printing
can make restrictions on authors, particularly in terms of length.
(Sometimes, however, one is advised to lengthen the copy in order to fill
up the required number of pages.)

Finally, we might observe that people who don't have access to the
technology may get excluded from the whole process. It must be almost
impossible, for example, for a ~~school teacher~~ *someone* who has not got easy access
to a manual typewriter, let alone an electric one, to prepare camera-ready
copy for a journal article. Written communication is becoming a technological business: it may make life easier for some but it won't do *it* for all.

Figure 3b. *An edited typescript of the same page. The final printed
version appears at the end of this introduction.*

once commented in conversation that the longer he sat on committees the more tortuous he thought his writing got!

Magnetic-tape systems (and text editors) make this revision process easier — at least for the typist. I am not so sure that they enable one to write better. Nonetheless one hopes that, given the chance to make revisions easily, more readable writing will result.

Finally, in this connection we may note that there have been interesting recent developments in computer-aided composition. At Bell Telephone Laboratories, for example, computer programs have been written which will detect spelling errors, compute the readability of text, indicate poor usage and style, and flag overly complex sentences. At present these programs (and others) are run after the original text has been written, but it is anticipated that they will soon be incorporated into the production process itself. In addition, programs are being developed which will aid the writer with the layout of his text as well as with its wording.

Computer conferencing

The final paper in this section, Paper 4.4, presents some intriguing material. In Britain the idea of computer conferencing seems remote. Nonetheless, there are interesting developments which might make us rethink our traditional ideas. Senders (1977) has described a journal without paper, and in Paper 4.4 Starr Hiltz describes a conference without a meeting.

The full paper (from which Paper 4.4 is an excerpt) describes a proposed evaluation of a technological innovation at the time of its invention.

The Electronic Information Exchange System (EIES) is trying to help a network of social scientists who wish to communicate with one another often and intensively. The idea stems from the fact that studies have shown that scientists rely heavily on informal channels of communication as a source of feedback as well as on more formal channels such as published articles or books.

The formal channels of scientific communication are very time-consuming. The time taken for an idea to see the light of day through such channels — and then for it to be read, assimilated and further assimilated — can be quite lengthy. (The proposal to publish this particular book was made in October 1978: these introductions are being written in July 1979: the book is scheduled for publication in March 1980.)

The aim of the EIES, then, is to link up and multiply informal channels of communication and to speed up the dissemination of ideas around the resulting network.

The main problems with this approach seem to be the need for a sufficient number of terminals to give adequate coverage, and the cost of the enterprise. The main advantages seem to lie in the speed of information exchange, and in the fact that each participant can benefit from the rapid responses of a large number of experts in the field. Hiltz's full paper outlines the techniques for evaluating EIES that she

197

plans to use, but the results are not yet available.

Concluding remarks

To carry out research in the field of written communication using modern technology, psychologists will have to widen their horizons. Few psychologists seem to know much about current technologies and how they impinge upon the production of text, let alone new ones. Much research on typography has been rightly criticized on the grounds that psychologists have remained in relative isolation from production problems. To be of help in designing, using and evaluating new technologies, psychologists will have to immerse themselves in new and different disciplines.

Here they will discover that textbooks, journals, magazines and newspapers each differ in their requirements, and that writers, journalists, typographers, editors, designers, publishers and printers all have their own technology, language and mystique. An additional problem is that these various people do not distinguish between types of psychologist (such as pure/applied, behavioural/analytical). We are all one to them. They do not know what psychologists do, or what contribution psychologists can make.

One consequence of this lack of shared vocabulary is that many people spend a lot of time doing things that could be done more effectively in other ways. Psychologists in the field of training, for instance, would be startled to find that with some systems of photocomposition, the operators do not see the output of their key-pressing until the paper has passed through the required chemistry. Similarly, with the word-processing systems, the typist's instructions to the computer are mixed in with the text that is being typed — thus making it difficult to see (a) if all the commands have been properly executed, and (b) if the text is correctly entered. There are further implications for training in the fact that first-class typists need to become computer programmers if they want to get away from using stored (straight-jacket) formats in their computer-aided typing. And even for those typists who are content to use stored formats, there are training manuals to be written.

A further consequence of a lack of common language is that many people spend a lot of time doing what others consider to be unnecessary. Thus, for example, writing a computer program to match a current composition routine requires a great deal of effort. Programs have to be meticulously conceived in order to match the capabilities of highly skilled craftsmen. Yet many people would question whether *all* of this work is necessary. Do we need to write programs in order to hyphenate words? And do we need both vertically and horizontally justified text?

In conclusion, we may note that technology can bring problems as well as benefits. The use of optical character recognition systems has had a profound — and detrimental — effect on the design of forms that are to be 'read' by computer (see Wright *et al*, 1977; Hammond and Wilson, 1979). Much automatic data processing (both input and output) ignores the basic rules of clarity. Much computer-generated text is printed in all-capital letters, and programs do not seem to be written to take into account the structural requirements of text: consequently the result is difficult to read (Poulton and Brown, 1968; and see Hartley, 1978 for illustrations). Preparing camera-ready copy provides new problems for authors and typists, and computer-assisted printing can make restrictions on authors, particularly in terms of length. Finally, we might observe that people who do not have access to the technology may get excluded from the whole process. It is almost impossible for someone who has not got easy access to a manual typewriter, let alone an electric one, to prepare camera-ready copy for a journal article. Written communication is becoming a technological business: it may make life easier for some but it won't do so for all.

References

Bork, A (1979) Tentative textual taxonomy. Discussion paper available from the author, Dept of Physics, University of California, Irvine, California 92717.

Hammond, R F and Wilson, P L (1979) Use of an optical mark reader in army selection procedures. In Q Whitlock and G T Page (eds) *Aspects of Educational Technology XIII*. London: Kogan Page and New York: Nichols

Hartley, J (1978) *Designing Instructional Text*. London: Kogan Page and New York: Nichols

Phillips, A H (1978a) Word processing and text handling devices. *Journal of Research Communication Studies* 1: 3-18

Phillips, A H (1978b) Printer's errors and author's corrections. *Journal of Research Communication Studies* 1: 243-51

Poulton, E C and Brown, C H (1968) Rate of comprehension of an existing teleprinter output and of possible alternatives. *Journal of Applied Psychology* 52 1: 16-21

Reynolds, L (1979) Visual presentation of information in library catalogues: a survey. Vol 1 Text, Vol 2 Appendices. *British Library Research & Development Report No 5472*. London: British Library

Reynolds, L and Spencer, H (1979) Two experiments in the layout of information on computer output microfilm. Graphic Information Research Unit, London: Royal College of Art

Reynolds, L, Spencer, H, and Glaze, G (1978) The legibility and readability of viewdata displays: a survey of relevant research. Graphic Information Research Unit, London: Royal College of Art

Senders, J (1977) An on-line scientific journal. *Information Scientist* 11: 3-10

Seybold, J W (1977) *Fundamentals of Modern Composition*. Seybold Publications Inc, Box 644, Media, Pa 19063, USA

Scholarly Publishers' Guide: New Methods & Techniques (1978) University of Leicester: Primary Communications Research Centre

Wright, P, Aldrich, A, and Wilcox P (1977) Some effects of coding answers for optical mark reading on the accuracy of answering multiple-choice questions. *Human Factors* 19 1: 83-7

Further reading

Phillips, A H (1968) *Computer Peripherals and Typesetting*. London: HMSO

Scholarly Publishers' Guide: New Methods and Techniques (1978) (2nd edition) Leicester University: Primary Communications Research Centre

A detailed, semi-technical journal on computer-assisted printing techniques and word processing is *The Seybold Report*, Seybold Publications, Box 644, Media, Pa 19063, USA

4.1 Factors affecting the acceptability of microforms as a reading medium

HERBERT SPENCER AND LINDA REYNOLDS

(Extracts from a report of the same title, published by the
Readability of Print Research Unit, Royal College of Art, London,
1976. Reproduced with permission of the authors.)

Introduction

As an information handling medium, microforms possess numerous
advantages over conventional alternatives and their use in the area of
information publishing is increasing rapidly. As a reading medium,
however, microforms have a number of disadvantages given the present
state-of-the-art. These disadvantages stem from the need for the use of
a piece of equipment for reading. This creates a reading situation very
different from that of print on paper, and has complex psychological
and physiological effects on the user. Psychologically, users may feel
remote from the information they seek, and physiologically the nature
of the reading situation may result in reduced speed and accuracy in
reading, and in subjective feelings of visual and bodily fatigue. User
resistance to microforms is often high, therefore, and the design of the
reading situation may influence the viability of a microform system as
a whole. If the potential of microforms as an information handling
medium is to be fully realized, it is clear that research is needed so
that the reading task may be made more efficient and less fatiguing.

What is not so clear, however, is the precise direction which such
research should take in order to have the greatest possible impact.
A great many factors are involved in the microform reading situation,
and some of these will be much more significant than others in terms
of their effects on the user. The purpose of this study was to identify
as many as possible of the factors influencing the acceptability of
microforms as a reading medium, and to assess their relative importance
on the basis of a review of past research and experience. The factors
which would best repay further research are those identified as the
most significant and least researched.

Methodology

Two main sources of information were used in identifying and assessing
the relative importance of factors affecting the acceptability of
microform as a reading medium. These were a series of visits to
representative microform users, and a survey of the literature relating

to problems of microfilm acceptability at the man-machine interface.

VISITS

Visits were chosen to cover as wide a range of applications as possible
within the time available. A variety of reading equipment, including rear
projection, front projection, hand operated and motorized models, was
observed in use in a number of different environments.

The visits were representative of a number of different patterns of
microform use. Some users were performing quick reference tasks for
short periods, for example those using library catalogues, British
Leyland parts catalogues and British Airways maintenance manuals,
while others were performing such tasks for relatively long periods,
as at the National Westminster Bank and in the Wadham Stringer
customer telephone enquiry department. British Airways and National
Westminster Bank staff in particular were under considerable pressure
to achieve speed and accuracy in their work. In some instances the
microfilm reader was used mainly as a means of locating the relevant
information and copying it, rather than as the primary reading medium.
Legibility of paper copies then became crucial, as at British Airways.
In other situations, users were reading microfilm more or less
continuously for varying periods of time, but at their own pace. This
was true of those using library materials such as abstracts, journals
and newspapers.

LITERATURE SURVEY

The literature survey had two main purposes: to identify any
additional factors not directly observed during the visits, and to review
past research and thereby identify those factors which have not so far
been adequately researched.

The survey revealed that there has been relatively little serious
research on factors affecting the acceptability of microforms as a
reading medium. Studies which have been undertaken fall into two
main categories: surveys of users' behaviour when offered microfilm
as an alternative or sole source of information and their subjective
opinions of it; and experimental studies of one or more factors using
objective measures of image quality and/or users' performance on some
given task. To date the emphasis in experimental work has tended to be
on factors relating to image quality, equipment design and work station
design, and that there has been very little work on the design of the
film image.

Apart from research reports, other types of literature were examined
in case they should reveal any additional factors which have not so far
been subjected to survey or experiment. There are, for example, several
thorough reviews of research on certain factors affecting user
acceptability, and some of these reviews make suggestions for further
research. There are also numerous papers discussing and making
recommendations on various factors, but in many of these the
recommendations are based on the author's experience or opinion

rather than on objective information obtained by experimentation.
Descriptions of microfilm systems in use in various organizations
yielded some additional factors, as did general descriptions of equipment
and techniques and practical handbooks for new users.

Conclusions

THE STATE-OF-THE-ART

Microform characteristics. It would seem that there is no shortage of
recommendations and standards in relation to certain microform
characteristics such as the production of source documents and the
preparation of graphics such as engineering drawings, although it would
appear that these are mostly based on physical measurements of the
resulting image quality which have not been validated by controlled
experiments with users.

There has been a considerable amount of experimentation on some
image quality factors, particularly on image polarity and reduction ratio,
but the results are often conflicting and difficult to extrapolate to
real life situations which may differ from the experimental conditions.
Recommendations as to optimum values for film resolution and
contrast are relatively few. There is a need for information which would
help the user in making decisions on such factors as image polarity and
reduction ratio in relation to other factors with which they are likely
to interact.

There has been relatively little research on factors relating to the
structuring and organization of information for microfilming, on the
advantages and disadvantages of the various possible microfilm formats
and layouts, and on the problems of indexing microfilm adequately.
It would seem that producers of microfilm are only just beginning to
realize that as an information carrying medium it has characteristics
very different from those of the printed book, and that the information
therefore needs to be structured, arranged and indexed differently. The
fact that the limitations and potential of microfilm as an information
carrying medium have not been fully realized by many publishers must
account for much of the observed user resistance to microforms.
Controlled research on these problems could do much to improve the
'useability' of microforms.

Perhaps the least researched aspects of microform design are
typography and layout. There have been surveys of the typography of
originals to be filmed for retrospective publications (in order to set
realistic image quality standards), but there has been little or no
controlled experimentation with a view to improving the design of
future publications. An assumption commonly made is that conventions
successfully used by designers and printers for the printed page will be
appropriate for microfilm images. This is not necessarily the case.
Typographic factors will interact in a complex way with one another,
and also with other factors such as direction of projection, image
polarity and screen brightness, which are unique to the microfilm
reading situation. Research on typographic factors could result not
only in images which are more legible in terms of the ease of character

recognition, but also in images whose structure is made clear by the use of those methods of information coding most suitable for microfilm presentation.

Equipment design. Although a number of studies have examined factors relating to screen characteristics and the performance of the optical system of readers, the results are sometimes conflicting, and often difficult to apply because the experimental conditions are inadequately specified or do not take into account other very relevant variables. In some cases it would appear that experimentation is needed to discover whether or not certain factors such as screen colour, screen curvature and scintillation do affect legibility or user acceptability, while in other cases it is obvious that there is an effect but optimum conditions have not been satisfactorily determined, as with screen luminance. Some factors, such as direction of projection and screen luminance, need to be investigated in relation to certain image characteristics, such as image polarity. Other basic characteristics of readers such as screen size and print size need to be considered more carefully in relation to standard paper sizes.

The aspect of reader design which possibly gives rise to most complaints and has apparently been least considered by manufacturers is that of in-use characteristics. Controls are often inconveniently placed, awkward to operate, and imprecise in their effects. Film loading and frame selection are two of the most significant factors. Many readers have undesirable in-use characteristics (such as excessive heat and noise generation) which might be avoided, while highly desirable facilities and accessories (such as retractable screen hoods and cursors) are omitted. The quality of printouts on many machines also leaves much to be desired.

A further, more fundamental, complaint is that reading equipment often appears to have been designed *in vacuo*, taking little or no account of the different types of environment in which it is likely to be used, or of the fact that in many cases the user will be performing some parallel task such as writing.

The need here would seem to be for technological and design research to improve optical performance and convenience in use. Some research has been directed at the overall problem of reader design, but the vigour with which the prototypes were assessed and the extent to which any new ideas have been adopted is unclear.

Work station design. The environment in which reading equipment is used can have a very significant effect on user acceptability. One of the most significant factors is that of ambient illumination. The effects of surrounding illumination on the screen image and on the user are complex, and although there have been numerous investigations on the subject, none of them seems to have taken into account all the relevant variables.

Apart from illumination, there is the problem of determining the optimum spatial relationship between the user, the screen, and the work surface on which he is performing any parallel tasks. The evidence suggests that ideally the position of the user and the screen should be variable in at least two dimensions. The ideal solution would seem to be a purpose-built work station or carrel, but as yet manufacturers have been slow to accept this as a need and users are obliged to be content with makeshift arrangements. Further research on the design of an economically feasible carrel would be of value.

Job characteristics. It would appear that in many instances the implications of introducing microfilm systems in terms of the way they change jobs are not fully considered. Experience indicates that for the successful introduction of any new system, specific consideration of the problems associated with using new materials and equipment must be backed up by a review of the organizational implications associated with its introduction. The system may require a certain type of staff, it may necessitate training of new and existing staff and it may require a reorganization of labour so that staff are not forced to perform a single task continuously. Relatively little has been written on this aspect of microfilm use, and the problems which users encounter in performing familiar tasks with a new information medium are worthy of more serious consideration.

User characteristics. Certain characteristics of the user may determine whether or not he will be prepared to accept microfilm as an information medium. At present there seems to be no evidence to suggest that his educational background will influence his attitude in any predictable way, but his level of motivation is very likely to affect his willingness or ability to overlook any less than optimal characteristics of the system, especially if he is making a direct comparison with a hard copy system. Much more research is needed on users' motivational levels. Factors such as eyesight and susceptibility to fatigue are likely to have a rather more predictable effect on attitudes.

In the final analysis, no matter how high the quality of the microforms and the equipment, it is often the user who determines the resulting quality of the screen image and of printouts. He may decide that he is content with an off-centre, slightly out-of-focus image on a dirty screen, and similarly that an off-centre, slightly out-of-focus print, streaky and lacking in contrast, is sufficient for his needs. Some users apparently not only need to be shown how to use microforms and equipment, they also need to be persuaded to attempt to get the best possible results from the system they are using. They may feel that fine adjustments are too much bother, and while this hardly suggests resistance to the medium, it may in fact mean that such careless users are strengthening their prejudices against microforms.

RESEARCH NEEDS

It would appear that two kinds of research are needed. Firstly, there is a need for controlled experimentation on a large number of factors, using objective measures of users' behaviour and performance at selected tasks relating to microform use. Such research would provide information for use in making recommendations and setting standards for image quality, equipment performance, work station design and job design. Secondly, there is a need for research of a more practical nature to establish ways and means of achieving the required standards of image quality and equipment performance, and of producing acceptable equipment and accessories (such as carrels) at reasonable prices. The most pressing research needs are summarized below.

Microform characteristics
Typography and layout for source documents and computer output microfilm (COM):

> character size in relation to character style and reduction ratio
> character style in relation to image polarity, reduction ratio and
>   image generation
> upper case only versus upper and lower case for COM
> character weight in relation to character style, image polarity
>   and image generation
> proportional versus non-proportional spacing for COM
> line spacing in relation to line length
> column spacing in tabular layouts in relation to line spacing
> single versus double column page layouts for COM
> typographic versus spatial coding systems

Organization of information content:

> repetition of figures and tables in simultaneous publications
> location of references in simultaneous publications
> location and frequency of contents lists and indexes

Microfilm formats:

> comic versus cine mode for continuous reading and search tasks
>   on roll film
> horizontal versus vertical frame progression for continuous reading
>   and search tasks on fiche

Indexing:

> the use of information units other than the page frame numbering
>   systems for fiche
> size and location of address numbers

Image quality:

> optimum reduction ratios in relation to type size
> the effects of image degradation in multi-generation systems
>   in relation to type style

Equipment design
Screen characteristics:

> luminance for front and rear projection screens in relation to image
>   polarity and ambient lighting

the effects of screen colour on reading performance
the effects of different levels of rear projection screen luminance
on type size, type style and type face

Optical system performance:

optimum magnification ratio in relation to character size and
reduction ratio
minimum and optimum screen image resolution
minimum screen image contrast values
the effects of loss of focus on reading performance

In-use characteristics:

film loading systems
frame selection systems
the size, shape and positioning of controls
the provision of a good portable reader

Printout quality:

optimum magnification ratio in relation to character size, film
reduction ratio, and print area available
print image polarity in relation to film image polarity and type
weight
minimum acceptable resolution in relation to character size
minimum acceptable contrast levels in relation to image polarity

Work station design

the effects of different levels of ambient lighting in relation to
projection type, screen brightness and image polarity
chosen viewing distance in relation to type size and screen
brightness

User characteristics

determinants of user motivation and the effect of motivation on
user attitudes and reading performance
the correlation between subjective feelings of fatigue and
measurable physiological changes and performance decrements.

Editorial footnote: For a detailed account of, and references to, the research
described in this paper, interested readers should consult the original report from
which these extracts are taken.

4.2 Teletext and Viewdata - a new challenge for the designer

LINDA REYNOLDS

(Paper from *Information Design Journal* (1979) 1 1: 2-14. Reproduced with permission of the author.)

Introduction

Teletext and Viewdata are both systems whereby a wide range of information held in a computer data base can be displayed in the home or the office on any domestic television receiver which has the necessary decoding device. The information is displayed in alphanumeric or simple graphic form, and the viewer is able to call up specific 'pages' or frames from the data base using a small remote control keypad. The visual characteristics of teletext and Viewdata displays are very similar. The main difference between them lies in the way in which the information is transmitted from the computer to the receiver. Teletext, as exemplified by the BBC's Ceefax system and the IBA's Oracle, is broadcast in coded form in four of the 625 horizontal scan lines which make up the normal television picture. The pages are broadcast sequentially in a continuous cycle, which means that the total number of pages in the system must be limited to about 200, or the user will have to wait an unacceptably long time for any given page to be transmitted. In Viewdata systems, such as the Post Office's Prestel, the information is transmitted via the telephone network. Pages are transmitted on request, rather than being cycled continuously, and are written up on the screen almost immediately. The total number of available pages is, therefore, much greater than with teletext because there is no limitation imposed by page cycling.

The design possibilities for pages of alphanumeric and graphic information generated in this way are severely limited in a number of respects. The shape, size and spacing of the characters are predetermined, as is the number of possible character positions on the screen. The designer therefore has little scope for the subtleties of typographic and spatial coding which he might normally employ in printed information. The medium does, however, offer one quite unprecedented freedom, which is the availability of seven colours at no extra cost. Teletext and Viewdata displays therefore have characteristics quite different from those of printed materials, and it cannot be assumed that design conventions which have been shown to be appropriate for print will necessarily be applicable. A set of conventions related to this particular medium is needed, but to date there has been little research of direct relevance to which the designer can turn for guidance. It is, however, possible to draw some general conclusions on the basis of research which has been carried out on other types of display, and from studies concerned with the optimum spatial organization of information and the perception of colour.

The aim here is to outline the visual features of teletext and Viewdata displays, to examine the significance of these features in terms of the legibility of the displays and the possibilities for visually indicating the structures of the information, and then to look at ways of displaying particular kinds of information such as text, tables, indexes and graphics.

The visual characteristics of teletext and Viewdata displays

CHARACTER GENERATION

Both teletext and Viewdata images are generated in the same way as a broadcast television picture. That is to say, they are built up by the movement of an electron beam across the phosphor-coated face of a cathode ray tube. The beam moves across the face from left to right and from top to bottom, building up the picture in a total of 625 horizontal scan lines. The characters are built up by blanking and unblanking of the electron beam to produce the required configuration.

Each page or frame of information consists of a maximum of 24 lines of up to 40 characters each, making a total of 960 character positions in all. Two types of character can be displayed. There are standard alphanumeric characters and graphics characters. These are illustrated in Figure 1.

STANDARD ALPHANUMERICS

Each alphanumeric character is formed on a 10 x 6 dot matrix, as illustrated in Figure 2. The characters themselves are a maximum of seven dots high by five dots wide for capitals and for lower case letters with ascenders or descenders, and five dots high by five dots wide for lower case letters without ascenders or descenders. The additional dot spaces serve to create space between adjacent characters and between successive lines of characters. On larger receivers, a character rounding facility is incorporated. This is illustrated in Figure 3. When the design of a character requires that two or more dots should be diagonally adjacent, half dots are added in appropriate positions. As a result, the individual dots making up the characters are much less noticeable.

The alphanumeric character set can be extended vertically on some receivers to produce double height characters. The size of the dot matrix remains the same, and so does the width of the character. Only 12 lines of such characters can be displayed on any one page.

GRAPHICS

In the graphics mode, each of the 960 character positions is divided into six cells, as shown in Figure 4. It may be seen that the two central cells

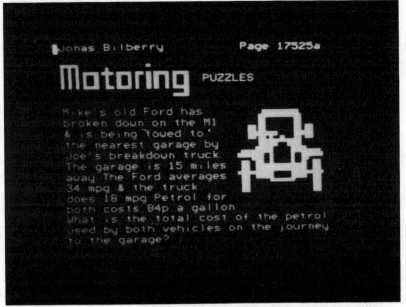

Figure 1. *A typical frame showing standard alphanumerics and graphics*

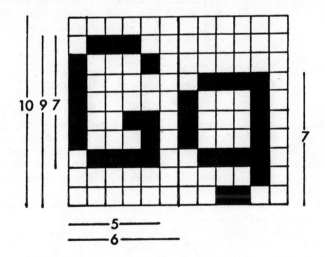

Figure 2. *The alphanumeric character matrix*

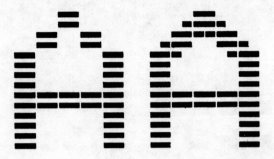

Figure 3. *A typical displayed character with and without character rounding (after Kinghorn, 1975)*

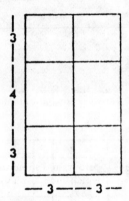

Figure 4. *The graphics mode character matrix*

are slightly larger than the top and bottom cells. This is because each character position occupies 20 scan lines, and this number is not divisible by three. Any combination of these cells can be displayed and each cell will appear as a solid block of colour. The variety of shapes which can be generated is illustrated in Figure 5. They can be used to construct character fonts for titling, for drawing simple graphs, charts and diagrams, and for rules and decorative borders. A standard alpha graphics font is available direct from the editing keyboard, but other fonts can be devised at will.

COLOUR

Both alphanumeric and graphics characters can be displayed in any one of seven colours. These are the primary colours, green, red and blue, the corresponding complementaries, magenta, cyan and yellow, and white. The complementary colours are obtained by mixing the two appropriate primary colours, and white is obtained by mixing all three primaries. As a result, images in complementary colours or white will

210

tend to have coloured rims around them and an uneven internal distribution of colour, particularly if the receiver is not perfectly adjusted.

There is no limit to the number of colours or colour changes possible on any given frame, but at present it is not possible on most receivers to change colour between horizontally adjacent characters. This is because the control code for the colour change occupies a character space. This limitation is likely to be removed shortly, however. It will also eventually be possible for a character of any chosen colour to be displayed on a background of any chosen colour.

Legibility

THE DESIGNER'S INFLUENCE

The 'legibility' of teletext and Viewdata displays in terms of ease of recognition of individual letters and words is affected by a large number of factors. Some of them are related to the nature of this kind of television display, some to the design of the characters and the availability of colour, and some to the conditions under which such displays are typically viewed. The designer has no control over the technical features of the display or the viewing conditions, and for this reason they are not considered in detail here. In the short term he is also unlikely to be able to influence the design of the standard alphanumeric characters, though in the longer term it is highly desirable that he should attempt to do so. For the time being, however, his greatest influence on the legibility of these displays is likely to be through the design of new alpha graphics fonts and the way in which he uses the colour facility.

CHARACTER DESIGN

Standard alphanumerics. Certain features of the characters are unlikely to be changed in the foreseeable future. These include the existence of a fixed number

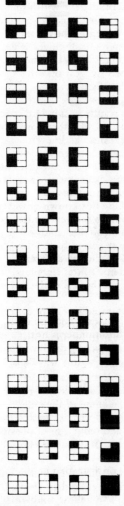

Figure 5. *Alternative cell configurations in the graphics mode*

of character positions on the screen and the use of the dot matrix method of character generation. It is, however, worth considering the implications of these before looking at the more detailed aspects of character design.

The number of rows of characters into which the screen is divided determines resolution, in terms of the number of scan lines per character height, and also the maximum physical size of the characters on a screen of given dimensions. Their visual size will, of course, be a function of screen size and viewing distance. The number of characters per row in relation to the number of rows determines the width to height ratio of the dot matrix on which the characters are constructed and this has considerable implications for the design of the characters themselves. None of these factors has been systematically investigated specifically in relation to teletext and Viewdata displays, but the results of experiments on similar kinds of display suggest that the present system is likely to give adequate — if less than optimal — legibility.

The fixed nature of the character positions results in standard spacing regardless of character width. Symbols such as *i, l* and *1* therefore tend to become isolated, and lengthy passages of text have an uneven texture. Word spacing is similarly inflexible, and it is therefore very difficult to justify copy, should this be required. Line spacing can only be varied by inserting whole line spaces, and this can sometimes create serious problems in the design of page layouts. The effects of these aesthetically sub-optimal features on legibility are not known however.

The use of a dot matrix for character generation severely limits the possibilities for character design. Research on similar kinds of display suggests, however, that a matrix of the size used for teletext and Viewdata is likely to give adequate legibility, though a larger matrix (in terms of the number of vertical and horizontal elements) would undoubtedly permit the design of more aesthetically pleasing characters, and possibly different fonts.

The character designs in current use are illustrated in Figure 6. It may be seen that for some characters the shape varies according to the manufacturer of the receiver. There would appear to be no published data on the relative legibility of these different shapes, and a comparative study, including other possible shapes, could prove very valuable. Research in slightly different contexts has suggested that as long as dot matrix characters are designed to look as much like roman characters as possible, it is almost inevitable that some of the characters will be confused with one another, but redesigning certain characters can often result in a favourable redistribution and reduction of possible sources of confusion. It is important, therefore, that designers should take an interest in the problem and attempt to persuade the manufacturers that small changes in character configuration could result in a more legible and more pleasing font.

In any future modifications of teletext and Viewdata characters, it is important that the implications of the self-luminous nature of the image should be taken fully into account. Such images are likely to require somewhat different width to height and stroke width to height

ratios and more generous character spacing than those which would be
optimal for characters on a printed page. The way in which the image is
built up is also significant. The on/off response of the electron beam is
not completely sharp and results in a degree of 'smearing' which has
implications for character design and spacing.

a a a a	q q q q	G G G G	W W W W W
b b b b	r r r r r r	H H	X X
c c	s s	I I	Y Y
d d d d	t t t	J J	Z Z
e e	u u u	K K	0 0 0 0 0
f f	v v v	L L	1 1
g g g g	w u	M M	2 2 2
h h	x x	N N	3 3
i i i i i i	y y y y	O O	4 4
j j j j	z z	P P	5 5
k k K	A A A A A A	Q Q	6 6
l l l l l l	B B	R R	7 7
m m m	C C	S S S	8 8
n n n n n n	D D D D D D	T T	9 9 9 9
o o	E E E	U U	
p p p p	F F F	V V U U U U	

Figure 6. *A comparison of the character fonts produced by various manufacturers (after Stokes, 1976)*

Graphics. In the case of alphanumerical characters built up from the
display rectangles of the graphics mode, the designer has every
opportunity of exerting an influence. Many of the fonts in current use
have been designed by editorial staff and are amateurish in appearance.
There is therefore a need for a series of related fonts designed by
professional type designers, possibly in collaboration with perceptual
psychologists. At present, however, there is no published research
relating to the legibility of characters of this kind. Certain basic
considerations, such as the importance of designing characters which
form a coherent font yet are easily distinguishable from one another,
will apply to the design of this kind of font as much as to any other,
but beyond this there is very little useful background information
available.

An important factor in the design of graphics alphabets for headings
is the amount of space that they consume. A display heading can
occupy as many as six of the available 24 lines, which may mean that
only about two-thirds of the frame area remains for the information
itself. There is therefore a need for a range of display faces which use
less space. Given the crudeness of the present graphics mode, the
possibilities are very limited however.

The use of colour. The way in which colour is used on these displays
will have a significant effect on legibility. The reasons for this are
related to the self-luminous nature of the image and the way in which
the colours are generated, and to the characteristics of the human
visual system (Kling and Riggs, 1972).

In relation to the screen image, one of the most important factors is the unequal luminance of the seven colours typically used. The white signal is obtained by mixing green, red and blue signals. If white is regarded as having a luminance of 100 per cent, then green has a luminance of 59 per cent, red 30 per cent and blue 11 per cent. The complementaries are each obtained by adding two primary signals, and thus yellow has a luminance of 89 per cent (green plus red), cyan 70 per cent (green plus blue) and magenta 41 per cent (red plus blue). The contrast which these colours make with the background therefore varies considerably. In terms of luminance alone, white, yellow, cyan and green in that order are likely to be the most legible colours, and magenta, red and blue the least. Red cannot, therefore, be used for emphasis in the same way as it is in print.

In addition to these differences in luminance, the fact that the human eye is not equally sensitive to all wavelengths of light must also be taken into account. When the eye is light adapted, as it normally would be when viewing teletext or Viewdata, it is maximally sensitive to wavelengths in the yellow/green area of the spectrum (Graham, 1965). Yellow is only 90 per cent as efficient a stimulus as green, and red is only 6 per cent as efficient. Blue in particular tends to have a lower subjective brightness than other colours, especially when viewed against a dark background (Ton, 1969). This differential sensitivity results in differences in acuity. Acuity is highest for white and green light. The eye's resolving power for red is only about 1/3 of that for white, and for blue it is only about 1/5 of that for white (Graham, 1965). On this basis it would seem that green and white are likely to be the most legible colours for self-luminous displays, and that red and blue should be avoided (Barmack and Sinaiko, 1966; Vanderkolk and Herman, 1975).

Yet another significant factor is the phenomenon of chromatic aberration. Different wavelengths of light are refracted by the eye to different degrees. This means that only one colour at a time can be in focus on the retina. If yellow/green or white are in focus, blue will be focused in front of the retina and red behind it. This not only results in reduced visual acuity for the out-of-focus colours, but it also causes differently coloured images to appear to be in different planes. This effect can be seen very clearly when red and blue are used in close proximity on a teletext or Viewdata receiver, and it can be disturbing. The same phenomenon also contributes to the apparent separation of the red and blue components of magenta. This is therefore not a good colour for substantial quantities of data.

If colour is to be used in a meaningful way, then viewers must be able to discriminate between and identify the colours used. Their ability to do this will depend on the luminance of the stimulus, its area, and the level of ambient illumination. Very high or very low stimulus luminance will cause difficulties in discrimination, as will very small areas of colour subtending less than 20 minutes of arc (Conover and Kraft, 1958). High levels of ambient illumination will interfere with discrimination of differences in saturation and hue. The eyesight of the viewer is also an important factor, since 8 per cent of men and

0.4 per cent of women suffer from some form of anomalous colour vision. Under suitable conditions, however, the average viewer should have no difficulty in discriminating between and uniquely identifying the seven colours in use on teletext and Viewdata. In one of the few experiments which are of direct relevance to televised alphanumerics, Haeusing (1976) found that at least six colour categories (excluding white) could be absolutely identified with an accuracy of 90 per cent or better for stimuli subtending 45 minutes or more. His six colours were red, yellow, green, cyan, blue and purple. He concluded, however, that for images subtending less than 30 minutes, cyan and yellow may become difficult to distinguish.

An additional factor which may become increasingly important is that of colour contrast. At present on most receivers it is only possible to display characters against a dark background, but in the future it will be possible to display a character of any colour on a background of any colour.

When two colours are presented in close juxtaposition in this way, the perception of each colour is modified by the presence of the other (Ton, 1969). Colours of relatively high and low luminances presented side by side appear respectively lighter and darker than if viewed alone, while adjacent colours of high and low saturation appear respectively more or less saturated than if viewed alone. The use of background colour will, however, result in considerable losses in luminance contrast between image and background, and this will almost certainly have a marked effect on legibility. Research on the implications of this new facility is therefore badly needed.

The evidence available therefore suggests that for large quantities of information, green is likely to be one of the most legible colours because it is produced by a single electron gun and the image is therefore sharp, it has adequate luminance, and it is one of the colours to which the eye is most sensitive and for which acuity is greatest. White, yellow and cyan are also likely to be highly legible, provided that the colour registration on the receiver is properly adjusted. Magenta is not recommended because of the tendency of its red and blue components to separate out visually, and red and blue are unsuitable because they have low luminance values, the eye is relatively insensitive to them, and the effects of chromatic aberration will result in a blurred image.

Ways of indicating information structure

INFORMATION DENSITY AND CODING

The display area available on each frame is relatively limited, especially as some of the 24 lines will be occupied by the page heading and other essential information. In some cases only two-thirds of the frame area may remain for the information itself. There is therefore a tendency on the part of editorial staff to want to include as much information as possible in the remaining area, particularly in situations where the viewer is required to pay for each frame he accesses. This aim is sometimes achieved at the expense of comprehensibility however.

The extensive use of symbols and non-standard abbreviations, the omission of space after punctuation and frequent non-standard word breaks are commonplace. In some cases this dense packing may offer the advantage of allowing a given amount of information to be accommodated in a single frame, thus giving the user an overview of the content. If, however, the display is incomprehensible as a result, the user's task would be quicker and easier if the information were presented more clearly over a larger number of frames.

The shortage of space means that only essential information can be given. Its structure must then be made clear by means of a coding system of some kind. If the information is visually coded in terms of its importance, this will allow the user to appreciate its hierarchical structure. If different kinds of information are coded, this will often allow him immediately to disregard information which is not directly relevant to his needs, thus reducing its apparent density. In printed materials, this kind of coding would, of course, be achieved by means of typographic variations or the use of space. On teletext and Viewdata the possibilities for both of these kinds of coding are limited, but there is the opportunity to use colour coding.

TYPOGRAPHIC CODING

Whereas in printed information changes in type size, style, weight or case might normally be used to indicate different levels or kinds of information, the only possibilities for typographic coding in standard alphanumerics on teletext and Viewdata are the use of double height characters or capitals. Either may be suitable for headings, though the double height characters will occupy two lines instead of one. Capitals are not suitable for extensive use, however, because they are almost certainly less legible than a mixture of upper and lower case. This is because the capitals are of uniform height, and they therefore result in less distinctive word shapes than the lower case letters with their ascenders and descenders. Large blocks of capitals tend to have a solid and impenetrable appearance, whereas lower case text has a more open texture as a result of the additional space created between the lines.

In the graphics mode there is more scope for typographic coding of headings, though these will occupy a considerable amount of space and will therefore be unsuitable for use in many situations.

SPATIAL CODING

In printed materials, spatial coding can usually be freely used to separate different levels and kinds of information or to relate similar kinds of information. On teletext and Viewdata, however, space cannot be used so freely because of the limited number of character positions available; an over-generous use of space will fragment the information into an unnecessarily large number of frames. It is important, however, that the information should be spatially coded to some extent so that the display does not become too dense and confusing. This is particularly important in view of the fact that some Prestel users will have monochrome receivers. A form of spatial coding which does not increase the use of space is positional coding. This is often used in the header lines of teletext and Viewdata displays, where the position of certain items of information is constant and provides a means of identification. Whatever the extent to which spatial coding is used over any given sequence of pages, its use should be consistent in relation to the structure of the information.

COLOUR CODING

The availability of colour can be used to compensate to some extent for the limited possibilities for typographic and spatial coding. As we have seen, however, the colours do not have equal legibility, and the number of colours which can safely be used for standard alphanumerics is four, ie white, yellow, cyan and green. Ideally, not more than three of these colours should be used on any one frame. Research has shown that if three or four colours are used in a target detection task on a CRT display, items of the same colour tend to form a *gestalt* and are easily distinguished from the rest of the display (Cahill and Carter, 1976). If more colours are used, the information becomes too fragmented and the *gestalt* is lost. The temptation to use as many colours as possible, simply because they are available, should be strongly resisted. The functional use of a small number of colours will be far more effective.

To date, the use of colour has often been indiscriminate and illogical. Shaw (1978) has noted that in some cases its use has been associative, the choice of colour being related to the meaning of the words rather than to the structure of the information. This can cause confusion because some colours will appear more dominant than others as a result of the differences in luminance. Thus a hierarchical relationship between items of information may be implied where none exists, or one which does exist may be misrepresented or not represented at all. It is important, therefore, that the choice of colours should relate to the structure of the information.

Colour coding can be used in a number of different ways to indicate structure. It may be used to give emphasis to particular words or phrases, in the same way that italics or bold might be used in print. It can also be used to indicate several categories of importance, for example in hierarchical systems of headings and subheadings or paragraphs and sub paragraphs. Alternatively it may be used to distinguish between different kinds of information which are of approximately the same importance. Finally, colour may be used to divide and relate information, as in tables and indexes for example.

Where colour is used to indicate levels of emphasis, the colours can be chosen to represent this hierarchy in the same way as typographic variations would be chosen for printed materials. Assuming that the brightest colours will be perceived as being the most dominant, the order of importance of the four most legible colours on teletext and Viewdata will be white, yellow, cyan and green. This would suggest that white or yellow might be used for headings and subheadings and cyan or green for text. If it is required to distinguish between items of information without suggesting any difference in importance, then two

217

colours as close as possible in the hierarchy might be used, such as white and yellow or cyan and green.

BLINK CODING

It is also possible to code items of information by causing them to flash on and off. This is extremely distracting, however, and likely to be very fatiguing over long periods. Its usefulness is very limited therefore.

Presentation of text, tables, indexes and graphics

TEXT

There are no directly relevant guidelines available for the presentation of text, but certain general principles can be derived from experiments on printed materials. For example, it is not advisable to fill every page to full capacity. Studies on printed materials have shown that text with a generous amount of space within it is rated as being 'easier' and more interesting than text which has a more solid appearance (Smith and McCombs, 1971). Jackson (1979) has reported that the ratio of page capacity to the number of displayed characters has been found to be typically about 3:1 for Viewdata displays, ie about 350 characters or 70 words.

Each page should be self-contained, because it will take several seconds for the next page to be written up. This will be sufficient for the viewer's concentration to be broken. The delay will be particularly disruptive if it occurs partway through a paragraph, or worse still, in mid-sentence. Ideally, page-breaks should correspond with a change of subject, even at the expense of leaving some pages short.

For most purposes, it would seem that a single-column layout will be preferable. The maximum line length of 40 characters is already shorter than the 50 or 60 characters which research has suggested is optimum for printed text (Tinker, 1963). Lines of less than 20 characters in length would result in a large number of word breaks, and a considerable wastage of space. It has been suggested in the past that a vertical sequence of words or phrases might allow the reader to grasp a whole concept at a glance, but it has not been shown that these arrangements are superior to the conventional horizontal sequence of words in terms of reading speed and comprehension (Coleman and Hahn, 1966; Carver, 1970). The wording itself will almost certainly be more legible in a mixture of upper and lower case than in capitals only.

The evidence on legibility discussed above suggests that large bodies of continuous text should be in green or cyan. In certain situations it may be desirable to emphasize certain words within the text. In print this would normally be done by the use of italics or bold. On teletext and Viewdata the alternatives are to use capitals or another colour. Words in capitals within upper and lower case text are not aesthetically pleasing, but on the other hand, use of a strongly contrasting colour is likely to attract too much attention and to interfere with the normal reading pattern. If emphasis of this kind is essential, the best solution may be to use a colour which is close to the text colour in the hierarchy, thus minimizing the effect. Cyan might be used for emphasis in green text, and yellow in cyan text. If such distinctions are made, however, it may then be difficult to limit the total number of colours used on a page to three. The value of this kind of coding must therefore be carefully assessed. Experiments on the use of typographic cueing devices such as underlining and colour in print suggest that cueing of particularly significant words or phrases may result in greater immediate retention of the material under certain circumstances, but in general it has no measurable effect (Klare, Mabry and Gustafson, 1955; Hershberger and Terry, 1965; Crouse and Idstein, 1972; Coles and Foster, 1975).

Given the existence of colour coding, teletext and Viewdata editors will sometimes omit normal punctuation where a colour change occurs. Besides being ungrammatical, this could cause considerable confusion on monochrome receivers. Where punctuation is used, the character space which would normally be left after a punctuation mark is often omitted. The result is aesthetically displeasing and it can give rise to confusion where the omission of a character space appears to relate words which are in fact unrelated. Hyphenation should also be kept to a minimum because its incidence seems much more noticeable and distracting in these displays than in print.

Ideally, paragraphs should be separated by a line space. This will prevent the text from forming a daunting solid block. Shaw (1978) suggests that paragraphs should be between three and six lines in length. This prevents the page from becoming disjointed, yet gives a sense of spaciousness and accessibility. Where line spacing is used, indentation of the first line of each paragraph will be unnecessary. Similarly, there will be no necessity for a change of colour between paragraphs simply to indicate that a new paragraph has begun. The use of colour in this way may cause the viewer to look for significance in the colour where there is none. Even where it is not possible to use a line space between paragraphs, the presentation of successive paragraphs in different colours should perhaps be avoided unless it has some special meaning. Instead, it may be possible, for example, to draw the first word of a new paragraph into the margin by one character. Alternatively, or in addition, the first word of a new paragraph might be in the next highest colour in the hierarchy.

In some cases it may be necessary to indicate a change of subject by placing headings between paragraphs. Double height characters will normally occupy too much space to be suitable for use in this way. The most satisfactory solution is likely to be a heading in upper and lower case which is distinguished from the text by its colour. The heading may be preceded by a line space, but it need not necessarily be followed by one. The selected colour should be more dominant than the text colour but less dominant than the main page heading, if there is one.

Headings should be ranged left. The centering of headings provides no advantage, and it tends to disrupt the normal pattern of eye movements. The eye naturally swings back to the left-hand margin at the end of each line, and centered headings may even be missed initially and necessitate regressive eye movements.

Where there is insufficient space for headings to stand alone on a line, it may be possible to incorporate them into the paragraph itself. Shaw (1978) has suggested that a change of subject might be indicated by stating the new subject in the first few words of a new paragraph and coding these words in a more dominant colour. This depends on the text being written so that the subject is encapsulated in the first few words of the paragraph however. It is therefore necessary for the editor and the designer to work in close collaboration.

TABLES

As in print, the case with which tabular material on teletext or Viewdata can be understood will depend on the logic behind the tabulation. The structure of the table should be as simple as possible, and should relate to the way in which it will be used. The information which the user already has should be given in the row or column headings, and the information which he seeks should be given in the body of the table (Wright, 1977). Where a table might be arranged either as a series of rows or as a series of columns, the choice will depend partly on how the information fits best into the frame area. Ideally, however, items which need to be compared, either in the headings or the body of the table, should be listed one below the other (Woodward, 1972).

As a general rule, only essential information should be given in tables designed for teletext or Viewdata. It is important, however, that the information is given as fully as possible so that the user has to do the minimum amount of work in extracting the information he needs. Abbreviations should be used sparingly, particularly if a key is required. Keys should always be given on the same frame as the abbreviations to which they refer. Using the minimum of abbreviations will sometimes mean that the information occupies a larger number of frames, but in many instances the added clarity will more than compensate for this.

The possibilities for the layout of tables are somewhat limited by the rigidity of the grid. Line and column spacing can only be varied in units of a whole character. Where users need to read across between columns the space between them should be sufficient to separate them but no more. Wide column spacing will increase the risk of error in adjacent columns. Unnecessary rules between columns will be distracting, tending to draw the eye down the columns instead of across them.

Colour coding can be useful as a substitute for, or adjunct to, spatial and typographic coding. In certain situations where relatively wide column spacing is unavoidable, the use of two colours on alternate lines may be useful in guiding the eye across from column to column. In this situation the two colours used should be as close together in the hierarchy as possible, to avoid any suggestion of dominance by one or other of the colours. Where column spacing is close, however, the colour coding will not be necessary and may introduce an unnecessary distraction. Colour coding of columns will not serve any useful purpose in tables where the user will be reading across each row, since it will be dividing associated items of information instead of relating them. It will tend to draw the eye down the page instead of across, in the same way as a vertical rule. Wording in tables should be in upper and lower case so that it can be easily distinguished from the numerical content.

LISTS AND INDEXES

One of the commonest forms of index, on Viewdata in particular, is the index to the data base. Routeing instructions usually consist of a three digit number on teletext pages and a single digit on Viewdata. These are often best placed to the left of the indexed item. Right-ranged numbers can result in mistakes in reading across unless adequate guidance is given, for example by leader dots. Research on tables has shown that the arrangement of two columns of information in a table is immaterial, so long as it is consistent (Wright and Fox, 1970). If there is a strong reason for not putting page numbers or routeing on the left, they can often be given immediately after the item in question rather than ranged right. This will eliminate the problem of reading across between columns.

The degree of distinction which should be made between successive items in a list will depend on the nature of the information. Where the entries are listed in some non-alphabetical order, the presence of the page number or routeing will often be sufficient to indicate a new entry. Line spaces between entries may be helpful if there is sufficient space available. The use of line spacing or colour to group items which are related in terms of subject matter may not be particularly beneficial however, unless the reason for the grouping is obvious or explicit. In lists and indexes where the entries are arranged alphabetically, it will be helpful if the first word of each entry is clearly distinguished in some way. This can be achieved by indenting the second and subsequent lines of each entry, or by colour coding the first word. The use of a two column format may be appropriate for lists and indexes with relatively short entries.

GRAPHICS

Logos and decorative devices. The place of decoration for its own sake needs to be carefully considered in relation to both teletext and Viewdata. In items which are essentially magazine material, the use of decorative graphics may be eye catching and attractive. In frames which are intended to convey serious information, however, excessive use of graphics may detract from the information itself and limit the amount of space available for it.

Where the use of logos and other decorative devices is appropriate, it is important that the design should be aesthetically pleasing and professionally executed. Given the limitations of the present graphics mode, considerable skill is required to prevent graphics from looking crude and amateurish.

Page headings. Headings in alpha-graphics are extravagant in terms of the amount of space they use. The information carried in the page heading will often be partially redundant because the user has deliberately accessed the page and therefore requires only a confirmation of its identity. Large headings tend to dominate the page and give a top-heavy appearance, and ordinary alphanumerics or possibly double-height characters will therefore be more suitable for most page headings. Sometimes headings are placed at the bottom of the page rather than the top. This allows the user to begin reading the information itself immediately.

Graphs, charts and diagrams. Any graph or chart presented on teletext or Viewdata must be kept extremely simple. Line graphs are difficult to produce satisfactorily, given the limitations of the graphics mode. Lines can be built up by the appropriate choice of graphics cells, but the discrepancy in cell sizes tends to be very obvious in this kind of display. Colour coding of the lines is likely to be extremely helpful, but even when contiguous colour is achieved, cross-over points will be difficult to represent accurately. The number of lines which can be represented will depend on how often they cross one another. In most cases, two or three lines per graph is likely to be the maximum.

Bar graphs are often a useful alternative to line graphs and are perhaps more suitable for the medium, given the limitations of the present graphics mode. Where the bars in a chart are made up of several different variables, these can be colour coded. The number of colours used on any one graph or chart should be kept to a minimum however, and care must be taken not to suggest non-existent relationships between colours in the chart and coloured wording elsewhere on the frame. The introduction of background colour will mean that bars can be banded in units smaller than a whole graphics rectangle if necessary. In vertical bar charts, however, the uneven division of the graphics rectangle is likely to become apparent.

Diagrams. The presentation of diagrams such as maps on teletext and Viewdata will be greatly enhanced by the introduction of contiguous and background colour. This will mean that more precise boundaries can be drawn between adjacent areas of colour, and captions can be superimposed directly on the coloured background. Careful studies of the legibility of the various colour combinations will therefore be necessary.

Conclusions

It may be seen from the above that teletext and Viewdata offer an almost unique set of problems in relation to the effective presentation of information. Yet because the medium is less than perfect for reading, it is all the more important that the presentation in terms of layout and the use of colour should be optimal. The design of these displays can present a challenging logical exercise which should surely appeal to many designers. A relatively small proportion of the information currently available on teletext and Viewdata has been influenced by designers, and the lack of their special expertise is often very obvious. Collaboration between editorial staff and designers would undoubtedly result in pages which would not only be more pleasing, but also easier to use. In the short term the designer could make a significant contribution simply by his approach to the problems and his experience with other media, but in the longer term there is a need for research on some of the problems specifically related to these displays.

References

Barmack, I E and Sinaiko, H W (1966) *Human Factors Problems in Computer Generated Graphic Displays.* AD-636-170 Arlington, Virginia: Institute for Defense Analyses

Cahill, M C and Carter, R C (1976) Colour code size for searching displays of different density. *Human Factors* 18 3: 273-80

Carver, R P (1970) The effect of a 'chunked' typography on reading rate and comprehension. *Journal of Applied Psychology* 54 3: 288-96

Coleman, E B and Hahn, S C (1966) Failure to improve readability with a vertical typography. *Journal of Applied Psychology* 50: 434-6

Coles, P and Foster, J (1975) Typographic cueing as an aid to learning from typewritten text. *Programmed Learning & Educational Technology* 12: 102-8

Conover, D W and Kraft, C (1958) *The Use of Colour in Coding Displays.* United States Air Force, WADC TR 55-471

Crouse, J H and Idstein, P (1972) Effects of encoding cues on prose learning. *Journal of Educational Psychology* 63: 309-13

Graham, C H (1965) Discriminations that depend on wavelengths. In C H Graham (ed) *Vision and Visual Perception.* New York: Wiley

Haeusing, M (1976) Colour coding of information on electronic displays. Proceedings of the 6th Congress of the International Ergonomics Association and Technical Program of the 20th Annual Meeting of the Human Factors Society, July 1976, 210-17

Hershberger, W A and Terry, D F (1965) Typographic cueing in conventional and programmed texts. *Journal of Applied Psychology* 49 1: 55-60

Jackson, R (1979) Television text: first experiences with a new medium. In P Kolers, M E Wrolstad and H Bouma (eds) *Processing of Visible Language 1.* New York: Plenum

Kinghorn, J R (1975) Character rounding for alphanumeric video display. *Mullard Technical Communications* no 126

Klare, G R, Mabry, J E and Gustafson, L M (1955) The relationship of patterning (under-lining) to immediate retention and to acceptability of technical materials. *Journal of Applied Psuchology* 39: 40-2

Kling, J W and Riggs, L A (1972) *Woodworth and Scholsberg's Experimental Psychology.* London: Methuen

Shaw, G (1978) A review of broadcast teletext as an information service. Department of Graphic Information, Royal College of Art, London (unpublished report)

Smith, S L and McCombs, M E (1971) The graphics of prose. *Journalism Quarterly* 48: 134-6

Stoke, S A (1976) Teletext. Department of Typography and Graphic Communication, University of Reading (unpublished BA dissertation)

Tinker, M A (1963) *Legibility of Print.* Ames: Iowa State University Press

Ton, W H (1969) Optimal visual characteristics for large screen displays. *Information Display* 6 4: 48-52

Vanderkolk, R J and Herman, J H (1975) *Dot Matrix Display Symbology Study.* TRC Report no T76-2172, July

Woodward, R M (1972) Proximity and direction of arrangement in numeric displays. *Human Factors* 14: 337-43

Wright, P (1977) Presenting technical information: a survey of research findings. *Instructional Science* 6: 93-134

Wright, P and Fox, K (1970) Presenting information in tables. *Applied Ergonomics* 1: 234-42

4.3 Publishing system equipment options: word processors

F LAURENCE KEELER

(First published as Appendix C of Keeler, F L (1977) An automated
publishing system for the US Naval Education and Training Command
Training Analysis and Evaluation Group: Report No 50, Orlando,
Florida. Reproduced with permission.)

A number of different options are available in the selection of the
equipment to be used in any publishing system. Not only hardware
costs, but its ease of use and relationship to other equipment
components are important. The following paragraphs describe briefly
various equipment components available for use, the functions for
which they are applicable, and the relative merits of their use in
accomplishing that function.

Monospaced typewriter

This is the conventional office typewriter. It is versatile in that it may
be used in the encoding, editing, and composing functions. Figure 1
depicts the information flow in a monospaced typewriter system. In
addition, the hardware cost is low and, if it is properly maintained, it
can produce clean copy in lieu of typesetting. However, it lacks several
features offered by other more sophisticated equipment, a deficiency
which seriously limits its effectiveness. In particular, the editing
function requires extensive re-keystroking which is eliminated in other
equipment by the use of a modifiable, magnetic storage medium. Of
equal importance in a large-volume publishing system is the composition
limitation imposed by the monospaced type. Monospaced type derives
its name from the equal horizontal spacing assigned to each character.
This equal spacing requires more space to accommodate the same
amount of text because each character is assigned a space equal to that
required by the widest character. This typically results in 20 to 25 per
cent less text per page or, conversely, requires 20 to 25 per cent more
pages for the same amount of text. In addition, the range of style and
sizes of typefaces is very limited with the monospaced typewriter.

Magnetic card equipped word processor

This is very similar to the monospaced typewriter with the exception
that it is equipped with a modifiable storage medium which permits the
operator to capture keystrokes on a mag-card during the encoding
process. This permits unchanged text to be read from the mag-cards
during the editing process, thus eliminating the necessity of re-
keystroking unchanged text. This has been shown to reduce the labour
required in editing up to 50 per cent. Figure 2 depicts the information

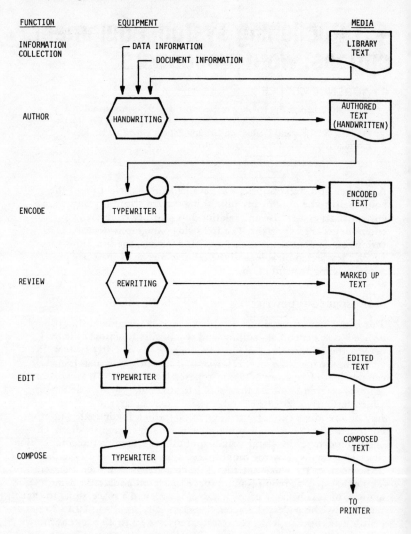

Figure 1. *Information flow in a typewriter based system*

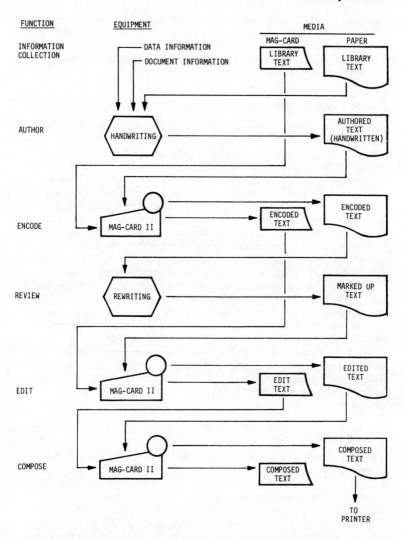

Figure 2. *Information flow in a mag-card II based system*

flow in a magnetic card based system. The hardware costs are greater than those for the monospaced typewriter but still moderate ($130 per month rental including maintenance). The other characteristics of the magnetic card equipped word processor are identical to those of the monospaced typewriter.

Video Display Terminal (VDT) equipped Word Processor

This is similar to the magnetic card equipped word processor, but is equipped with a cathode ray tube video display which provides a window into the memory. This allows the operator to see what is stored on the modifiable magnetic medium without having to wait for it to be printed out as is required with less sophisticated machines. As a rule, the modifiable medium used for storage is a floppy disc, instead of a magnetic card, which results in further labour savings because a floppy disc will accomodate approximately 100 pages of text as opposed to the single page stored on a magnetic card.

The VDT machines are usually equipped with automatic search, replace and move capabilities so that a particular string of text may be manipulated anywhere within a page, greatly facilitating the editing process. The labour-saving features offered by the VDT word processor reportedly result in twice the overall output of the magnetic card equipped word processor and up to six times the output of a standard typewriter. Figure 3 depicts the information flow in a VDT word processor based system. The hardware costs of the VDT word processor are significantly higher than those of the magnetic card equipped word processor ($610 per month including maintenance). The remaining characteristics of the VDT word processor are the same as those of the monospaced typewriter and the mag-card II word processor.

Text editor system

The text editor system is a multi-terminal device, similar to the VDT word processor. Its primary usefulness also lies in the encoding and editing functions. It differs from the other encoding/editing devices discussed in that the terminals are not stand-alone devices. The text editor system has a central processing unit (CPU), which acts as a controller for all of the terminals, input/output tape devices, a printer, and an on-line memory device. Figure 4 depicts a typical text editor system hardware configuration and the typical information flow in a text editor system. Because of each terminal's ability to share the same CPU without interfering with each other, a result of the inherently high speed of electronic computers, more powerful editing features may be built into the text editor system than could be cost-justified in stand-alone devices. Two such features are global search and replacement of text strings in multi-page documents and moving text from any place in a file to any other file in memory. An important distinction between word processors and text editor systems lies in their approach to document maintenance. The word processor maintains the document in pages. The text editor system maintains the document as a continuous

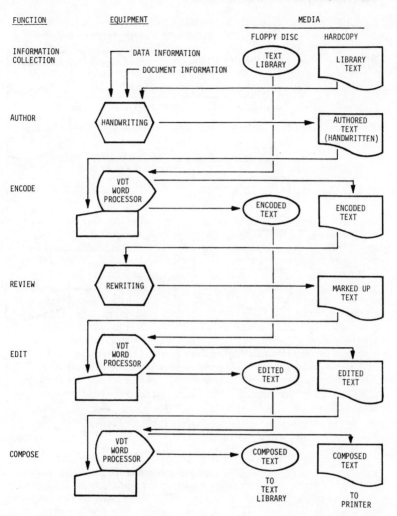

Figure 3. *Information flow in a VDT word processor based system*

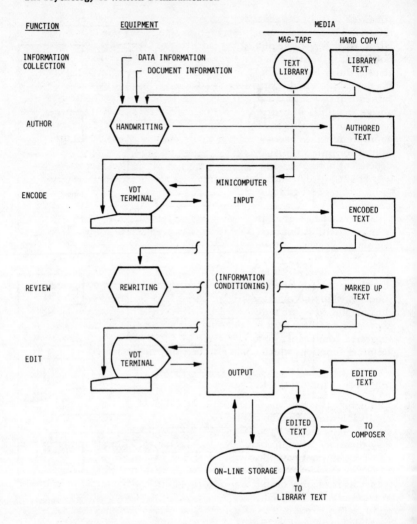

Figure 4. *Information flow in a text editor based system*

stream of text. In the general office environment, this makes little difference because the usual document is generally a one or two page letter. However, in the publishing environment, the typical working document is the size of a chapter, and it is more convenient to be able to use editing features which operate on the whole document. Thus, if a paragraph is added, it will not be necessary to reformat all subsequent pages, or if a stream of text is to be replaced, to 'search' a page at a time. Of course the text editor system should (and does) have an automatic means for breaking the continuous text stream up appropriately into pages whenever a hard copy is produced by the printer for review. The hardware cost of a text editor system is dependent upon the number of terminals. A text editor system would cost about $77,000 with four terminals, or about $92,000 with nine terminals. (A text editor system can support up to 32 terminals with a single CPU.)

An important feature of the text editor system which has not yet been discussed is that the CPU is in reality a general purpose mini-computer. Because of this, it is flexible, thus new user-defined functions may easily be incorporated by a change to the software. One user defined function which might be useful would be an automatic dictionary look-up of all words as a check for spelling. Another useful function would be an automated measure of the readability index, thus helping to assure that the published material is written at an appropriate reading level for the reader. The two special functions suggested could easily be incorporated by a software change, and there are other functions which could also be easily implemented.

Magnetic tape selectric composer

This is similar to the magnetic card word processor in that it has a modifiable storage medium, but many pages of text may be stored on one magnetic tape as opposed to one page per magnetic card. Its use may therefore result in some labour savings in the editing function. However, it is not equipped with a VDT, so it does not offer the labour-saving advantages of a VDT word processor. Its major advantage is that its hard copy output is proportional-spaced typing. That is, the horizontal space assigned to each character is proportional to the width actually required by that letter, with the result that the same text may be printed in 20 to 25 per cent less space than that required with monospaced type. In addition, proportional spaced type is more easily read and aesthetically pleasing to the eye. Like the monospaced typewriter and word processors, the range of sizes and styles of type-faces is still limited. The hardware cost ($380 per month) is only slightly more than that of the magnetic card word processor.

Typesetter

A typesetter is an opto-mechanical or electro-opto-mechanical device which is capable of optically generating proportionally spaced characters from the text stored on a magnetic medium. The range of different styles and size of typefaces available is usually in the hundreds.

231

Text which has been typeset can be easily read and, at the same time, be the most aesthetically pleasing. But the major advantage of typesetting is in the savings in paper and printing costs which may be had through its use. The hardware cost of a typesetter is relatively high ($100,000 plus $8,000 a year for maintenance), but the resulting savings in paper and printing costs might offset this expense.

Composers

The high speed typesetter discussed may not read the text to be typeset directly from the magnetic storage medium produced by the text editor or word processor but must have typesetting command codes inserted into the text stream by a device called a composer. These typesetting commands convey the information required to format the text into pages; eg information to change typefaces, add leading (space between lines), reverse leading (move up the page to start a new column), as well as inter-letter and inter-word spacing information. The composer must have width information stored for each character of each style and size of typeface used by the typesetter so that it may automatically make end-of-line and end-of-page decisions.

Two types of composer are available: a stand-alone single-terminal version, and a multi-terminal or cluster version. The multi-terminal composer has a CPU which acts as a controller for all of the terminals, input/output tape drives, printer and on-line memory device. The single-terminal stand-alone composer has a smaller CPU which controls a single terminal and the other peripheral devices. Dollar for dollar, a multi-terminal composer is usually more powerful than a stand-alone single-terminal composer, but this is applicable only if the work load is sufficient to require the operation of several terminals. On the other hand, some of the manufacturers of the stand-alone composers have attempted to capture the market of stand-alone word processor users by designing their stand-alone composers to accept word processor floppy discs or mag-tapes as input text. Such a stand-alone single-terminal composer costs about $60,000. By way of comparison, a multi-terminal composer would cost about $125,000 with two terminals, or about $195,000 with 12 terminals. (A multi-terminal composer is limited to about 12 terminals per CPU in order to avoid processing delays.)

4.4 A computerized conferencing system

STARR ROXANNE HILTZ

(Excerpt from Hiltz, S R (1978) Impact of a computerized conferencing system upon scientific research specialities. *Journal of Research Communication Studies* 1: 117-24. Extract reproduced with permission of the author and the publishers.)

The Electronic Information Exchange System (EIES)

A computer conferencing system uses a computer to store, process, and deliver written communications among the members of a group. Each participant uses a computer terminal, which is like an electric typewriter, with either a hard copy or a TV screen-like (CRT) display, to communicate with other members of the system. The terminal is connected to a telephone, and the communication is sent over telephone lines to be stored in the computer. The information is then delivered on the terminals of the persons to whom it is directed, either immediately, if they happen to be 'on line', or the next time that they connect into the system. Thus, the computer can bridge both time and space barriers, enabling group members who are dispersed around North America to communicate at their convenience.

There are four main communications capabilities or structures within the EIES system, designed by Murray Turoff at the New Jersey Institute of Technology for different types of scientific communications. These are displayed in Table 1.

A *message* may be addressed to one individual, many specific individuals, or to a whole group. The time and date of receipt of the message by each individual recipient is confirmed to the sender; two or three months later it disappears from the system. The content, like that of the informal one-to-one communication channels that it is meant to replace, can vary from chatty 'How are you? What's new?' messages to a request for assistance or information related to a specific problem in one's research.

For the experimental phase of use of EIES, the scientific user groups are seen as varying from about ten to fifty individuals, though such systems could conceivably accommodate a scientific specialty group of two hundred or more. One sends a message to the whole group by simply listing its name or number when asked who the message is to. One thing that group messages seem to be used for at present, besides broadcasting general requests for information on a research problem, is for announcements of the availability of drafts of preliminary research findings, or of completed but as yet unpublished papers.

As with all other entries in EIES, one may choose not to divulge one's identity by signing a message, but instead have the message sent anonymously, or with a pen-name. This is meant to enable people to feel free to say critical or controversial things.

A *conference* is a topic-oriented discussion in which a permanent transcript is built up of the proceedings. A conference will typically last from a week to a few months. Participants enter and leave the discussion at their convenience, taking as long as they need to reflect on previous entries or to consult references or data before responding.

A conference entry can be given an association number, noting the earlier items to which it is related. A participant can be helped to review and organize the proceeding by asking to see all of the entries that are associated with a specific one. One can also review the entries by asking to see, for instance, any that contain a certain keyword or phrase, such as 'side-effects', or 'validity'.

The *notebook* is the scientist's private on-line space for composing, storing and reorganizing items on which he or she is working. Within it, there are extensive computer-assisted editing routines (also available for conference or message or Bulletin entries). One can, for instance, delete a word or a part of a line and replace it with new text; switch lines or paragraphs around; make long inserts; use automatic formatting for tables. One can open designated pages of one's notebook to others for reading. For instance, after completing a draft of a paper, the scientist could send a group message inviting anyone interested to read it and comment. One can also open parts of the notebook to others to write in, thus facilitating remote co-authoring.

Structure and Feature	Replaces
Messages	
Individuals	Letters
Group	Telephone
Pen names or anonymous	Face to face conversations, visits
Conferences	
Permanent transcript	Face to face conferences or
Review	meetings
Association	
Voting	
Notebooks	
Editing	Sending of drafts or preprints
Formatting	Necessity for co-authors to be co-located
Bulletin	
	Newsletters
	Eventually perhaps journals and abstract services

Table 1. *EIES communication features*

The *Bulletin* is a public space, like an on-line newsletter. Any user of the EIES system can request the titles of Bulletin entries; and then the abstract and/or the full text, if something is of interest. The Bulletin feature is not yet operative, but it is expected that it will initially be used to publish short papers or discussions, 'letters', announcements of meetings or grants or job opportunities of interest to the specialty, etc. Eventually, it might carry full papers and abstracts of papers published elsewhere, thus becoming an on-line journal which facilitates the speedy review and publication of research results, and their selective dissemination to interested persons.

The current cost of the EIES facility (which will be covered by the US National Science Foundation for the scientific user groups) is $5.00 per hour for the computer and $3.50 per hour for the US nationwide Telenet communication link. These costs are expected to drop substantially during the next four years. The system is currently operational only for North America; however, within the year, access will be extended to European and perhaps other nations.

Part 5: Some Aspects of Scientific Communication

5.0 Introduction

'Ninety per cent of the world's scientists who have ever lived are alive today . . . two-thirds of scientific knowledge known to man has been discovered since the second world war . . . the sum total of knowledge will soon be doubling every year.' *Radio Times*, 3 November 1966

'Since the seventeenth century the literature of science has been growing at a steady and rapid rate (Price, 1975). The number of scientific journals has increased from one in 1665 to a current total of over 100,000. The number of scientific papers published annually has doubled every 12 to 15 years for the past 250 years. If science continues to grow at its current rate one million scientific journals will be available by the end of the century. To keep informed, researchers in the year 2000 will have to read four times as many papers as today's scientists read.' Kulik *et al* (1979)

'For a variety of reasons it seems very probable that learned journals will become obsolete in the future. Scientific information will be distributed in abstracts and stored in a form available for mechanical processing so that it can be automatically retrieved. But this will not make the scientific paper obsolete, although it may change its conventions.' Wason (Paper 5.1)

These quotations encapsulate the concerns of this part of this book. In Paper 5.1 we look at how one person views the writing of a scientific paper; in Paper 5.2 we examine different strategies for writing review articles; in Paper 5.3 we consider some of the biases present in the editorial and review practices of different journals; and in Paper 5.4 we consider the problems of simplification and condensation necessary in the writing of popular introductory textbooks.

Writing scientific papers

In Paper 5.1 Peter Wason expresses a personal point of view that strikes sympathetic chords with the editor of this text. We both indulge in a great deal of revision, and we both believe that writing helps the thinking process. However, it must be said that the dynamics of the writing process described by Wason are idiosyncratic. There may be similarities between writers but there are a great many differences too.

239

	Colleague A	Colleague B	Colleague C	Colleague D	Colleague E
Method of composing the 1st draft	typewriter	longhand	longhand	longhand	longhand and typewriter, revising as goes along a page at a time
Method of revising the 1st draft	typewriter and longhand	longhand	longhand	longhand	
Method of producing the 2nd draft	typewriter	typewriter	longhand	typewriter	longhand and typewriter as above, leading to final version
Method of revising the 2nd draft	typewriter and longhand	longhand	longhand	longhand leading to final version	
Method of producing the 3rd draft	typewriter	typewriter	secretary		
Method of revising the 3rd draft	typewriter and longhand	longhand	longhand – after receiving readers' comments		
Method of producing the final version (not necessarily the 4th draft)	secretary	secretary	secretary	secretary	secretary sometimes, but not always
Method of sequencing	Introduction first, of prime importance	Main elements in sequence	Main elements in sequence	Methods and results first, introduction last	Main elements in sequence

Table 1. *Simplified accounts of different strategies used by the writer's colleagues when writing scientific papers*

To assess the variety that might occur between individuals I asked several colleagues in my department at Keele about their methods of writing scientific papers. Some of the differences that emerged can be seen in Table 1, and some points of contrast are as follows:

Colleague A composes directly with a typewriter (with triple spacing and wide margins at the top, bottom and sides). He revises his manuscript, using a mixture of longhand and typewritten corrections, and continues by this procedure until he has a version (scissored and pasted, if necessary) from which a secretary can produce a clean, final version.

Colleague B, like the writer, composes and revises his first draft in longhand. He then types out his second draft, and revises it in longhand. This process continues until a meticulously prepared version, with only one or two corrections per page, is ready for a secretary to produce the final copy.

Colleague C is very similar to the writer. He composes and revises his first and second drafts in longhand. The resulting version is then given to a secretary for typing. Once the text is 'in print', consultation with others takes place, leading to major revisions, retyping, and further minor revisions before a final version is produced. Figures 3a and 3b in Paper 4.0, pp 195-6, illustrate this approach.

In addition to these global strategies we may note other differences of approach. Most colleagues write with specific journals in mind, but Colleague A does not ('They all have roughly the same format'). All would like to get the whole article done at one sitting (Wason's approach) but often time prevents this; so they work on one section at a time (eg introduction, method, results, discussion). Colleague A pays great attention to the introduction and does it first — to clarify his thinking. Colleagues B, C and E prefer to do the sections in the order in which they come, but Colleague D prefers to write first the method and results, then the discussion and finally the introduction, although, as he says, it is 'in his head' from the beginning. In all cases, the summary and abstract are the last sections to be written.

These accounts are simplifications. Writers to not proceed directly in stages or in sequence. There is much going to and fro. Most of my colleagues wanted to add the word 'usually' to my description of their strategies. Colleague E, in particular, found it difficult to think in terms of a numbered sequence of drafts. Furthermore, these procedures may strike our American colleagues as odd. In the United States, it is more common to compose on a typewriter and, these days, to use a word processor from the start.

Writing scientific articles can thus be seen as a goal-directed, hierarchically-organized activity. Editing frequently interrupts at any stage, and sections may be written at different times in different sequences. Indeed, goals may be modified as writing proceeds. The accounts given above fit in well with the model of writing proposed by Hayes and Flower (1979).

NEW DEVELOPMENTS

In concluding his article Wason comments that scientific progress is likely to change the conventions for writing scientific articles in the future. In a useful review, May Katzen (1978) has documented some of the changes that are now happening in this respect, and what we might expect to see in the future. The current economic situation is likely to result in more publishers trying various expedients, such as camera-ready copy (which eliminates the costs of setting and of proof-correcting); photocopied articles and theses on demand; microfilm; synoptic publications (eg the publication of lengthy abstracts rather than full articles); and journals of abstracts and critical commentaries. In the United States advances are being made with computer-based editorial processing centres, and with electronic journals with on-line transmission of text and print-out facilities. More humbly, there are developments with poster-sessions in conventional conferences (see Eisenschitz *et al*, 1979). Katzen (1978) documents these developments in the United States and Western Europe, and indicates the size and scope of international work in this field.

Writing reviews

The quotations given at the beginning of this introduction suggest that it is already difficult, and it will become even more difficult, for research workers to keep up with scientific developments. Despite the advent of computer-based retrieval systems, computer-conferencing and the like, there is a need for broad integrative reviews of work that has been done in particular areas. Journals such as *Psychological Review* and *Review of Educational Research* provide a valuable function in this respect. Citation studies have shown that review articles frequently become milestone papers, comparable in importance with experimental or theoretical papers in the same field (Garfield, 1977).

The strategies that writers use, however, in producing such reviews vary. The aim of Paper 5.2 is to describe and comment on these strategies and to highlight some of the problems that arise when reviewing a particular field. This paper was written in 1978, and if we were writing it today we would revise it slightly to emphasize more the review strategy that rejects the 'arithmetic summation', 'scoreboard', or 'tug-of-war' approach in favour of a more critical assessment of the studies involved (see, for example, the review by Macdonald-Ross, 1977). We would also stress further the use of reviews to test out new hypotheses and to make constructive suggestions (see, for example, the reviews by Klare, 1976, and Hartley and Davies, 1976, 1978). Finally, we would draw more attention than we did to the importance of secondary analysis and to meta-analysis (Glass, 1976). By meta-analysis is meant the analysis of analyses. (In other words, all the data on a particular issue is pooled in some way and a statistical analysis made of the results.) This approach, it is argued, is especially valuable where there are a great many studies on a particular topic.

The problem with meta-analysis is whether to include every study, however badly done, and face the accusation that 'garbage in leads to garbage out', or to be selective and get accused of bias. We would favour the latter approach, provided the criteria for selection were made clear. (Since the preparation of Paper 5.2 two interesting reviews using techniques of meta-analysis have appeared: Hall (1978) analysed the results of 75 studies that investigated the accuracy of males and females at decoding non-verbal communication, and Kulik *et al* (1979) examined the outcomes of 75 studies of Keller's Personalized System of Instruction.)

Editorial practices

One of the less pleasant experiences of academics is to have their papers —their progeny — rejected by journal editors and their referees. It is of interest, therefore, to report that editorial practices are now becoming the subject of research themselves.

In a recent monograph Michael Gordon (1978) examines the editorial arrangements of 33 British journals. The diversity revealed is somewhat eye-opening. The rejection rates for articles appear to be related to the subject matter of the journals. Journals in the physical sciences have the lowest rejection rates (about 20 per cent), followed by the life-sciences (about 50 per cent), social sciences (about 80 per cent) and finally philosophy —with *Philosophy* having a rejection rate of 92 per cent. These British results are similar to those found in the USA by Zuckerman and Merton (1971).

Psychologists will be interested to know that there are similar variations in psychology journals (which Gordon did not study). The average rejection rate of the journals published by the American Psychological Association is 76 per cent, but this varies from the *Journal of Comparative and Physiological Psychology* (55 per cent) to *Developmental Psychology* (90 per cent). (Figures from the *American Psychologist*, **34** 6: 537.) Data provided by the British Psychological Society is more obscure, but is reasonably similar. The average rejection rate (in 1978) appears to be about 80 per cent, with the highest being the clinical section of the *British Journal of Social and Clinical Psychology* (87 per cent) and the lowest the *British Journal of Psychology* (63 per cent).

Perhaps of more interest than rejection rates are the descriptions that Gordon provides of the editorial practices of different journals. The editor of *Philosophy*, for example, only used referees twice in five years, despite a submission rate of 300 articles a year and a rejection rate of 92 per cent. Similarly, the *Lancet* deals in-house with 95 per cent of its 3000 submissions a year.

Unfortunately, as noted above, Gordon did not include psychology journals in his sample. Bitter personal experience suggests that the editors of different psychology journals operate in different ways: it might well be helpful if they could discuss together the advantages and disadvantages of their various procedures.

Paper 5.3 provides an extract from Gordon's (1978) report which is concerned with what Gordon terms the 'unwitting bias' of referees. The biases that Gordon deals with in this paper are national and institutional. The possibility of sexual bias (which is not discussed by Gordon) is now also receiving attention. Teghtsoonian (1974), for example, examined the representation of men and women on the editorial boards of psychology journals, and found that the women were not as well represented as one might predict from their numbers as authors. Mischel (1974) found that journal articles attributed to women authors were evaluated less positively than when they were attributed to men in such fields as law and city planning, but that the opposite was true for articles written in areas of primary education and dietetics. Thus bias tended to occur in the direction of the judged appropriateness of the field. (Mischel found these results with American high school and college students, but was unable to replicate them with Israeli high school students.) More recently, Moore (1978) found that book reviewers in *Contemporary Psychology* (a journal of reviews) were biased towards authors of their own sex. Moore also found that women reviewers were more critical of books by male authors, but that the reverse did not hold true.

One way of attempting to avoid referee bias is, of course, to use the technique of 'blind reviewing'. Here papers are sent for refereeing without the authors' names or affiliations. At the time of writing, eight journals published by the American Psychological Association use blind reviewing, and so too do a number of journals published by the American Educational Research Association.

One study of blind reviewing is that of Tobias and Zibrin (1978). These authors selected out every third paper submitted for consideration for part of the programme of an American educational conference. Two versions of each paper (192 in all) were sent blind and two complete to independent referees. No significant differences were found between the judgements of the manuscripts which were refereed blind and those same manuscripts which were refereed normally. Tobias and Zibrin note, of course, that is is probably unwise to generalize from their results on refereeing conference submissions to refereeing journal articles. Finally, in connection with blind reviewing, we may note that it is difficult, especially if the authors are prominent ones, to delete references to them and their previous work.

So far, in this section on editorial practices, we have considered the problem of referee bias without considering the issues of consistency of judgement between referees, whether or not referees should be named or even the desirability of having referees at all. There is debate about the consistency of judgement between referees (see, for example, Scarr and Weber, 1978) and criteria have been suggested for aiding decision-making in refereeing journal articles (Gottfredson, 1978). One commentator has argued that referees would work more speedily and more diligently if their names were acknowledged (Garfield, 1973). The general opinion, however, seems to be that if referee bias is present it is not overly serious, and that it is preferable to have referees than to be without them. What appears to be needed most is a more open discussion and exchange of ideas about editorial practices between editors, referees and authors.

Writing textbooks

If journal editorial practices seem somewhat obscure (to writers), the same is true of publishing practices in general. There are a number of books about the process, but most of them seem to be more concerned with fiction than with academic publishing. Benjamin (1977) provides an entertaining commentary on the process (as well as a useful annotated bibliography) and Altbach and McVey (1976) present a number of useful chapters on textbooks, written by different specialists. An article by Powell (1978) describes publishers' decision-making in the context of the social sciences.

Whitten (1976) depicts a changing pattern in textbook production. Until the 1960s, he maintains, there was the 'traditional' text. An author would submit a proposal to a publishing house, perhaps with a synopsis and a draft chapter. The proposal would be sent for peer review and, if it was accepted, a contract would be drawn up. The author would agree to deliver the manuscript by a certain date (eg in a year's time) and he would receive an advance against his anticipated royalties, first for signing the contract and later for delivering the manuscript. The manuscript (rarely delivered on time) would generally contain few graphics, and those provided would be of poor quality. The text would be given to an in-house editor for checking and revision, and the publication process would then take about a year. The whole cycle would take, on average, from about four to six years.

The next stage, according to Whitten, was the introduction of the 'synthetic' text. The primary difference was that this text was commissioned from a prominent scholar by the publishers. Most of the content was known before the text was written, and what was required was a conventional treatment of the basic issues with one or two innovatory sections in order to outdo the opposition. The quality of the presentation and the graphics were much improved, and production was quicker. Such texts were typically revised every three to four years so that the latest innovations could be included and sales maintained.

The third stage (which arrived in 1970) was that of the 'managed' text. The chapters in the book, commissioned by the publishers on the basis of market research, were written by different authors and rewritten by professional writers. The book had no author, as such, but a prominent scholar might be named as editor. The time needed to produce the text was drastically reduced, and lower royalty rates were paid.

The first managed text in psychology was CRM's *Psychology Today*. It was a resounding success, selling over 186,000 copies in its first year at two dollars more than its competitors. As Whitten points out, however, there were a number of reasons for the success of the book other than the fact that it was a managed text: (a) *Psychology Today* was the title of an already well-known monthly magazine published by the same company; (b) 38 well-known psychologists acted as consultants for the book; (c) there was an exceptional use of coloured graphics and full-page colour illustrations; and (d) new marketing techniques (telephone sales and direct mailing) were employed.

Although Whitten depicts textbook production as going through evolutionary changes in America, I think it fairer to say that all three kinds of textbook are now being produced side by side. Aronson's (1972) *The Social Animal*, for example, is a classic example of a 'traditional' text which has sold over 260,000 copies at the time of writing. There are several 'synthetic' introductory textbooks in psychology and education and, indeed, these seem to be the most popular form, regularly being revised and vying with each other. There have been other 'managed' texts since 1970 but none has enjoyed the success of that first *Psychology Today*. The reasons for this are hinted at in Paper 5.4, written by James McConnell who was the overall editor of *Psychology Today*. McConnell describes this alarming experience, and how he learned from it to produce his own 'synthetic' text — *Understanding Human Behavior*.

References

Altbach, P G and McVey, S (eds) (1976) *Perspectives in Publishing*. Lexington, Mass: Heath

Aronson, E (1972) *The Social Animal*. New York: Freeman

Benjamin, C G (1977) *A Candid Critique of Book Publishing*. New York: Bowker

Eisenschitz, T M *et al* (1979) Poster sessions as a medium of scientific communication. *Journal of Research Communication Studies* 1: 235-42

Garfield, E (1973) Publishing referees' names and comments could make a thankless and belated task a timely and a rewarding activity. *Current Contents* 5 17: 5-7

Garfield, E (1977) Proposal for a new profession: scientific reviewer. *Current Contents* 9 14: 5-8

Glass, G V (1976) Primary, secondary and meta-analysis of research. *Educational Researcher* 10: 3-8

Gordon, M D (1978) A study of the evaluation of research papers by primary journals in the UK. University of Leicester: Primary Communications Research Centre

Gottfredson, S D (1978) Evaluating psychological research reports. *American Psychologist* 33 10: 920-34

Hall, J A (1978) Gender effects in decoding non-verbal cues. *Psychological Bulletin* 85: 845-57

Hartley, J and Davies, I K (1976) Pre-instructional strategies: the role of pre-tests, behavioural objectives, overviews and advance organizers. *Review of Educational Research* 46 2: 239-65

Hartley, J and Davies, I K (1978) Note-taking: a critical review. *Programmed Learning & Educational Technology* 15 3: 207-24

Hayes, J R and Flower, L S (1979) Identifying the organization of writing processes. In L W Gregg and E R Steinberg (eds) *Cognitive Processes in Writing Skills*. Hillsdale, NJ: Erlbaum (in press)

Katzen, M (1978) Trends in scholarly publications in the United States and Western Europe. Leicester University: Primary Communications Research Centre

Klare, G R (1976) A second look at the validity of readability formulas. *Journal of Reading Behavior* VIII 2: 129-52

Kulik, J A, Kulik, C C and Cohen, P (1979) A meta-analysis of outcome studies of Keller's Personalized System of Instruction. *American Psychologist* 34 4: 307-18

Macdonald-Ross, M (1977) How numbers are shown: a review of research on the presentation of quantitative information. *Audio Visual Communication Review* 25 4: 359-409

Mischel, H (1974) Sex bias in the evaluation of professional achievements. *Journal of Educational Psychology* 66 2: 157-66

Moore, M (1978) Discrimination or favoritism? Sex bias in book reviews. *American Psychologist* 33 10: 936-8

Powell, W W (1978) Publishers' decision making: what criteria do they use in deciding which books to publish? *Social Research* 45 2: 227-52

Price, D J (1975) *Science since Babylon.* New Haven, Conn: Yale University Press

Scarr, S and Weber, B L R (1978) The reliability of reviews for the American Psychologist. *American Psychologist* 33 10: 935

Teghtsoonian, M (1974) Distribution by sex of authors and editors of psychological journals, 1970-1972. *American Psychologist* 29: 262-9

Tobias, S and Zibrin, M (1978) Does blind reviewing make a difference? *Educational Researcher* 7 1: 14-16

Whitten, P (1976) The changing world of college textbook publication. In P G Altbach and S McVey (eds) *Perspectives in Publishing.* Lexington, Mass: Heath

Zuckerman, H and Merton, R C (1971) Patterns of evaluation in science: institutionalisation, structure and function of the reference system. *Minerva* IX 1: 66-100. (Reference and data cited by Gordon, 1978.)

Further reading

Altbach, P G and McVey, S (eds) (1976) *Perspectives in Publishing.* Lexington, Mass: Heath

O'Connor, M (1978) *Editing Scientific Books and Journals.* London: Pitman

The Journal of Research Communication Studies (Elsevier) which commenced publication in 1978, carries articles highly relevant to this section of the book.

5.1 On writing scientific papers

PETER WASON

(First published in the *Physics Bulletin* (1970) 21: 407-8.
Reproduced with permission of the author and the Institute
of Physics.)

'The relation of thought to word is not a thing, but a process, a
continual movement back and forth from thought to word and
from word to thought.' L S Vygotsky

At one time I believed that people who could think clearly could also
write clearly. This essay is about my disenchantment with this belief,
and about my own method of writing papers. First of all, its
limitations must be made explicit.

I am an experimental psychologist concerned with thinking and
language. Unlike physics, psychology is not yet an exact science, and
there is little agreement about which of its explanatory concepts are
likely to be most fruitful. This means that a psychological paper may
have a very different character from a physics paper. So when I was
invited to write on this problem I was acutely aware that my
experience may be totally irrelevant for the reader. I shall ignore this
apprehension and assume that scientific writing does present
difficulties which are not specific to any one science.

Clarity

Confusion is readily recognized in the writing of others. When writing
goes wrong we can usually find the fault but when it goes well we are
not conscious of any mechanisms which ease its progress: we attend
directly to what is said. For many years I have kept a file of 'golden
sentences', drafted by my research students, or noted in papers or
grant proposals which I have refereed. Here are sentences in which the
writers seemed blissfully unaware of their lack of clarity, sentences
in which obscure and pedantic expressions seemed to have been
deliberately chosen (for reasons best known to the authors), and long
sentences so 'embedded' that the memory is placed under an intolerable
strain. It would be unethical to quote examples. Instead, I shall content
myself with a single observation.

Sometimes people only have to be reminded that they are unclear in
order to liberate them from the words to which they were committed.
In supervising several PhD theses, I was struck by the fact that, when I
remarked on a bad sentence, the student would often immediately

utter a perfectly acceptable substitute for the monstrosity which had been perpetrated. This suggests, doesn't it, that when pen is put to paper something odd may happen to the expression of thought. But the crucial question is this: did these individuals know what they were trying to say, when they *originally* tried to say it, or only when its expression was subsequently queried? There is no simple answer to this question.

The dynamics of writing

My own practice, which may have some generality, is to write the complete first draft of a paper at a single sitting, as quickly as possible, even if it is disjointed and lacking in cohesion. I have then exteriorized my thoughts and can work upon them. Only then do I seem to grasp what I was really trying to say by noticing the errors in what I have in fact said. I suspect, however, that this is an illusion: it implies that I had failed to capture something which I already knew, but in fact the process is more like discovery than recollection.

The second draft is a critique of the first, but now unexpected connections and relations are spontaneously seen between the thoughts which had been written down first of all. The critical process of examining what has been said apparently induces the creative process of generating ideas. The cycle then repeats itself — a third draft may lead to further insights and to increased clarity. Thus a goal is both formulated and clarified *by* the process of writing; in striving to express ideas more clearly we learn more about them. How does one know when this goal has been reached? It might seem that successive drafting could degenerate into a never ending, obsessional ritual. There is, of course, no objective test for completion, but an intuitive criterion is acquired for the unity of a paper and the balance between its parts. Contrary to expectation, this criterion can be fulfilled quickly.

I first imagined this delayed feedback (as opposed to the immediate feedback which occurs when individual sentences are written) as a kind of dialectical relation between language and thought, the one changing the other and being changed by it. While error is corrected, a new synthesis seems to emerge from the tension aroused between words and thoughts. This crude analysis is misleading for technical reasons, but its practical consequences are compelling: if you want to think, then write. Martin (1957) has put this better: 'We do not *know* until we have *told*'.

This process leads to a hypothesis about the relation between interiorized and exteriorized thought. It owes something to the theorizing of cognitive psychologists such as Bruner, Piaget and especially Vygotsky, and its main point may be understood by considering what would make it wrong. It would be wrong if there were no correlation between successive drafts and the amount of relevant information they contained. It would not, of course, be sufficient to show that successive drafts were merely expressed better. And it would be necessary to show that the thoughts in the final draft would not have been reached (or reached so quickly) by simply pondering the first draft. The technical problems of testing this hypothesis are not insuperable, but other variables, such as the subject matter involved and the time interval elapsing between drafts, must also be investigated.

Planning

It is difficult to say more at the moment about the creative aspects of these dynamics. Their critical aspects, however, are more tangible. They consist to a large extent in correct planning. At about the stage of the second draft the critical scrutiny of the material coincides with the effort to impose organization, or form, upon it. How is this done?

Hebb and Bindra (1952) point out that the fundamental difficulty of verbal communication is 'to get an overview of a complicated structure that must be apprehended bit by bit'. A temporal pattern has to be transposed into a spatial one. This perspective is gained by making a series of decisions about the raw material in the first draft. It has to be decided what is really salient and what is merely corroborative; what inferences are warranted and from what evidence; what may be left implicit and what must be made explicit. And above all is the problem of seriation: the best order in which the different parts of the paper follow each other, and yet cohere into a single whole. Without this organization the reader feels as if he is walking through a wood, where no track is apparent and there is no landmark to be seen.

Organization is essential, but at the planning stage it is only a conceptual framework. Looked at sceptically, it is nothing but a list of headings and subheadings — directives about what to say and when to say it. These directives have to be executed. The paper has to be written.

Execution

Textbooks on expository writing prescribe rules of different kinds — rules of composition, of sentence structure and of usage. But as Hebb and Bindra point out, one does not know for certain how these rules are to be applied in a particular case. They are unlike the algorithmic rules of mathematics and logic and more like the heuristic principles underlying the tactics and strategy of chess. They are crutches which may sometimes provide support, but not substitutes for the practice which alone develops an intuitive feeling for a fitting way to describe the aim of an investigation, the conditions and results of experiments, and the speculations about further lines of enquiry.

Each individual may acquire his own style of writing, based on the rhythms within and between his sentences. The scientist may react against this concept because of its vagueness and its literary connotations. One of its strengths, however, is utilitarian. It makes prose not just intelligible, but also memorable, and when it does this we ascribe aesthetic properties to it. But the selfconscious cultivation of style may lead to expressions which conceal, rather than illuminate, the content. What is wanted is a balance between content and expression, and this is most likely to come about as a function of the organization imposed on the paper and a feeling for the use of language.

Finally, it is essential to invoke the aid of two agents, one imaginary and the other real. To report research objectively it is necessary to become temporarily detached from it. And a good way to do this is to imagine a listener, who is checking the sense and euphony of our words while we are writing them. But this imaginary listener, being a projection of oneself, cannot detect those blind spots from which we all suffer. Hence one's paper must be given to a colleague for thorough criticism. As we gain experience, we learn to enjoy altering a paper to do justice to another's point of view, or to meet objections raised by a rival theory which we had overlooked. It frees us from the egocentric stance we often adopt towards our own work. In addition, saying something in different ways, like describing an object seen from different angles, may be one of the best ways of learning to use words effectively.

Conclusions

For a variety of reasons it seems very probable that learned journals will become obsolete in the future. Scientific information will be distributed in abstracts and stored in a form available for mechanical processing, so that it can be automatically retrieved.

But this will not make the scientific paper obsolete, although it may change its conventions. If I am correct in my arguments, the act of writing has consequences for thought. It suggests new ideas and interpretations, just as carrying out research on a problem often changes the way we see the problem. In both cases, doing something changes our consciousness, whereas thought which remains interiorized risks being caught in repetitive tendencies which stultify its growth. Writing is a modest form of action. It not only clarifies thought but also enlarges it.

References

Hebb, D O and Bindra, D (1952) Scientific writing and the general problem of communication. *American Psychologist* 7: 569-73

Martin, H C (1957) *The Logic and Rhetoric of Exposition.* New York: Rinehart.

5.2 Writing reviews: some problems of reviewing research in the social sciences

JAMES HARTLEY, ALAN BRANTHWAITE AND ALEX COOK

(First published in the *Journal of Research Communication Studies* 1: 211-23. Reprinted with permission of the publishers.)

Whether it be for the initial chapter in a PhD thesis or for the introduction to a paper written for publication, it is common practice for authors to begin by reviewing related research. Such reviews have a variety of functions, and the way they are tackled depends upon the purpose for which they are written. Reviews may show the history of research in a field (eg Macdonald-Ross, 1977) or the work done in a particular year (eg Weintraub *et al*, 1976-77); they may plot the development of a line of reasoning (eg Sternberg, 1975) or they may integrate and synthesize findings from different research areas (eg Hartley and Davies, 1976); and, of course, reviews may be used to generate new hypotheses (eg Klare, 1976). In certain cases, where a single hypothesis has been subject to a large number of tests by several different researchers, then the aim of the review may be to draw together the results and evaluate the current state of that hypothesis. Thus, for example, Kohlberg (1963) evaluated Piagetian theory, Hartley (1966) evaluated programmed versus conventional instruction, and Smith and Glass (1977) evaluated behaviour therapy versus psychotherapy.

In these last cases it is usual — and helpful for the reader — for the authors to summarize the results of their labours in a tabular form. This paper is concerned with some of the problems of producing and interpreting such tables or 'scoreboards': in particular it is concerned with the problems of what can be communicated in such scoreboards and what conclusions can be properly drawn from a certain area of research enquiry with the information provided. Our method of approach is to list certain strategies that have been used in the past (with examples) and to comment on them as we proceed. Finally we shall suggest some guidelines — based on our comments — for authors writing literature reviews.

However, before we begin we need to distinguish here between 'statistical significance', 'theoretical significance', and 'practical significance'. A result may be statistically significant (ie it did not happen by chance), but it might have no theoretical interest or practical application. Conversely, a result may be practically useful even if it is not statistically significant (eg it may be useful to know that different teaching methods might be equally effective on certain criteria). There is a need, therefore, for reviewers to tie their arguments to a theoretical or practical argument. It is presumably this, after all, that inspires a review.

How have reviewers tackled the task?

STRATEGY 1: THE SIMPLE SCOREBOARD

With this approach authors simply cite the results of their survey of relevant studies in a tabular 'scoreboard'. Table 1 from Kulik *et al* (1976) provides a typical example.

	Comparisons favouring PSI		Comparisons favouring lectures	
	Significant difference	*Non-significant difference*	*Significant difference*	*Non-significant difference*
End of course	39	4	0	1
Retention	9	0	0	0
Transfer	4	1	0	0
Overall evaluation	7	1	1	0

Table 1. *A summary of comparisons between PSI (personalized system of instruction) and lecture groups (from Kulik et al, 1976)*

Such scoreboards are useful — they show the state of the game — but they do not provide details of how the score got that way. Nothing is said concerning the sources of the studies or their validity and the reader must take it on trust that the writer has fully surveyed the relevant field and drawn the pertinent inferences.

A variation on Strategy 1 is to present a scoreboard with footnotes. Kulik and Jaska (1977) in a subsequent article presented a table similar to Table 1 with the following remark: 'A list of the studies summarized in this table is available from the authors . . . ' This strategy indicates that details are available in some form, but that the reader will have to make an effort to retrieve them.

STRATEGY 2: SCOREBOARD PLUS DETAILS

Table 2 shows a summary of the results obtained in a review of studies comparing programmed with conventional instruction which was first presented by Hartley (1966). The format of this scoreboard was repeated for school, military and industrial studies, and the references to all 112 studies were provided in the article, classified in the same way.

An alternative, but similar technique (commonly used, for example, by authors in the *Review of Educational Research*) is to present a list of references classified in terms of their results, together with accumulated totals. Table 3 illustrates this approach. These strategies, then, have the advantage that readers can trace the quoted studies if they wish.

Measures recorded	No of studies recording these measures	Programmed Instruction Group		
		Significantly superior	Not significantly different	Significantly worse
Time taken	90	47	37	6
Test results	110	41	54	15
Retest results	33	6	24	3

Note: The figures in the first column differ because not all three measures were recorded for every one of the 112 studies.

Table 2. *The results from 112 studies comparing programmed with conventional instruction (from Hartley, 1966)*

Studies indicating Yes (N=17)	Studies indicating no significant difference (N=16)	Studies indicating No (N=2)
Jones 1923 (1 study)	Jones 1923 (2 studies)	Peters 1972
Crawford 1925b (2 studies)	Crawford 1925b (3 studies)	Thomas *et al* 1975
McHenry 1969 (4 studies)	Freyberg 1956	
Berliner 1969	McClendon 1958	
Berliner 1971	Eisner & Rohde 1959	
Berliner 1972	Pauk 1963	
Peters & Harris (undated)	McManaway 1968	
DiVesta & Gray 1972	Howe 1970	
DiVesta & Gray 1973 (2 studies)	Fisher & Harris 1974a	
Fisher & Harris 1973	Fisher & Harris 1974b	
Baker *et al* 1974 (1 study)	Baker *et al* 1974 (1 study)	
Fairbanks & Costello 1977	Aiken *et al* 1975	
	Carter & Van Matre 1975	

Table 3. *A summary of findings with respect to the question whether taking notes helps subsequent recall (from Hartley and Davies, 1978)*

Furthermore, by comparing different reviews on the same topic readers can judge whether or not the coverage of the field of concern is representative, and — perhaps more interesting — whether or not different reviewers classify the same studies in the same or different ways.

Thus, for example, Barnes and Clawson (1975) reviewed 32 studies on advance-organizers, and Hartley and Davies (1976) reviewed 28. However, the Barnes and Clawson review included 11 studies not mentioned by the Hartley and Davies review, and the Hartley and Davies review included nine studies not mentioned by Barnes and Clawson. Fortunately there was agreement between the two sets of reviewers concerning the studies that they reviewed in common — but their conclusions concerning the overall picture were different. These differences appeared to reflect the fact that different additional studies had been reviewed, and the fact that the authors had organized their reviews in different ways.

Such differences in conclusions should not be too surprising. The problem is that different studies are being compared — all of which may purport to be examining the same hypothesis — but many of them will have used different ways of interpreting and testing this hypothesis. Reviewers have to interpret further these studies and to equate the findings. In doing this they may interpret the evidence selectively to support the case they are presenting, and one study might be interpreted in many different ways or even excluded on the grounds of inadequate methodology. The authors of some studies in fact may be surprised (or even horrified) by the statements made by reviewers concerning their particular studies. (See, for example, Ford, 1976, or Ausubel, 1978.) Finally, of course, one has to consider that reviewers may make mistakes, or (later) change their minds. Kohlberg's (1963) table, for instance, contains several errors, and Cronbach and Snow (1977) apologize to readers for having misled them in their influential review of 1969.

Factors such as these suggest that current reviewers should consult primary source material, and not rely on earlier reviews and computer-based retrieval systems — except for references — in their survey of a field. When the references in earlier reviews are checked out then distortions may be found and remedied. For example, Hartley *et al*, (1971) examined the studies of achievement motivation cited by Heckhausen (1967) and discovered that even though he had provided many references, Heckhausen had been partial in his presentation of their results. Similarly Ausubel (1978) complained that many of the reviewers of the research on advance-organizers had not read his original papers, and that the errors made by one reviewer appeared in subsequent reviews. Clearly then, secondary source materials (as well as some of the interpretations made in primary source materials) should be considered with caution. Table 4 illustrates the problem.

Finally, in this section, we may note that some reviewers may feel a wish to re-analyse original data in different ways. Such 'secondary analysis' has had some profound effects on certain segments of the educational profession (see, for example, Burstein, 1978).

STRATEGY 3: SCOREBOARDS INCORPORATING MINIMAL CRITERIA: SOME STATISTICAL CONSIDERATIONS

A major problem of pooling studies together in order to obtain an overall picture is that invariably the studies differ in their sample sizes, materials, dependent variables, experimental procedures and in the statistical treatments of their results. There seem to be no satisfactory ways of handling this problem although, as we shall see below, various kinds of solution have been attempted.

First, however, it is necessary to point out some of the assumptions that are often made here — assumptions which may or which may not be necessarily true. These are:

1. It is (reputedly) easier to publish a study that has a significant result than one which does not. Should one, therefore, give more weight to published experiments that have statistically

non-significant results?

2. On the other hand, it is easier to find a non-significant result than to find a significant one. Should one, therefore, give more weight to experiments with statistically significant results?

3. Levels of significance, however, are only conventions which are rather arbitrarily based. Results which fall just outside the accepted level of significance cannot be considered completely worthless. One cannot escape the feeling that if ten studies provide ten barely non-significant results all pointing in the same direction then this would be almost as surprising as obtaining ten heads when tossing a coin ten times. So, should one pool non-significant results that point in the same direction?

4. Relatedly, if, as R A Fisher believed, the repetition of significant results forms the basis of scientific truth (Tukey, 1969) then should studies which have been replicated be given more weight than studies which have not been replicated? (We may note here, of course, that most studies in psychology have not been replicated and that replication is difficult to do: of the 112 studies reviewed by Hartley (1966) less than ten had been repeated once in the same or similar conditions.)

Secondary source (extract)

Another way of eliminating a conditioned response is to train an incompatible response to the same stimulus. This is the way that Albert was cured of his fear of the white rat. First the caged rat was brought into the same room as Albert but moved away until Albert could tolerate its presence without whimpering. While Albert kept track of the rat out of the corner of his eye, he was plied with his favourite dessert. The next day the rat was moved a little bit closer while Albert happily ate . . . After a number of sessions the rat and Albert were happily re-united. Mednick (1964)

Primary source (extract)

iv. Detachment, or removal of conditioned responses
Unfortunately Albert was taken from the hospital the day the above tests were made (1 year 21 days). Hence the opportunity of building up an experimental technique by means of which we could remove the conditioned emotional response was denied us. Watson and Rayner (1920)

(Note: Mednick has concatenated the separate experiments of Watson and Rayner (1920) and Jones (1924) in his account. That Mednick is not alone in doing this is amply confirmed by Harris (1979).)

Note: In the original draft of this paper we included four examples of contrasts between secondary and primary sources designed to illustrate bias, error, and over-simplification. Colleagues were quick to provide us with more, so this may be a greater problem than we thought.

Table 4. *A contrast between a secondary and a primary source*

5. Large-scale studies are often assumed to be superior to small-scale ones — but need this necessarily be so? If the results could have been equally well-obtained with a small-scale study then a large-scale one may simply be a testament to inefficiency. In general the main reason for sampling is to do an investigation efficiently (ie with the minimum of cost and the maximum of relevance to the theoretical and/or practical issues involved). Should one, therefore, comment on the quality of the research designs of different studies which purport to examine the same hypothesis?

6. There is much discussion over the problem of *how* one can, or *if* one should, pool together studies which vary in quality. Glass (1978) for instance, opposes the *a priori* judgement that 'weak designs' or 'methodological inadequacies' render worthless the findings of such studies. He argues that one needs to examine this question *a posteriori*. Eysenck (1978), on the other hand, objects strongly to the notion of feeding into the computer for further analysis the results from good, bad and indifferent studies. Eysenck argues simply, 'garbage in leads to garbage out'. Clearly the quality of relevant studies can vary a great deal. Lawton and Laska (1977), for instance, rejected Barnes and Clawson's (1975) conclusions on the grounds that an overly large proportion of the data came from trivial studies. Similarly, Hartley (1966) rejected 106 of the 112 studies he reviewed on the grounds that they did not meet the minimal criteria necessary for them to be regarded as adequate studies of the problem in question. (The whole focus of Hartley's article — rarely commented on by subsequent reviewers when they reproduce Table 2 — was to question the quality of the research in this area and to set forth criteria for a different approach to comparison studies in education.)

7. Finally we need to remind readers here of some further fundamental points — or *assumptions* — that are made when pooling experiments in psychological research. Without going into more detail these are:

   (a) that different dependent variables (manipulated by different investigators to test the same hypothesis) are of equal importance;
   (b) that the results obtained from limited samples (eg university students) apply to wide populations (eg all adults); and
   (c) that the results obtained in experiments apply to natural situations.

   Reviewers may wish to make their position clear on each of these assumptions. In addition they may want to make it clear whether they consider that the research they have reviewed has theoretical and/or practical significance — and how they reached this conclusion.

Thus, there are a great many problems in pooling studies in a review. How have different investigators gone about it? Robert Rosenthal (1978),

Method	Advantages	Limitations	Applicable when
Adding logs	Well established	Cumulates poorly; can support opposite conclusions	N of studies is small ($\leqslant 5$)
Adding ps	Good power	Inapplicable when N of studies (or ps) is large, unless complex corrections are introduced	N of studies is small ($\Sigma p \leqslant 1.0$)
Adding ts	Unaffected by N of studies given minimum df per study	Inapplicable when ts are based on very few df	Studies are not based on too few df
Adding Zs	Routinely applicable, simple	Assumes unit variance when under some conditions Type I or Type II errors may be increased	Any time
Adding weighted Zs	Routinely applicable, permits weighting	Assumes unit variance when under some conditions Type I or Type II errors may be increased	Whenever weighting is desired
Testing mean p	Simple	N of studies should not be less than four	N of studies $\geqslant 4$
Testing mean Z	No assumption of unit variance	Low power when N of studies is small	N of studies $\geqslant 5$
Counting	Simple and robust	Large N of studies is needed; may be low in power	N of studies is large
Blocking	Displays all means for inspection, thus facilitating search for moderator variables	Laborious when N is large; insufficient data may be available	N of studies is not too large

Table 5. *The advantages and limitations of nine methods of combining results of independent studies (after Rosenthal, 1978) [Table reproduced with permission of the author and the American Psychological Association © American Psychological Association, 1978]*

in an interesting article, compared nine ways of combining the results of independent studies. His summary table is reproduced here as Table 5.

Most of the ways of combining studies discussed by Rosenthal are concerned with combining a small number of studies. When this number is large then the most common procedure that investigators seem to use is the one that Rosenthal calls 'counting'. Here reviewers seem to accept the original investigator's conclusions and simply to tabulate the number of studies reporting significant findings in one direction, the number reporting significant findings in the opposite direction, and the number of studies reporting non-significant findings. This method sometimes yields a clear conclusion (as shown in Table 1) but such conclusions might be biased by the presence of studies with large sample sizes. Furthermore, an unlikely but additional problem here might be that all of the studies reviewed have the same error(s) in common!

Other investigators have used more sophisticated procedures (see, for example, Anderson and Biddle, 1975; Dubin and Taveggia, 1968; Smith and Glass, 1977) but clearly there are no firm rules about how to pool experiments which have different sample sizes, materials, procedures and levels of significance: flexibility seems needed, together with a clear statement of the criteria used by reviewers in their decision-making. In most instances where the number of studies is large, one might in fact question Rosenthal's notion of applying a significance test to the overall results: significance tests are only significant if they are relevant to change.

A subsequent article by Rosenthal (Rosenthal, 1979) raises what he calls the 'file-drawer' problem: this is the argument that for all the published studies there must be hundreds of unpublished ones filed away. The aim of Rosenthal's article is to show how one can calculate the number of studies with non-significant results that is required to reject an overall conclusion that points to a significant finding. Rosenthal concludes that more and more research workers in the future will need to estimate the average effect sizes and the combined significance of the studies that they summarize.

STRATEGY 4: EXAMINING ACTUAL MATERIALS AND DISSERTATIONS

An unspoken assumption of this paper so far is that it is possible to write a review article by simply surveying published papers. It is now time to question this assumption. In our experience it is remarkable how one's view of the validity of an experiment changes when one sees the actual materials, the methods, and the tests used in a particular experiment. Other investigators have reported similar observations. Thus, for example, Macdonald-Ross (1977) concluded — after examining the materials used in her study of graphics — that Vernon's (1946) results were largely a consequence of using poorly designed diagrams. Similarly, Elashoff and Snow (1971) were able to write a devastating critique of *Pygmalion in the Classroom* after examining the tests and procedures used by Rosenthal and Jacobson (1968).

In our experience few reviewers seem to have adopted the strategy of going back to an original dissertation that formed the basis for a published article — or, indeed, back to the dissertations that never got that far. Yet such an approach seems to hold much promise.

In 1976 George Klare published the results of his analysis of 36 experimental studies carried out since World War II on the effects of readability variables upon the reader's comprehension of text. Most of these studies were dissertations (including theses) and most were on microfilm. (Klare reported that reading such dissertations was not exactly his favourite pastime, but that financial inducement from the US Navy somewhat sweetened the task!) Some of the results found by Klare are shown in Table 6.

Klare commented that the zero in Table 6 was not quite as significant in its implications as it seemed, since three of the dissertations were later published as journal articles and one as a report. Klare reported that the studies with non-significant differences were more valuable to him than were those with the significant differences

	Statistically significant	Mixed	Not statistically significant
Published studies	6	3	0
Theses or dissertations	13	3	11

Table 6. *The results of 36 experimental studies of the effects of readability variables upon comprehension (from Klare, 1976)*

because the former were more informative in indicating which readability variables were or were not associated with comprehension. He also remarked that he much preferred reading the dissertations to the published articles, largely because of the amount of detail they included. By examining these dissertations Klare was able to draw up a model to account for those factors which were most likely to affect the predictability of readability measures — a model that could not have been arrived at from a consideration of the published research alone. New experiments — devised to test the model — are now successfully being carried out (Entin and Klare, 1978; Fass and Schumacher, 1978).

Clearly then, this approach seems of value. Unfortunately, however, to check out the validity of Klare's judgements, we too would have to read the dissertations! Klare remarks, however, in this connection, that no author has yet written to him to complain about the classification of his articles (Klare, personal communication).

Guidelines for reviewers

The results of our survey suggest eight important guidelines for reviewers:

☐ Set the review firmly in a theoretical and/or practical context.
☐ Provide references to all of the studies cited. (If space does not permit this, then make the references available on request.)
☐ Group, if possible, all of the references in terms of the classification of the results used in the review.
☐ Make explicit the criteria used for classifying and commenting on the experiments in particular ways.
☐ Use original papers, and not secondary source material if possible. (If secondary sources are being discussed, make this clear to the reader.)
☐ Try to locate copies of the actual materials, tests, etc, used in experiments, especially those which appear critical to the conclusions being drawn.
☐ If a published paper is based on an unpublished thesis, then try to get hold of the thesis too.
☐ Consider Rosenthal's (1979) criteria for testing how well-established a combined significance level might be.

Clearly some of these guidelines are harder to follow than others, and to follow them all would be to follow a counsel of perfection. Nonetheless, if research workers wish to have accurate scoreboards which reflect the state of play in a particular research area, then we feel that the more of these guidelines that can be followed, the better. The final review, of course, will still be like a portrait — painted at one point in time and from one particular perspective. And, like all portraits, it will be perceived differently by different people.

References

Anderson, R C and Biddle, W B (1975) On asking people questions about what they are reading. In G H Bower (ed) *The Psychology of Learning and Motivation* 9. New York: Academic Press

Ausubel, D P (1978) In defense of advance organizers: a reply to the critics. *Review of Educational Research* 48 2: 251-7

Ausubel, D P, Novak, J D and Hanesian, H (1978) *Educational Psychology: A Cognitive View* (2nd edition). New York: Holt, Rinehart & Winston

Barnes, B R and Clawson, E U (1975) Do advance organisers facilitate learning? *Review of Educational Research* 45 4: 637-59

Burstein, L (1978) Secondary analysis: an important resource for educational research and evaluation. *Educational Researcher* 7 5: 9-12

Cronbach, L J and Snow, R E (1969) Individual differences in learning ability as a function of instructional variables. Unpublished Report ED 029021, School of Education, Stanford University

Cronbach, L J and Snow, R E (1977) *Aptitudes and Instructional Methods*. New York: Irvington

Dubin, R and Taveggia, T C (1968) *The Teaching Learning Paradox*. University of Oregon: Center for the Advanced Study of Education

Elashoff, J D and Snow, R E (1971) *Pygmalion Reconsidered*. Worthington, Ohio: Charles A Jones

Entin, E B and Klare, G R (1978) Some inter-relationships of readability, cloze and multiple-choice comprehension scores on a reading comprehension test. *Journal of Reading Behavior* X 4: 417-36

Eysenck, H J (1978) Correspondence section. *Bulletin of the British Psychological Society* 31: 56

Fass, W and Schumacher, G M (1978) The effects of motivation, subject activity and readability on the retention of prose materials. *Journal of Educational Psychology* 70 5: 803-7

Ford, J (1976) Facts, evidence and rumour: a rational reconstruction of 'Social class and the comprehensive school'. In M Shipman (ed) *The Organisation and Impact of Social Research*. London: Routledge & Kegan Paul

Glass, G V (1978) Reply to Mansfield and Busse. *Educational Researcher* 7 1: 3

Harris, B (1979) Whatever happened to little Albert? *American Psychologist* 34 2: 151-60

Hartley, J (1966) Research report. *New Education* 2 1: 29-35

Hartley, J and Davies, I K (1976) Pre-instructional strategies: the role of pre-tests, behavioural objectives, overviews and advance organizers. *Review of Educational Research* 46 2: 239-65

Hartley, J and Davies, I K (1978) Note-taking: a critical review. *Programmed Learning & Educational Technology* 15 3: 207-24

Hartley, J, Holt, J and Hogarth, F (1971) Academic motivation and programmed learning. *British Journal of Educational Psychology* 41 2: 171-83

Heckhausen, H (1967) *The Anatomy of Achievement Motivation*. New York: Academic Press

Jones, M C (1924) A laboratory study of fear: the case of Peter. *Pedagogical Seminar* 31: 308-15

Klare, G R (1976) A second look at the validity of readability formulas. *Journal of Reading Behavior* **VIII** 2: 129-52

Kohlberg, L (1963) Moral development and identification. In H W Stevenson (ed) *Child Psychology*. Chicago: NSSE

Kulik, J A and Jaska, P (1977) PSI and other educational technologies in college teaching. *Educational Technology* **XVII** 9: 12-19

Kulik, J A, Kulik, C L C and Smith, B B (1976) Research on the personalised system of instruction. *Programmed Learning & Educational Technology* 13 1: 23-30

Lawton, J T and Laska, S K (1977) Advance organisers as a teaching strategy: a reply to Barnes and Clawson. *Review of Educational Research* 47 2: 233-44

Macdonald-Ross, M (1977) How numbers are shown: a review of research on the presentation of quantitative information. *Audio Visual Communication Review* 25 4: 359-409

Mednick, S A (1964) *Learning.* Englewood Cliffs, NJ: Prentice-Hall

Rosenthal, R (1978) Combining results of independent studies. *Psychological Bulletin* 85 1: 185-93

Rosenthal, R (1979) The 'file-drawer' problem and tolerance for null results. *Psychological Bulletin* 86 3: 638-41

Rosenthal, R and Jacobson, L (1968) *Pygmalion in the Classroom.* New York: Holt, Rinehart & Winston

Smith, M L and Glass, G V (1977) Meta-analysis of psychotherapy outcome studies. *American Psychologist* 32: 752-60

Sternberg, S (1975) Memory scanning: new findings and current controversies. *Quarterly Journal of Experimental Psychology* 27: 1-32

Tukey, J W (1969) Analysing data: sanctification or detective work? *American Psychologist* 24: 83-91

Vernon, M D (1946) Learning from graphical material. *British Journal of Psychology* 36: 145-59

Watson, J B and Rayner, R (1920) Conditioned emotional reactions. *Journal of Experimental Psychology* 3: 1-14

Weintraub, S, Smith, H K, Pessas, G P, Roser, N L and Rowls, M (1976-77) Summary of investigations relating to reading July 1, 1975 to June 30, 1976. *Reading Research Quarterly* **XII** 3: 231-565

5.3 The role of referees in scientific communication

MICHAEL D GORDON

(A revised version of Chapters 4 and 5 of Gordon, M (1978) *A Study in the Evaluation of Research Papers by Primary Journals in the UK.* University of Leicester: Primary Communications Research Centre © British Library Board. Reproduced with permission of the author and the British Library.)

The use, selection and performance of referees

EDITORS' EXPECTATIONS AND CRITERIA FOR SELECTION OF REFEREES

Journals differ quite considerably, one from another, with respect to (a) their editorial organization, (b) the types and numbers of submissions they receive, and (c) the amounts of journal space they have available. Furthermore, editors differ in their views of the role of journal publication within the social and intellectual activity of their discipline, and so in the criteria they seek to satisfy as preconditions to the acceptance of papers. As a consequence, referees are used in different organizational contexts in different journals, and editors' expectations of the scope of referees' tasks similarly vary. It is not, therefore, surprising to find that the criteria editors apply in selecting referees also differ from journal to journal, and that the selection process fits in with the patterning of factors outlined above.

When editors in the earth, physical and chemical sciences are asked what criteria they apply in selecting referees, they typically answer that a referee should be both up-to-date and competent in the specialism covered by the paper. This should ensure that the referee can make a thorough technical criticism of the scientific content of the paper. The adoption of these criteria simply reflects implicit editorial assumptions concerning the nature of science and the role of research journal publication within it. This perspective can be characterized as depicting disciplines in terms of arrays of specialisms that are only partially integrated with one another. These specialisms advance incrementally and relatively independently in a self-correcting fashion. In accord with this view, earth, physical and chemical science editors appear to see the role of the research journal as (a) ensuring that papers do, indeed, report advances (ie guaranteeing the contents are original); and (b) ensuring that they satisfy the technical scientific criteria of their particular specialism (ie making sure that the methodology and modes of interpretation which papers report are error-free and legitimate in relation to the consensus upheld by the appropriate community of specialists).

Biological science editors appear to share the views of editors in the

263

'harder' sciences concerning the nature of their discipline and the role of journal publication within it. This is demonstrated by their acceptance of similar editorial decision rules and in their citing similar criteria as appropriate for the selection of referees. Specialist medical editors, meanwhile, were found to adhere to different editorial decision rules as compared with editors in the natural sciences, and they are similarly found to differ slightly in the criteria they apply in selecting referees.

We may quote, by way of example, the editors of two specialist medical journals: 'A referee must be a specialist in his field, recognized and accepted as an expert.' 'A referee must be someone who is regarded as an authority in the specialist subject of the paper.' These two quotes typify medical editors' responses to the question of criteria for the selection of referees, because, firstly, they reflect the same requirement of scientific competence demanded by editors in the natural sciences, but secondly, they go beyond this to identify as necessary the clearly recognizable social status of 'expert' or 'authority'. The citing of this additional criterion can be interpreted as having association with two related factors. Firstly, medical editors display greater intellectual caution. This showed itself in the specialist medical editors' rating of publication of incorrect papers as more serious than the rejection of high quality ones (*cf* all natural science editors' rating of the latter as more serious than the former). The second, and related factor, is the differing perception of the distribution of expertise and intellectual authority in medicine as compared with the academic scientific world.

The medical profession has a regular professional interaction with the general public, involving a great amount of responsibility on the part of its members. The profession has therefore evolved a far more highly structured hierarchy of professional authority than has the more isolated world of academic science. As a result, medical editors' perceptions of the distribution of authority to make competent evaluations appear to be influenced by a comparatively strong association of such competence with an individual's position in the formal professional hierarchy. In the less formally hierarchical, predominantly academic world of the natural sciences, the necessary expertise for the evaluation of papers is not assumed to be distributed in the same way. Natural science editors' identification of competent referees is influenced rather more by the recognition individuals' research work receives from their peers, and rather less by individuals' status in the formal social hierarchy of the academic community. As a consequence, it would appear that medical referees tend to be somewhat more senior than are referees in the pure sciences, and their evaluations may reinforce the greater intellectual caution which medical editors show in their adherence to more conservative editorial decision rules.

Mathematical editors differ from both medical and natural science editors in the criteria they cite as relevant to the process by which referees are selected. This difference can be accounted for in terms of the distinctive nature of the editorial evaluation required for mathematical papers. Each of the mathematical editors indicated that the evaluation of the papers they receive has two aspects. The first of these is the examination of consistency, accuracy and correctness of the mathematical arguments; the second is that of assessing the mathematical importance of the paper as a whole. It takes good technical mathematical ability and a willingness to give a considerable amount of time and attention to detail to perform the former assessment, and extensive mathematical experience to perform the latter. All the mathematical editors found that, as a result, young, relatively less eminent referees are better able to perform technical criticism, and older, more experienced referees are better able to give evaluations of the mathematical importance of a piece of work. Thus, one mathematical editor said that if a paper's author were established and confident, he would send that paper to a recent post-doctorate mathematician for technical criticism; while, if the author were less experienced, he would select an experienced, rather more eminent referee to judge the paper's importance. Another mathematical editor said that he sought referees who had both enough experience to evaluate the papers' importance and enough interest in the subject area of the papers to devote effort to their technical criticism. When, however, he felt capable of assessing a paper's mathematical importance himself, he would choose a fairly junior referee to evaluate the mathematical accuracy.

The remaining journals we examined come from the high rejection end of the spectrum and fall into two categories; firstly, those in the social sciences and philosophy, and secondly, those with high circulations and weekly publication. In the examination of editors' attitudes and editorial organization in both these categories of periodicals, high rejection rate journals were found to be distinguished from lower rejection rate publications by their editorial policies of imposing criteria additional to those of scholarly competence as a pre-condition for acceptance.

In the high circulation journals (*Nature, British Medical Journal* and *Lancet*), those referees who accept a role as adviser, have a knowledge of the journal's interests, and reply promptly, are preferentially chosen. The citing of these criteria clearly indicates the editors' concern with preserving their own editorial control over the selection of manuscripts, as opposed to distributing this control throughout the relevant research communities. The objective of this emphasis, and the reason why these criteria are applied in the selection of referees, lies in the editorial requirement that papers must be speedily published, and should be not only 'sound', but also conform to a particular concept of 'significance' which the editors feel papers in their journals possess.

The imposition of additional criteria as pre-conditions for accepting papers also occurs in social science and philosophy journals, but the additional requirements cited here are different. They are, firstly, that referees should be capable of making 'balanced' judgements, and, secondly, that they should be capable of assessing a paper's interest both to researchers working in the same specialism, and to the general journal readership. The first of these additional considerations perhaps indicates a recognition on the part of journal editors in the social sciences and philosophy of the prevalence of 'schools' of thought within their areas of coverage. The second reflects an additional criterion concerning the expected readership of papers in these subjects. The breadth of audience for which a paper is expected to have a general interest is, of course, journal dependent, being narrower for, say, *Population Studies*, and comparatively broader for the *British Journal of Sociology*. But the overall trend of editorial concern, nevertheless, provides an insight into the type of communications role allotted to journals in these disciplines. This role finds its rationale within a perspective viewing journal publication as a complement to monograph publication in the formal dissemination of research findings, and also as providing a reader-orientated current awareness function. This contrasts with the natural science and mathematical editors' depiction of the roles of their journals, which views them as considerably more author-orientated, with archival and priority recognition functions given greater weight.

In taking an overview of similarities and differences in the criteria applied by editors for the selection of referees, a pattern is thus seen to emerge which corresponds with that found to characterize the distribution of editorial decision rules for the evaluation of manuscripts. And, further, it is seen that this correspondence in distributions can be accounted for in terms of the relations of the formulations of both sets of preferences to editors' views of the social and intellectual roles of their journals.

HOW SUITABLE REFEREES ARE IDENTIFIED

With very few exceptions, editors claim that they are able to select referees for the majority of papers they receive purely on the basis of their own personal knowledge. The extent to which editors are able to make such selections varies, depending on the nature of the subject area of their journal, its editorial structure and their own research and journal editing experience.

The subject area dependence appears to be related both to the breadth of subject area covered by the journal and the subject breadth within that area which individual referees are capable of evaluating. This latter factor, which is associated with the extent to which journals' areas of coverage are differentiated into networks of specialisms, and the relative degrees of closure of those specialisms, dictates the degree of specificity required in the matching of referees to papers.

When a journal's subject area is both broad and highly fragmented into relatively 'closed' specialisms, the editorial task of matching referees to papers primarily on the basis of personal knowledge becomes unmanageable for the part-time editor. Such journals have therefore evolved editorial systems to overcome this problem. The first system is that of maintaining a board, or panel, of editors, each of whom deals with a particular area within the journal coverage (eg *Monthly Notices of the RAS, Geophysical Journal, Journal of the Geology Society, London Mathematical Society, Biometrika, Journal of Physiology, Journal of*

Medical Microbiology) The second method is that of maintaining a staff of full-time assistant editors who select referees using specially developed files containing the names and areas of specialized competence of researchers approved of by their senior part-time editors (eg *Journal of Physics, Faraday Transactions*). Journals using the latter system are the only ones for which editors' personal knowledge is not the most common means by which referees are identified.

The third factor affecting the frequency with which editors are able to select referees without reference to any other source is the extent of the editor's experience; both as an editor of the journal in question and as a member of the research community served by that journal. From the experience of being a practising researcher an editor develops an awareness of 'who is doing what, where'. Through experience as an editor, this awareness is heightened; and further, editors acquire an ever-growing personal record of which possible referees with the appropriate research competence actually perform as referees in a satisfactory fashion. Many editors thought that, although they are now normally able to think of a suitable referee for each paper they receive, this was not the case when they first took on their editing job. New editors, it seems, rely heavily on records and files left by outgoing editors and on the advice of the many colleagues they regularly contact on professional matters.

Most of the editors interviewed were part-time, being also members of the research communities served by their journals. As such, they maintained an extensive network of professional contacts whom they could call upon for advice in the selection of referees. For such editors, the advice of colleagues is normally placed second as a means for identifying referees. For editors of journals associated with particular academic departments, consultation with colleagues is found to be particularly common and these colleagues are normally to be found within the same department. The editors of *Mathematika* and *Economica*, for example, placed such consultations as second in frequency to those made 'off the top of the head' as a means for identifying referees. The editor of the *British Journal of Sociology* reported that 80 per cent of the referees they use are selected as a consequence of consultation with colleagues at the London School of Economics. The editors of these departmentally-based journals explained that the papers they attract tend to be aligned with the intellectual interests and tastes of the university departments publishing the journal. As a result, colleagues within these departments are well situated intellectually, as well as physically, to assist both in the evaluation of submissions and in the recommendation of referees.

Editors mentioned a variety of means by which they assist themselves in the selection of referees. Such means include checking through the list of references in papers and/or through abstracts journals to identify who does similar work; use of such directories as *Scientific Research in British Universities and Colleges* (found to be out-of-date and of limited help); and in the case of some society journals, checking through lists of society members and their interests. All these documented sources are, however, only used as an aid in the selection of referees in a comparatively small minority of cases. While useful to relatively inexperienced assistant editors, all other editors rely in the vast majority of cases upon their own, or on trusted colleagues', evaluations of the suitability of particular referees for particular papers.

REFEREE PERFORMANCE

Editors reported that they find different referees vary considerably in the way they perform their task. The variations are evident in such aspects of referee performance as promptness of response, length and specificity of criticism, and clarity of editorial recommendation. While variation is found in the way different referees perform, individual referees appear to be consistent in their own performance. Editors find, for example, that some referees are always prompt, whilst others are always slow; some always give pages of detailed comments, whilst others always give shorter comments on a limited number of aspects.

Editors find that this widespread variation in referees' attitudes can present them with difficulties, particularly when these variations reflect misunderstandings of the scope of the referee's task. For example, an extensive list of technical criticisms without any recommendation as to whether a paper is worth accepting or not, may sometimes be useful, but is often almost useless to the editor. Equally, a referee who offers firm recommendations to accept, or reject, with little or no substantiating arguments may well be useless. Editors normally want reports which fall somewhere between these two extremes, but the actual balance required varies not only from editor to editor, but also from paper to paper for particular editors. It is thus not surprising that referees differ in their understanding of what editors expect of them.

These variations in referee performance are, of course, not only based on referees' differing comprehension of editors' expectations. They are also associated with the relative importance which referees attribute to the task of refereeing. Variations in the opinions held by referees in respect of these two aspects of their task would seem to affect considerably the ways in which they perform it. It appears from editors' comments that these variations in opinion are, further, associated with the stage referees have reached in their own careers. A selection of quotes from editors working in a variety of disciplines illustrates this:

Multidisciplinary: 'Younger referees review more critically and take their task more seriously. They are also more competitive, and so like to be thorough with the work of their competitors.'

Chemical sciences: 'Most variations are idiosyncratic, but newer, younger referees tend to take more trouble.'

Biological sciences: 'Perhaps the more eminent referees have less time, and so show less attention to detail.'

Medical sciences: 'Juniors tend to give more time, but lack the judgement of seniors who will recommend what is to be done.'

Mathematics: 'Younger referees are meticulous in technical criticism and quicker [in returning reports], but older men have more definite opinions.'

'The young are obsessed by detail, but do not give enough attention to purpose and significance.'

Social science: 'The longer at it, the more decisive.'

Philosophy: 'Younger referees give longer and more detailed reports and are generally more conscientious — returning their reports in less time. More eminent referees send shorter reports and general editorial advice and tend to recommend acceptance.'

It can be inferred from the above comments that younger referees in all disciplines tend to put more effort into refereeing, as they are less busy than their seniors and so have more time to give. They are also more likely to be flattered by being asked to referee and rather more eager to display their critical abilities, since they are at a stage in their careers when they are still trying to establish themselves professionally. As a result, they more often return extensive, detailed criticisms. Older referees, on the other hand, more often have very tight time schedules and, having already established their professional reputations, are less willing to sacrifice the hours required to give extensive detailed criticism. They compensate for this, however, by being able to draw on their greater experience to place papers within the perspective of on-going work in their discipline, and so offer firmer editorial recommendations.

Referees' personalities, critical abilities and ordering of professional priorities will, of course, vary to a considerable extent independently of the age-experience variable. Indeed, this independent variation is marked enough to render the age-experience dependence of referee performance undetectable to half our sample of editors. The responses of the other half, however, in having a high area of overlap while being independently offered by editors in a wide variety of disciplines, indicate that there is an underlying association between the stage which referees have reached in their careers, and the way they approach and perform their refereeing task.

The patterning of referees' evaluations

Editors and referees comprise the two crucial decision-making elements within research journals' systems for manuscript evaluation and selection. As has been shown, the division of labour and responsibility between these two types of participant in the system varies from journal to journal. In all journals, however, ultimate responsibility for intellectual content and reputation (and to a varying extent economic viability) lies with editors. In consequence, the main topic of investigation up to this point has been editorial policies, practices and preferences, viewed in terms of the editors' depiction of their own journal's functions and organization. We have also looked at the editors' differing expectations and degrees of satisfaction with the performance of their referees, and the differing procedural contexts within which they use them. A direct analysis of referee performance has clearly not been possible on the basis of the interviews conducted. Such an analysis is, however, necessary if we are to obtain a fuller view of the mechanisms involved in the selection of manuscripts for publication.

We may note, in particular, that it is the activities of referees which often precipitate the most heated discussions within research communities. Thus, it is sometimes suggested that referees abuse their protective anonymity and the privileges of their position by adopting deliberately obstructive tactics (eg in order to suppress the work of their rivals). Such accusations of so-called 'refereemanship' are typically presented by aggrieved authors. They may be found not only in the relative privacy of informal discussions, but also in the printed pages of such high circulation scientific publications as the *British Medical Journal* and *New Scientist.*

This type of critical stance found can best be exemplified by quotation:

> Almost every working scientist can illustrate from his own experience the virtues and perils of the traditional principle that referees or assessors of work submitted for publication remain anonymous. In general, the existing refereeing system, practised by the great majority of scientific journals, works well. But it necessarily depends for its success on the consistently high moral fibre of all referees. Unfortunately, the presumption is not always justified.
>
> On occasion, the act of submission of a paper can place the author at the mercy of the malignant jealousy of an anonymous rival. Manifestations of antipathy can take many forms, which range from contemptuous mockery (often self-damaging in the long run, because those who indulge in such capers rarely possess the self-control adequate to avoid betraying themselves to the editor) to outright theft. To have suffered such an experience generally induces sympathy from colleagues, but condolences are not enough. What is needed is justice; and justice can be secured only by altering the system. (Jones, 1974)

A more extreme position is taken by some critics:

> Why should an apparently counter-productive institution like reviewing exist? It does not and cannot succeed in its supposed function of protecting journal readers against error. Reviewers, chosen by editors, are seldom as well matched to articles as the eventual readers. Reviewing's real function is what it does successfully, to deny innovators direct access to publication. People fear change. It lowers the value of anyone who does not exploit it. It puts us all on a down escalator, where we climb just to stay even. Innovation occurs faster than society will use it, perhaps faster than it can possibly be used. As the guilds controlled progress in the middle ages, so the scientific and technological establishments slow the pace of change to a rate they can accommodate to. Reviewing is part of the mechanism for doing this. (McCutchen, 1976)

This depiction of refereeing as 'An Evolved Conspiracy' is at variance with the attitudes of the majority of authors, referees and editors who feel that deliberate bias does not occur very often and that, when it does, an experienced editor can normally detect it with, or without, a second referee's report and author's letter of appeal. If this is so, then the influence of deliberate 'refereemanship' upon the overall pattern of growth or a discipline's literature can be considered minimal.

That deliberate bias is not frequently displayed by referees does not, of course, preclude the possibility that all referees may evaluate papers in a way which reflects their own personal sets of intellectual predispositions. The evaluations and recommendations which they offer may thus be systematically patterned in accord with their affiliations.

One would expect that, if this type of bias does operate, it will show itself most clearly in the performance of referees who are evaluating the work of authors identified with rival schools of thought (ie who hold different beliefs in relation to their areas of research).

The fragmentation of research communities into competing schools adhering to different sets of research beliefs is considered quite regular in areas of the social and behavioural sciences, though it is a much less common feature of the natural sciences. Some recent research has set out to assess the nature and extent of bias in referee evaluations, when the referees were affiliated to identifiable schools of thought in such an area of the behavioural sciences (Mahoney, 1976).

Seventy-five anonymously authored manuscripts were distributed to the referees of a US psychology journal, all papers having the same bibliography, introduction and methods sections. The data sections were, however, adjusted to give results which were either congruent with, or contradictory to, the referees' presumed theoretical standpoints. When the referees' reports were returned, evaluations were seen to be dramatically affected by the particular slant of the data. Manuscripts which were identical in topic and procedure were recommended for publication when their results were congruent with referees' theoretical positions, but were consistently rejected when the results were opposed. Referees were also found to rate the same experimental procedures as significantly more adequate when they were alleged to yield the preferred type of data. Finally, referees were seen to scrutinize much more closely those manuscripts that bore results conflicting with their preconceptions.

Thus, it appears that when non-complementary theoretical positions co-exist within a given research area, referees sometimes quite discernibly return evaluations which are biased by their own predispositions. In consequence, the selection of referees can be critical in dictating which papers are recommended for publication.

This situation has also been illustrated by a study of three American social science journals: *American Sociological Review, American Economic Review and Sociometry* (Crane, 1967). Analyses of the past and present institutional affiliations of authors and evaluators were made for each of these journals over a number of periods. For each journal it was then found that, as the proportion of evaluators chosen from certain groups of institutions increased, so the proportion of successful authors from those groups of institutions similarly increased.

271

Crane concluded that the evaluation of papers is 'affected to some degree by non-scientific factors', and two possible interpretations were offered:

(a) As a result of academic training, editorial readers tend to respond to certain aspects of methodology, theoretical orientation and mode of expression in the writings of those who have received similar training.

(b) Doctoral training and academic affiliations influence personal ties between scientists which in turn influence their evaluation of scientific work. Since most scientific writing is terse, knowledge of details may influence the reader's response to an article.

The data were found to support the first of these interpretations more strongly than the second. In all three journals, the majority of authors and evaluators had degrees from major US universities. This suggested that evaluators and contributors shared common viewpoints based on training, rather than personal, ties. However, as the academic affiliations of evaluators became more diverse the academic affiliations of successful authors became more diverse also. This suggested that personal ties may play a secondary role.

One might, of course, look at the findings of the two studies above and suggest that the systematic biases which have been observed are only characteristic of social and behavioural sciences, where a plurality of non-complementary methodological and theoretical positions can co-exist. Some might argue that such findings as have just been presented could not have emerged from studies of evaluation in the natural sciences, where such fragmentation is assumed not to occur.

Data comparing the frequency of agreement between pairs of referees do not, however, reflect totally uniform objective criteria being applied in the evaluation of research papers in natural sciences. Rather they show that varying degrees of subjectivity enter all evaluations of the quality of scientific work. Consequently, one can enquire about 'biases' in refereeing judgement even in the area of science with the highest levels of consensus — physical science.

It would seem that even in this area, where clearly identifiable schools of thought are far less commonly in evidence, different sets of evaluators display slightly differing sets of preferences, predispositions and preconceptions of what constitutes 'good science'. While these non-concurring attitudes may reflect only small departures from the consensus of the discipline, they are, it seems, still detectable. During the series of interviews which we conducted, the editor of a prestigious journal covering the physical sciences offered the opinion that: 'Scientists cluster in schools of varying degrees of visibility. The problem resulting from this clustering comes when an evaluation is required on a paper's interest value, degree of novelty and breadth of implication . . . When it is a matter of straight scientific soundness, referees may still have their objectivity impaired, but to a lesser extent.'

Another very experienced editor of the same journal commented:

'If a referee is a member of the same school as the author, he will likely as not be under-critical of methodology and over-emphasize the importance and relevance of the problem area to those working in adjacent areas. If, on the other hand, the referee is a member of a rival school, he might then assume an opposite stance.'

In the light of these informed opinions, it is of interest to investigate whether the biases referred to can be detected in a statistical analysis of refereeing judgements.

We have conducted such an investigation by analysing data obtained from the records of a society which publishes research journals in two prestigious areas of the physical sciences. Each paper received by the society, during a six-year period, was coded to record the number, nationality, institutional affiliation, response time and editorial recommendations of referees, and the specific points of criticism they offered. A data base was thus compiled which contained a record of 2572 referee reports completed in the evaluation of 1980 papers, along with information on the professional characteristics of authors and their referees. Using SPSS programs, an analysis was then conducted to identify the relationship between referees' evaluations and the pairing of author-referee characteristics.

The hypotheses which the analysis set out to test were firstly, that particular sets of research styles, values and beliefs would command higher levels of consensus within national and institutional groups than across them, and secondly, that this situation, compounded perhaps by the influence of personal ties, would result in authors receiving less critical evaluations from referees with similar national and institutional identities.

Nationality: Looking firstly at the relationship between authors' and referees' nationalities and resulting evaluations, the following data emerged:

	UK authors	N American authors	Totals
UK referees	70% of 600 papers	65% of 307 papers	907
N American referees	66% of 35 papers	75% of 20 papers	55
Totals	635	327	962

Table 1. *Percentage of papers rated 'good' by referees*

These results are not statistically significant, with the number of North American referees being so small, but it is apparent from the above table that UK authors are, on average, less critically evaluated by UK referees than they are by North American referees ($x^2 = 0.29$), while North American authors are less critically evaluated by North American referees ($x^2 = 0.81$). Or, UK referees evaluate UK authors' papers less critically than they do those of North American authors ($x^2 = 2.27$) and North American referees evaluate North American authors' papers less critically than they do those of UK authors ($x^2 = 0.51$). So it is seen that while the results are not significant (x^2 must exceed 3.8 to be significant at p $<$ .05), a higher frequency of favourable evaluation of papers by co-nationals is indicated in each of the four possible cases. And, in aggregate, co-national pairings are found more frequently to produce favourable evaluations but not at a level quite reaching 5 per cent significance (x^2 = 2.51).

Institution: UK universities were split into two groups. The first group, which can for convenience be called 'major universities', consists of those which stand apart from the rest in terms of the outstandingly high levels of funding they receive from the Science Research Council. The second group, 'minor universities', consists of all the other UK universities. The use of these labels is purely for analytical convenience and is not intended to place a value judgement on the work carried out at either group of institutions.

Having established such a dichotomy, the table of authors, referees and their evaluations then appears as follows:

	Minor university authors	Major university authors	Totals
Minor university referees	65% of 120 papers	67.5% of 80 papers	200
Major university referees	50% of 110 papers	82.5% of 309 papers	419
Totals	230	389	619

Table 2. *Percentage of papers rated 'good' by referees*

It can be seen that there is little difference between the frequencies with which minor university referees evaluate minor and major university authors' papers as 'good' (x^2 = 0.13); but a massive difference between the frequencies with which major university referees favourably evaluate major and minor university papers (x^2 = 44.56 p$<$.001).

From the perspective of authors, minor university authors are more frequently evaluated favourably (ie less critically) by minor university referees (x^2 = 5.30 p$<$.05), while major university authors are more often evaluated favourably by major university referees than they are by those affiliated to minor universities (x^2 = 8.78 p$<$.01).

It would therefore appear that when referees and authors in these areas of the physical sciences share membership of national or institutional groups, the chances that the referees will be less critical are increased. This can be put down primarily to there being higher levels of consensus on research beliefs within these groups than there are across them. There may also be preferences for particular areas, or types, of research existing within particular national or institutional groups. These problem areas, or types, of research (eg experimental/theoretical) may by their nature, lead to the possibility of higher levels of consensus being shared on standards of satisfactory work and so to a higher frequency of recommended acceptance.

Personal ties and extra-scientific preferences and prejudices might, of course, be playing a part as well. But it appears that, even in the absence of these personal factors, the scientific predispositions of referees still bias them towards less critical evaluation of colleagues who come from similar institutional or national groups, and so share to a greater extent sets of beliefs on what constitutes good research.

A quotation from a refereeing form completed by a referee at a 'major' UK university 'A' reporting on a paper by an author from another 'major' UK university 'B' further illustrates the point.

> I was recently talking to (a non-UK professor) about refereeing and he volunteered the suggestion that some 'B' papers (and other UK papers) should be sent to 'C' for refereeing. He thought that there were some deficiencies which tended to recur, and which he and others at 'C' (and elsewhere) might be able to point out. There is a natural exchange of washing between 'A' and 'B' and I am concerned that I may too easily be giving papers a completely clean bill of health.

This quotation illustrates how even the most conscientious referees can be limited in their critical perspective when evaluating the papers of colleagues who work in similar institutional environments and who, in consequence, often share similar sets of research beliefs. Correspondingly, it shows how criticism may be more forthcoming from referees who do not share these institutional and intellectual affiliations.

It can therefore be argued that biases systematically operate within refereeing systems in such a way as to give advantage to those elements of a research community which supply the largest proportion of the referees used by the editors of its journals. The papers of such authors may on occasion be less demandingly evaluated than those of authors outside the group. Hence, access to publication may sometimes be easier for them. The accurate identification of group members may be difficult, since they may display a variety of professional characteristics beyond those investigated above. Nevertheless, the institutional and national categorizations used in this study have proved to be significant for the distinguishing of preferential patterns of evaluation. They thus serve to illustrate how groups preferred on 'intellectual' grounds overlap with 'socially' connected groups, and how this may lead to a degree of relativism in the evaluative criteria which are applied by referees.

References

Crane, D (1967) The gatekeeper of science: some factors affecting the selection of articles for scientific journals. *American Sociologist* 2: 195-201
Jones, R (1974) Rights, wrongs and referees. *New Scientist* 61: 758-9 (21 March)
McCutchen, C (1976) An evolved conspiracy. *New Scientist* 70: 225 (29 April)
Mahoney, M J (1976) *The Scientist as Subject: The Psychological Imperative*, Chapter 5. Cambridge, Mass: Ballinger

5.4 Confessions of a textbook writer

JAMES V McCONNELL

(Excerpts from Confessions of a textbook writer, *American Psychologist* (1978) 33 2: 159-69 © American Psychological Association, Inc. Reproduced with permission of the author and the American Psychological Association.)

Dallenbach's anecdotes

I suppose that I first began to think about writing my own introductory psychology text during my last year as a graduate student at the University of Texas, when I was a teaching fellow for Karl M Dallenbach. Dallenbach was, at that time, the Chairman of the Psychology Department, and he became not only my mentor but a role model of sorts. Dr Dall — as we all called him — was iconoclastic, authoritarian, and often irascible. He was also a marvellous human being who, more than any of my other professors, tried to teach me how to be both a gentleman and a scholar. I learned a great deal from him — although what he taught me wasn't always what he hoped I would learn.

The first point about good teaching that he made was a most important one, though. Dr Dall always insisted on teaching the introductory course himself — in part because it was the only contact that most students would have with scientific psychology. He saw the first course as an entry point into the field as well, and would trust the teaching of the class to no one but himself, since he wanted to attract to psychology as many good students as he could. There weren't many people around with that viewpoint in those days; unfortunately, there still aren't. But as Dr Dall and I talked extensively about the class, I came to share his opinion, and still do. For if the first course doesn't excite and challenge the best students available to us, how will our discipline prosper as it should?

The second point that Dr Dall made was equally critical, for it had to do with a style of teaching that I now attempt to follow. Dr Dall believed that psychology was the scientific study of *people* — not of behaviour, or of concepts, or of the nervous system, or of personality. Rather, psychology was about real, live human beings — and about what went into making them humans. It is true that he was more interested in sensation and perception than in anything else — at least in his own laboratory. But in the classroom, he delighted his students with anecdote after anecdote about the famous names in the field of psychology. He talked about Wundt and Titchener, both of whom he knew personally. He hinted at the sexual problems that led to Watson's dismissal from Johns Hopkins. Dr Dall even told stories about Freud, whose theories Dr Dall didn't really approve of, but whose genius was readily apparent.

As Dr Dall's assistant, I would sit in class, making notes on what the great man was saying, and then would go over the material with the introductory students in their discussion sections. I suppose I recognized unconsciously the great pedagogical value of the anecdotes, but Dr Dall was not one to trust the unconscious. Almost as soon as I had begun working for him, he called me into his office and asked to see the notes I had taken on the day's lecture. He looked over my scrawlings, then asked, 'Where's the story about Titchener?'

'That wasn't data', I replied defensively. In truth, I had been so interested in the story that I had simply forgotten to take notes on it.

'Don't be foolish,' Dr Dall said gruffly. 'The facts and data you can find in any stupid textbook. But the stories are priceless. They don't appear in print anywhere. If you want to capture the imaginations of young people, you have to tell them stories! Forget the facts, and copy down the anecdotes!'

Karl Dallenbach was ahead of his time. As his teaching assistant, I had at first wanted to cram the students' craniums with facts, facts, and more facts. I was comfortable with facts, for they were proven entities that could be demonstrated and pointed at and trusted. But Dr Dall realized then — as I did belatedly — that students remember and use facts only when these dull bits of data are placed within a memorable and interesting context. Ebbinghaus had made the same point almost 100 years earlier, of course, but who other than a few magnificent scholars such as Dr Dall ever read Ebbinghaus in the original German? And who other than people like Dr Dall ever tried to put Ebbinghaus's conclusions into practice in the classroom?

Lowell Kelly's hitchhiker

Shortly after I left Texas and came to the University of Michigan, I had the pleasure of team-teaching with E Lowell Kelly. I learned many things from Lowell, not the least of which was the importance of enthusiasm for one's subject matter and deep concern for one's students. Of all the interesting things that Lowell said to me, however, perhaps the thing that impressed me most was an anecdote that he related shortly after I got to Michigan.

Lowell said that years earlier he had been driving through California and had picked up a hitch-hiker. Lowell got to talking with this young man and discovered that the hitch-hiker had not only been to college but had taken an introductory psychology course while there.

'What do you remember of the course?' asked Lowell. The young man thought seriously for some time, then finally replied. 'To tell the truth, the only thing I remember is this. If you ring a bell, a dog will salivate like hell!'

At a surface level of interpretation, the story is certainly amusing. But at a deeper level, it is so disturbing that it left a life-long mark on me. I was teaching the introductory course at the time, and I got to wondering how many of my own students took into their later lives so little of what I said, and so little of what they read in the textbook we were using at the time?

Is psychology memorable?

But how does one go about making a textbook memorable? To begin with, as teachers and writers, we must take into account the needs and abilities of our students. When a young man or woman enrols in the introductory course, that person is typically educable but ignorant. If we are to help them learn, we must first of all give them an overview of the field that somehow makes sense and seems worthwhile to them. We must be as complete as possible, within these constraints, but we must give our students an aerial map of psychology, not merely a series of unrelated photomicrographs. Yet there are tremendous market pressures on the textbook writer to throw everything into a text, including the sodium pump and the kitchen sink. Let me give you a specific example of what these pressures are like.

As some of you know, my text, *Understanding Human Behavior*, (UHB), has a bit more biological detail in it than do many other texts. Since I believe that some knowledge of physiology is necessary for a student to appreciate why we think, feel, and act as we do, I don't apologize for including the biological side of human nature in my text. However, I have frequently been taken to task by teachers who believe that I haven't put enough 'facts' about physiological psychology in the text. No fewer than five critics have reminded me that, in my discussion of the so-called 'hunger' and 'satiation' centres in the brain, I describe these centres as being 'in the hypothalamus'. These critics informed me that such information isn't specific enough — that I should have put the 'feeding' or 'hunger' centre in the lateral hypothalamus, and the 'satiation' centre in the medial ventral hypothalamus.

Now, I ask you, how much detail do you expect the average introductory student to remember of all this a year later? If all that Lowell Kelly's hitch-hiker could recall was Pavlov's salivating canines, do you really expect most students to remember the term *hypothalamus* 12 months later — much less *medial ventral hypothalamus*? And even if the students could recall those three complex words — medial, ventral, hypothalamus — of what possible good could this knowledge be to them unless they have chosen a career in medicine or biology?

Frankly, I believe we should be overjoyed if our students recall — a year after taking the introductory class — that there are parts of the nervous system that influence both the onset and the offset of eating behaviour. For it is the *interactions* among body, mind, behaviour, and environment that are the real stuff of psychology, and it is the principles underlying these interactions that we should teach in the introductory course.

The itch for integration

How does one teach principles? Only by taking an integrated approach
to the field, I feel sure. There are probably thousands of different ways
to organize the various areas of psychology, and every single one of
them is right. My own preference has been for General Systems Theory,
because it is broad enough to include everything one might wish to
include yet vague enough so that it offends few people and seldom
gets in the way. Perhaps the best thing about General Systems Theory,
though, is the fact that it constantly brings one back to the
interrelations between and among physiological, mental, and
environmental processes.

But integration across the various fields of psychology is not enough.
It seems to me that the textbook author — and the teacher — must
integrate *within areas* as well. How can one discuss physiological
psychology sensibly and meaningfully without bringing in perception,
motivation, learning, developmental, personality, and social psychology?
And how can one discuss personality without touching on physiological
and social psychology, as well as on motivation, perception, learning,
and developmental processes? Unless our students see the connective
tissues in the body psychological, how can they be expected to
remember much of anything other than a series of unrelated facts
about dogs and salivation?

For better or worse, UHB is integrated not merely from front to
back, but within each major topic area as well. Yet as sensible as that
approach may seem on paper, it is not an approach that all teachers
subscribe to. Disregarding all the pioneering work on human memory
by Ebbinghaus and so many other scientists, many teachers wish an
author to confine the blasted nervous system to one or two chapters,
or to restrict that Freudian nonsense to a short section which may
conveniently be omitted. The problem with my text — as I have been
warned many times — is that there is no way in the world a teacher
can ignore any of the major areas in psychology, since each area
appears and reappears a dozen times.

I suppose I cannot really fault a teacher who wishes to emphasize
only certain aspects of psychology. When I was first teaching the
introductory course at Michigan, I too tended to pontificate about
those areas of the behavioural sciences that were obviously the most
important — that is, about those things I knew something about and
hence liked. Given the narrow focus of most graduate training
programmes, perhaps it is only to be expected that most young
teachers lack the breadth of view that someone like Dallenbach had in
his later years. And perhaps that is why Dr Dall insisted on teaching
the introductory course himself at Texas.

Frames and feedback

Another major obstacle that any textbook writer has to overcome is
the reluctance of most of us to obtain and utilize feedback from our
students in a creative and positive way. And little wonder, since most
of us were never taught the importance of feedback when we were either

teaching assistants or newly fledged instructors.

I was more fortunate than most, I suppose, thanks to the good offices of Allen Calvin. Back in the late 1950s, when Allen was teaching at Hollins College, he set up a Center for Programmed Instruction. This Center eventually metamorphosed into the Britannica Center for Research on Teaching and Learning at Palo Alto. Allen was Director of the Britannica Center; I was one of three Associate Directors. It was our primary task to create, test, and market programmed instructional materials for elementary and high school students. We hired subject-matter experts to draft materials in programmed form and then tested the first drafts on real, live students.

It was our assumption that if any frame in the programme had an error rate of about 5 per cent or greater, the programmer had somehow missed the mark. Thus the programme would have to be rewritten and retested until the error rate for each frame fell below the magic 5 per cent mark. Now, this procedure sounds like an easy one to follow, and often it was. The students we used gave us no trouble at all. They either learned, or they didn't, and it was up to us to change things until most of them had mastered the material. But oh, those programmers! I can still recall quite vividly a discussion we had with a mathematics expert who had prepared a programme on simple algebra. When we tested it out, we found that a very large percentage of the students simply couldn't handle the material the way it was organized and presented. So we dumped the programme back on the expert's desk and told him to redo it. He read through the frames, answered all the questions correctly, and then threw the programme back to us. 'I won't change a word of it.' he said angrily, 'because it's perfect. I got all the answers right. If your dumb students can't comprehend what I've written, they deserve to flunk and shouldn't be taking mathematics anyhow.'

The viewpoint this man expressed is, sadly enough, a very common one among most professors. Many of us who teach the introductory course have our doctoral degrees and years of experience in the field. There's almost nothing in any introductory text that we don't know. We have long since organized the whole field of psychology to suit our own needs, and thus we can assimilate new findings rapidly. We can give rambling disconnected lectures and write unorganized texts because the cognitive connections between one part of psychology and another are painfully obvious to us and our peers.

But consider the poor sophomore whose knowledge of psychology is limited to the sort of watered-down Freud presented on the soap operas. For such students, rambling lectures and encyclopaedic textbooks are a veritable nightmare. Long-term retention depends not merely on rote memory, but on organization. A programmatic approach to psychology is most necessary for these students if they are to remember anything at all about the field years later — other than that 'if you ring a bell, a dog will salivate like hell'.

Who's reinforced?

Twenty years ago, programmed textbooks seemed the answer to a pedagogue's dreams, because a good programme had built into it the type of organization that promotes long-term retention. Programmes are also classroom-tested and demonstrably effective. And yet, the frame-by-frame approach seems to have diminished in popularity over the years. Why?

There are many reasons for this diminution, not the least of which is that programmes are very expensive to prepare — and not all subject-matter experts are willing to accept feedback from actual learners. A more important reason, I feel sure, is that research soon showed that a semi-programmed approach — in which the material is presented in prose form rather than in frames to which the student must respond — is just as effective a way of imparting knowledge. But most important of all, most of the programmes written in the 1960s were downright dull. They worked — in test situations where students were paid to complete the work. But in real-life classrooms, the programmes just were not interesting enough to compete with reasonably well-written texts. Programmed textbooks work very well with those few students for whom 'the job of learning' or 'the thrill of achieving' is a powerful reinforcer. But for the bulk of the students, the frame-by-frame approach is too often a tedious chore that is more than mildly punitive.

The split brain story

My first attempt at writing a major section of an introductory book came in 1960, when Allen Calvin asked me to prepare the material on sensation and perception for a text he was editing. This book, entitled *Psychology* and published in 1961 by Allyn and Bacon, sold about 17 copies and soon disappeared from the scene. However, I learned a lot from preparing the manuscript. As I wrote, I tried to picture an average student sitting across the desk from me, and I attempted to 'speak' to the student as I typed. I soon found myself resorting to several devices that have, consciously or subconsciously, been a part of my writing style ever since. First, I organized the material in as logical a sequence as I could and presented the facts in a step-by-step manner that would (I hoped) reveal the underlying theoretical structure as well as the facts themselves. When my mythical student behind the typewriter started to fall asleep in the middle of a paragraph, I started slipping in analogies, anecdotes, and even hypothetical situations that might create a little more emotional involvement and hence keep the student awake and reinforced. Unfortunately, I still used 'big words' that weren't well-defined; my analogies were too heavily intellectual in content; and my anecdotes were those that pleased me and not necessarily my student. God knows, I didn't bother to test out the material on real live readers before I shipped it off to Calvin, so my section richly deserved the obscurity into which it almost immediately sank. But at least I had made a move in the right direction.

A decade later, I received a call from Dick Roe, who in 1969 was vice president of the CRM publishing group. Dick and his colleagues had decided to create an introductory textbook to be called *Psychology Today — An Introduction.* They had commissioned some

30 psychologists to write first-draft chapters that were later supposed to be synthesized into a coherent whole. As the chapters began rolling into the CRM offices in Del Mar, California, Dick suddenly realized that they had no one to edit and pull the material together. So, one cold night in January, he called and asked me to fly out to sunny California to take on the job. It would be a simple matter, he assured me — one that wouldn't take much time at all. I would thus be able to spend most of my time on the beach, sunning and swimming, but might have to put in a couple of hours a day at the office doing a little rewriting and stuff like that. Since I had sabbatical leave at the time, since Michigan winters are notoriously cold, and since I despise ice and snow, I agreed to fly out almost at once.

I spent about seven weeks in Del Mar trying to create order out of chaos. Some of the chapters we received were reasonably well-written, some were poorly written, and some we never got at all. But a book written by 30 different people simply has no internal organization or consistency to it, so that was what I had to supply — as best I could under the circumstances. I wrote several of the chapters 'from scratch'. I rewrote others extensively, and I tried to weave the rest into a meaningful text. Need I say that I spent 12 hours a day at the office seven days a week, that I seldom saw the sun, and that I never once got close to the ocean or to a swimming pool? Ah well, it was a 'learning experience', as they say.

My first real crisis with the *Psychology Today* text came early on, when we received a chapter on physiological psychology from a noted scientist. The material was factually correct, adequately organized, but frankly it was dull as dishwater. I puzzled over it for a couple of hours, trying to figure out how to make it palatable to undergraduates. Then I noticed that this scientist had buried the material on split brains in a single paragraph in the middle of the chapter. 'Now, that's silly,' I told myself. 'This split-brain stuff is by far the most exciting and intriguing data in the whole chapter. What will the students think and feel when they learn that they actually have two minds buried away in their skulls? Why don't we emphasize this research by building the whole chapter around it?'

A marvellous idea, I suppose, but I simply didn't have time to go back to the original research papers to pull out the fascinating details. So, in a sense, I invented them. Which is to say that I began the chapter with a brief vignette, which went something like this:

> You are a 30-year-old housewife with a husband, two children, and a fairly happy life. But about five years ago you began having severe headaches. The headaches turned into epileptic seizures, and eventually the seizures became so frequent that they were occurring a dozen times or more each day. You felt so bad that you wanted to die. Then one day the doctors told you about a new operation that might help. The surgery involved separating one half of your brain from the other. The doctors warned you that, even if the operation was successful, there might be rather peculiar side-effects. You were so desperate that you told them to go ahead. After the surgery, the epileptic seizures stopped almost

entirely. Aside from some problems in coordinating your movements, you seemed to be getting along quite fine. You felt good for the first time in years. But then, you noticed that your left hand had started doing some very strange things . . .

As you can see, I was trying to present some fairly complex brain research from a point of view the introductory student could understand and identify with. I assumed that once the student got interested in the housewife, the student might be motivated to master the technicalities of the brain well enough to comprehend why the woman's left hand was doing all those crazy things.

I liked the idea of using this little story so much that, when I encountered dull stretches of prose in other chapters, I often created similar vignettes based on the scientific material covered in that particular chapter. Some of my colleagues who read the book in manuscript form were distressed at this sort of 'popularization', but since the CRM people were in a great hurry to get the book into print, the vignettes survived — at least in the first edition.

A year later, I found myself teaching an honours section of the introductory course at Michigan. Naturally, I assigned the *Psychology Today* text. Since all of us associated with the book wanted to know the students' viewpoints toward it, I asked my class to keep reading logs as they went through the text — telling me what they particularly liked and disliked. The students knew that I had edited the book, but they didn't know which parts I had written myself. To my amazement and delight, there was near-unanimous approval of all the vignettes — and similar unanimous derision of the duller passages and for the fact that we used 'so many big words'. Now, honours students at Michigan are not exactly dullards, but they turned out to have much more limited vocabularies than I had imagined. More than this, some 90 per cent of the students either never discovered that there was a glossary at the end of the book or found it too late to do them much good. What a difference student feedback makes if you're really interested in finding out what use the students actually make of a text!

All of which brings us back to the thorny question of what our goals should be in the introductory course. Knowledge and skills, of course — although we might well disagree among ourselves on how best to inculcate knowledge and to teach these skills. But surely there is more to psychology than rote memory and motor behaviours. For instance, I believe it absolutely necessary to impart to my students some of the excitement, the thrill of intellectual wonder, and the emotional rewards that come with a growing understanding of the complexities of the behavioural sciences. Thus, from my biased point of view, it is just as important to shape our students' attitudes and emotions as it is to train their cognitions, perceptions, and behaviours.

The author's dilemma

Changing one's own behaviours to meet one's students' needs is not the easiest thing in the world to accomplish. But when I began writing my text, I decided to give it a try. So I deliberately set out to draft the simplest, most logically presented, most interesting, and motivating book that my own feeble powers could create. I thought the first draft of the text rather a good one but took the precaution of testing it on more than 100 students to see if the book accomplished their goals as well as mine. And what an eye-opening and ego-devastating experience that was! Because I tried to be honest with these first readers, and because I rewarded them for any comments they made — no matter how punitive — the students opened up to me in a way I had never quite seen before. They told me frankly and bluntly what they didn't like — where I was dull, trivial, unclear, or far off the target of interesting them in learning about psychology. In the process, they ripped my elegant prose to shreds and punctured many of the grandiose notions I had about my ability to communicate. But they also told me what they liked most about what I had written, and to improve those many sections of the book that didn't meet their high standard of pedagogical excellence. In brief, they taught me that writing for introductory students is quite different from writing for one's peers who have spent 20 years working in the field of psychology.

One of the most important things I learned from this feedback is that — whether the students were taking the course at Michigan or at a nearby community college — they were all bright enough to learn the material if I were bright enough to find a way to present the facts simply and logically, and if I could discover devices to keep them motivated throughout the book. Most young people — even honours students at Michigan — have rather limited vocabularies as compared to the vocabularies of those people who write, edit, and teach from introductory texts. Until UHB came along, few writers (and, I suspect, few teachers) bothered to define terms by giving the students a 'feel' for where the words came from and what the terms actually meant. Thus my students responded with great joy to the idea of a 'running vocabulary' in the margins of my text that would define terms as they appeared, rather than gathering the words and phrases into a rather useless glossary at the end of the book. The students appreciated as well the short stories I wrote and the anecdotes I told, for these dramatizations gave the students a sense of the emotional undertones of psychology that simply cannot be gained from many textbooks. But best of all, the students perceived the text as my attempt to share with them my passionate involvement with the field of psychology.

Authors, teachers and publishers

Unfortunately for textbook authors, the students are not the only audience that must be pleased or catered to. Students don't generally select the texts they will read — the instructors do. Thus, in a sense, the teachers are the major audience for whom most texts are written. But the author must also consider those psychologists who teach more advanced classes and who demand that any introductory text prepare the student for what these teachers want to cover in their higher level courses. The author must also take into account the needs of the publisher who prints and distributes the text. And the writer must deal as well with his or her own feelings about what is or is not important in the field of psychology.

These five different audiences — students, instructors, peers and colleagues, publishers, and one's inner feelings and needs — make very different and often conflicting demands on the writer of an introductory text. Satisfying them all is something of an impossibility.

For example, our surveys show that the vast majority of students prefer a simple, well-organized, coherent but interesting textbook that covers the whole field of psychology. But our surveys also indicate that many teachers either dislike or even distrust such a book. The major complaint that I have had from teachers about my own text is that the level of presentation is too simple. The problem seems to be that these teachers know too much about psychology — and perhaps cannot therefore put themselves easily in their students' places. These instructors forget what it is like to be a freshman or sophomore and to run smack up against the parts of the brain or the complexities of Freudian theory for the first time. Some of these teachers seem to expect near PhD-level performance from their introductory students and become punitive when their students don't meet this criterion of excellence. I can sympathize with these teachers, for my own expectations were rather high when I first taught the introductory course, and I too was disappointed at how little my students seemed to be learning. What I found eventually was that the fault was more mine than that of my students — and that if I took the time to explain things in terms the students understood, they were more than capable of achieving at a high level. However, perhaps it is a bit unfair for a textbook writer to ask that teachers change their pedagogical styles in order to use a text oriented more toward the student than toward the instructor.

New approaches to teaching — such as that found in UHB — sometimes disturb one's publisher at least as much as one's colleagues. When the manuscript for UHB first arrived at the editorial offices of Holt, Rinehart and Winston, it created something of a stir. The compositional problems involved in having chapters that began and ended with short stories, and that had the glossary stuck in the page margins, were difficult enough to solve — although the people at Holt did a marvellous job of handling these difficulties. But the very differentness of the approach — the simplicity of the language, and the book's attempt to cater to student needs — was actually a grave financial threat.

Publishers must make money in order to survive, and this need for a decent profit often brings out a kind of fiscal conservatism in business people. It is much safer to copy a product that has already succeeded in the marketplace than it is to pioneer a new approach. Fortunately, the people at Holt were willing to take a gamble with my text, and just as fortunately, the gamble paid off — with some rather unexpected benefits.

For instance, let us be blatantly truthful about certain financial matters. Most best-selling introductory texts are on a three-year revision cycle. The ostensible reason for revising these books every third year is to make sure that they keep up with current events in a fast-changing world. But the actual reason for frequent revisions is a financial one. The first year that a new book or new edition appears on the market is almost always the best year of the cycle, as far as sales are concerned. The second year of the cycle, the text typically sells about 60 per cent of what it did the first year. And by the third year, sales are often 30 per cent of what they were the year the edition first appeared. The reason for this precipitous sales decline is that the students tend to sell their texts back to their local college bookstores at the end of each semester. Thus by the third year there are more used books floating around than there are new copies. Well, publishers don't make any money on used books — and neither do authors — so it behoves both the writer and the publisher to think of ways to get rid of all those used copies.

Somehow it never occurred to us back in 1969 to ask *why* students sell back their texts. We just assumed — as publishers have always assumed — that it was the logical thing for the student to do. Yet when I first tested my own text on my 'sample students', I discovered an interesting phenomenon. Most of the students said it was so interesting that they'd like to keep a copy. Many of them said that they wanted to give the book to their parents or to friends to read. And when the first edition appeared, it turned out that we had found a new and very delightful solution to the used-book problem. For second- and third-year sales of the text were at least 50 per cent higher than we had expected simply because the students enjoyed the text so much that they tended to keep it rather than sell it.

The very success of UHB has caused Holt and many other publishers to re-examine some of their basic tenets about the college market. For it has occurred to them — as to me — that perhaps the best financial strategy of all is to satisfy the basic needs of the consumer. I now believe that the day will soon come when book companies are required to guarantee prior to publication that their texts really teach. Of course, such guarantees would have to be based on firm, empirical data of some kind. Thus the people at Holt are beginning to discuss the possibility of providing financial support for research aimed at discovering what it is about a text that really does enhance learning, and what it is about texts and teaching that turn students off and bias them against educational growth.

Education research — in good conscience

The ultimate audience that any writer must please is his or her own conscience. And I must say that my conscience finds this new turmoil in the publishing world very pleasing. Most of us involved in teaching have realized for years that we really know very little about the educational process and that we don't always use wisely the few crumbs of knowledge that we have. I have searched the literature in vain for studies on what we can do in the classroom or in texts that will promote long-term retention among our students. All I find is ample evidence that most students forget about 90 per cent of what they are taught within weeks after taking the final examination in any particular course. I have hopes that the students who read UHB do a little better than average as far as long-term retention of the facts and theories of psychology are concerned. But frankly, I cannot yet prove that this is the case. To coin a phrase, more research needs to be done on this problem — and I do hope that the publishers will help underwrite some of this work.

Reference

McConnell, J V (1977) *Understanding Human Behavior* (2nd edition). New York: Holt, Rinehart & Winston

Authors' Addresses

J De Ajuriaguerra
Chaire de neuropsychologie du
developpement
College de France
Place Marcelin Berthelot
75231 Paris, France

Richard C Anderson
Center for the Study of Reading
University of Illinois
51 Gerty Drive
Champaign
Illinois 61820, USA

David P Ausubel
262 Central Park West
New York
New York 10024, USA

J Alan Branthwaite
Department of Psychology
University of Keele
Keele
Staffordshire ST5 5BG, UK

Peter Burnhill
Design Department
Stafford College of Further Education
The Oval
Stafford, UK

Andrew S C Ehrenberg
Graduate School of Business Studies
Sussex Place
Regents Park
London NW1, UK

Michael D Gordon
Primary Communications Research
Centre
University of Leicester
Leicester LE1 7RH, UK

John D Gould
IBM T J Watson Research Center
PO Box 218
Yorktown Heights
New York 10598, USA

James Hartley
Department of Psychology
University of Keele
Keele
Staffordshire ST5 5BG, UK

Starr R Hiltz
Department of Sociology
Princeton University
Princeton
New Jersey 08540, USA

F Laurence Keeler
US Naval Training Analysis and
Evaluation Group
Orlando
Florida 32813, USA

James V McConnell
Department of Psychology
University of Michigan
Ann Arbor
Michigan 48104, USA

Linda Reynolds
Graphic Information Research Unit
6A Cromwell Place
London SW7 2NJ, UK

Ernst Z Rothkopf
Head, Department 1222
Bell Telephone Laboratories
600 Mountain Avenue
Murray Hill
New Jersey 07904, USA

Richard J Shavelson
Department of Education
University of California
Los Angeles
California 90024, USA

Herbert Spencer
Graphic Information Research Unit
Royal College of Art
6A Cromwell Place
London SW7 2NJ, UK

Robert H W Waller
Institute of Educational Technology
The Open University

Walton Hall
Milton Keynes MK7 6AA, UK

Peter Wason
Department of Phonetics and
Linguistics Annexe
University College London
Wolfson House
4 Stephenson Way
London NW1 2HE, UK

Patricia Wright
MRC Applied Psychology Unit
15 Chaucer Road
Cambridge CB2 2EF, UK

Index

Index

Index